# Success in

# COMMERCE

## FOURTH EDITION

**Success Studybooks**

Accounting and Costing: Problems and Projects
Book-keeping and Accounts
British History 1760–1914
British History since 1914
Business Calculations
Chemistry
Commerce
Commerce: West African Edition
Communication
Economic Geography
Economics
Economics: West African Edition
Electronics
Elements of Banking
European History 1815–1941
Geography: Human and Regional
Information Processing
Insurance
Investment
Law
Management Accounting: An Introduction
Management: Personnel
Office Practice
Physics
Principles of Accounting
Principles of Accounting: Answer Book
Principles of Catering
Statistics
Twentieth Century World Affairs
World History since 1945

# Success in

# COMMERCE

## FOURTH EDITION

**Derek Lobley,** B.A.

Department of Business and Management Studies

Barking College

John Murray

To David and John

First published 1975
by John Murray (Publishers) Ltd
50 Albemarle Street, London W1X 4BD

Reprinted 1977, 1978, 1980
Second edition 1982
Reprinted 1983, 1984, 1985, 1986, 1987
Third edition 1988
Reprinted (with revisions) 1990 (twice), 1991, 1992
Fourth edition 1993

Typeset by Fakenham Photosetting Ltd, Fakenham, Norfolk
Printed in England by Clays Ltd, St Ives plc

A catalogue entry for this title can be obtained from the British Library.

ISBN 0–7195–5157–9

# Foreword

*Success in Commerce* is intended for anyone following a basic course in commerce. This edition has been prepared during the transition from GCE and CSE to GCSE, and it covers the principal requirements of the syllabuses of the GCSE examining groups. Students preparing for first commerce examinations and the commerce content of secretarial examinations set by other bodies such as the London Chamber of Commerce and Industry, the Pitman Examinations Institute and the Royal Society of Arts will also find that the text covers their work.

Each Unit of the book is followed by a series of questions for students' use. In previous editions these questions were divided into three rather arbitrary groups. This division has now been abandoned, since many of the items can be used in a variety of ways. While it is not possible in the space available to include many structured questions, an attempt has been made to provide a wider variety of questions than before, in acknowledgement of the requirements of the new syllabuses.

Commerce books are inevitably to some extent out of date before they reach the consumer. There is a steady stream of legislation which affects commercial and financial activity; new institutions emerge in response to changing circumstances; the Government expands some activities and reduces others. The only way to keep up to date with these developments is through the financial and economic press. Most students will not have time (or perhaps the inclination) to do this, but a useful and informative annual summary is provided in the Government publication *Britain, an Official Handbook*, published annually by Her Majesty's Stationery Office. It is recommended that students refer to this where necessary, for more up-to-date information.

For this new edition the text has been thoroughly revised and updated, and more illustrations and tables have been included to back up the text. The influence of new technology has been acknowledged throughout, and a new Unit has been added to summarize its effects. The basic structure of the book has been retained, however – while the Units are each self-contained, so that they can be taken in almost any order, I believe that the progression from familiar retail institutions, through the financial organizations and on through commercial organizations to international trade is the most appropriate for the majority of students.

D.L.

# Acknowledgements

The author and publishers would like to thank the following organizations for their kind permission to reproduce illustrations:

Shell Photographic Service (fig. 1.1); *Market Trader* (fig. 3.2); *Retail Newsagent* (figs 3.3 and 8.3); Brent Cross Shopping Centre (The Hammerson Group) (fig. 3.4); Tesco Stores Ltd (fig. 3.5); J. Sainsbury plc (fig. 3.6); Nurdin & Peacock Cash and Carry Ltd (fig. 4.1); Consumer Credit Trade Association (figs 6.3, 6.5 and 6.6); British Standards Institution (fig. 7.1); *Super Marketing* (fig. 8.1); Barclays Bank PLC (fig. 11.2); Lloyds Bank Plc (figs 11.3, 11.9, 11.14 and 11.16); Midland Bank plc (figs 11.4 to 11.8 and 11.13); National Westminster Bank PLC (figs 11.11 and 11.12); the Bank of England (fig. 12.1); *Financial Times* (fig. 13.6); Kleinwort Benson Ltd (fig. 13.7); the Post Office (fig. 15.1); British Telecommunications plc (fig. 16.1); Mercury Communications Ltd (fig. 16.2); The Advertising Standards Authority (fig. 17.1); Pickfords Removals Ltd (fig. 18.1); Freightliners Ltd (fig. 18.2); Skyfotos Ltd (fig. 18.3); Lloyd's of London (fig. 19.3); Manpower Services Commission (fig. 22.2); Richard Turpin and IBM United Kingdom Ltd (fig. 23.1); Sally & Richard Greenhill (fig. 23.2); Sagesoft PLC (fig. 23.3).

The principal statistics quoted are based on information from the following sources:

*Annual Abstract of Statistics* (HMSO) (fig. 1.3); *British Business* (HMSO) (Table 3.1 and fig. 6.7); *Times 1000* (Times Books Ltd) (fig. 8.6); *Bank of England Quarterly Bulletin* (Tables 10.1 and 12.1); *Financial Statistics* (HMSO) (Table 11.1 and figs 11.15 and 13.3); The Building Societies Association (fig. 13.2); The Unit Trust Association (fig. 13.4); the Department for National Savings (fig. 13.5); the Department of Transport and *Annual Abstract of Statistics* (Table 18.1); British Railways Board and *Annual Abstract of Statistics* (Table 18.2); the Department of Trade and Industry (fig. 20.1); the Central Statistical Office (Tables 21.1, 21.2 and (with *Financial Statistics*) 21.3); *Economic Progress Report* (Central Office of Information) (fig. 22.1).

The article on in-store credit cards in question 11 of Unit 6 is reproduced by kind permission of *The Telegraph Sunday Magazine*.

# Contents

# UNIT 1

# The commercial world

## 1.1 Introduction

Did you buy a newspaper today? If so, did you stop to think how it reached you? Like so many of the things we use, the newspaper is taken for granted. We read it and discard it, perhaps within an hour, with scarcely a thought for the complex network of industry and enterprise needed to bring it to us punctually and regularly. Hundreds of people working in different occupations combine, often unknowingly, in producing a newspaper. For this reason, the production of a newspaper is a good illustration of the complexities of *commerce*.

The first requirement for producing a newspaper is the paper. This may be manufactured in the United Kingdom or overseas, but in either case its production will have required a large number of workers to undertake various specialized jobs. Next, this paper must be delivered to the site where the newspaper is produced. A large number of commercial functions are already involved: *transport* must be arranged to deliver the newsprint to the printer; the newsprint must be *insured* against loss or damage while in transit; financial transactions take place (sometimes the newsprint manufacturer delivers the material before payment is made, sometimes the printer pays in advance of delivery), and the *banks* may be called upon to make loans; *marketing* facilities including *advertising* will probably be used; and the newsprint will certainly have been held in a *warehouse* pending its dispatch for use.

Meanwhile, other workers produce the other physical components of a newspaper – the ink and the printing presses, for example. This means more commercial activity, like financing the purchase of machinery which may cost hundreds of thousands of pounds.

Leaving aside these physical components, think about the way the news itself is gathered. Journalists all over the world contribute to a single edition of a newspaper, so means of *communication* are vital. Without these communication facilities, which include both the postal services and telecommunications, news might be weeks or even months out of date before being published. More contributions arrive from photographers, advertisers and many other sources. When all these individual contributions have been received, teams of editors and sub-editors have to prepare copy to be set, while designers plan the layout of the paper. Then the printers and their staff – some highly skilled, others less skilled – get to work. When the papers roll off the presses they have to be packed before they can be delivered by road, rail and air transport to local centres. There, wholesale and retail newsagents, together with their staff, and street corner newsvendors provide the final links in the chain.

Before this stage is reached the skills of advertising agencies may have been used in various ways to attract our attention to the forthcoming edition. And by the time we come to read today's edition, production of tomorrow's will be well under way.

The process by which raw materials are transformed into a finished product suitable for use and delivered to consumers is known as *production* and constitutes a large part of the subject matter of economics. *Commerce* is concerned with one section of this process: it is the system by which raw materials are distributed to industry, and the finished products to consumers. We must look briefly at the economic system as a whole, in order to see exactly where commerce fits into the economic picture.

## 1.2  The economic system

Every weekday about 25 million people in the UK go to work. What is the object of their being at work? The obvious answer is that they want to earn an income, but this is not an end in itself. They need the income to buy goods and services of all kinds – some that are essential and many others that they feel that they should or would like to have – and this is their real reason for working. The combined efforts of these millions of workers convert raw materials into forms that are useful and valuable to the whole population. In this way they are helping to produce the goods and services which ensure a high standard of living for the community in general.

Most workers concentrate on producing a narrow range of goods, often only one item. The result could be that producers accumulate huge surpluses of goods which they do not require for themselves. It is an essential feature of modern society that these surpluses are *exchanged* for money which workers can then use to purchase the goods produced by other groups of people. Without facilities for exchange, there is no point in producing surpluses.

It is convenient to divide production into three stages – primary, secondary and tertiary (fig. 1.1) – in each of which the value of the raw materials is increased.

### 1.2.1  Primary production
This is the first stage of production and includes workers employed in mining, quarrying, fishing, forestry and farming – the *extractive* industries. The output

**Fig. 1.1** Shell's activities cover all three stages of production: (i) extraction of oil (*top*), (ii) processing or refining of the raw material (*centre*) and (iii) distributing the finished products to customers (*bottom*)

of such workers, especially those in mines and quarries, is likely to be in the wrong place and the wrong condition to meet the needs of the final consumer. (There are a few exceptions, of course, such as fruit growers or poultry keepers, who can sell their products – apples, strawberries, eggs – to the final consumer at the farm gate.) Most of the output of primary production is in a raw unusable state, however, and has to be moved on to the *secondary sector*.

### 1.2.2    Secondary production

In this secondary stage of production, people working in all kinds of manufacturing processes transform raw materials into the thousands of goods and products that we need. The word *manufacturing* once meant literally *making by hand*, but today a great deal of work is performed by machinery. It is unlikely, however, that raw materials will go in at one end of the factory and come out as finished products at the other. It is much more probable that the raw materials are turned into semi-manufactured goods in one factory and then sent on to another to be finished off or incorporated into a larger or more complex product. While this is happening the value of the materials is increasing as they are being converted into more useful forms. Also included in the secondary sector is the building and construction industry.

### 1.2.3    Tertiary production

The process of production may still be incomplete, even when the goods have passed through the secondary stage, for they will almost certainly be in the wrong place for most consumers. A factory in the north of England, for instance, may produce goods which are destined to reach consumers all over the country – north, south, east and west. The transfer of goods from the factory to the consumer is where the activities of the *tertiary sector*, the third stage of production, are needed.

In the tertiary sector there are two broad groups of workers, those providing *commercial services* and those offering *direct services*. The former include those in communications, finance, insurance, wholesaling and retailing; they are all involved in getting the finished goods to the final consumer. It is with this group that we shall be mainly concerned in this book.

People in the second group work to provide a direct service, rather than to ensure the delivery of goods to consumers. Teachers, doctors and nurses are examples of people providing direct services. They are not remote from the process of production, however; indeed production is facilitated by having a well-educated and healthy workforce. Other kinds of direct services include those provided by actors and professional sportsmen, civil servants, policemen and lawyers.

## 1.3    Commercial occupations

The main purpose of commercial activity is to facilitate the trading of goods, either between people and organizations within a country or on an inter-

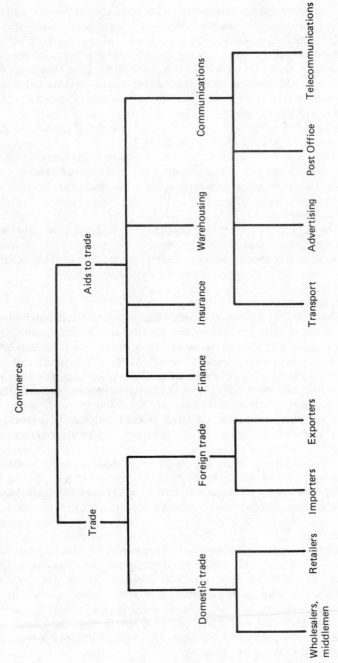

**Fig. 1.2** Commercial occupations

national basis. The full range of commercial activities is summarized in fig. 1.2. At the centre of commerce is *trade*, which may be defined as buying and selling with a view to making a profit.

International trade involves exporting and importing and is more complicated than domestic trade; we will defer a study of this until Unit 20.

In domestic trade, methods of buying, selling and distributing goods are continually changing. Traditionally goods reach consumers via wholesalers and retailers, but since about 1960 the growth of large-scale retailers has often led to the omission of the wholesaler. We shall examine the structure and development of domestic trading in Units 2 to 4.

However efficient manufacturers and traders may be individually, they can do nothing without the *aids to trade* provided by the *service industries*. These are summarized below and examined in more detail later.

### 1.3.1    Transport
The importance of transport in getting goods to the right place at the right time is self-evident. When large quantities of goods are produced in one place everything depends on the suppliers of transport – by land, air and sea – getting them safely transferred to the consumer (see Unit 18).

### 1.3.2    Finance
The machinery that helps to produce and distribute the goods has to be bought in the first place. The goods themselves are often sold on credit (that is, the purchaser receives the goods now and pays later); in any case, there may be a long interval between the purchase of the raw materials and the sale of the finished product at a profit. Therefore the producer or purchaser will almost certainly need to borrow money. The *banks* and other financial organizations play an important part in providing the necessary finance, and making it possible for trading to take place. In Units 6, 11 and 12 we examine the ways in which money can be borrowed for different purposes and for different periods of time.

The need for cash to pay for everyday items such as food, fares and clothes is even more fundamental, and in Units 10 and 11 we shall look at the way in which money and other means of payment have developed and are made available to the customer through the banks.

### 1.3.3    Insurance
There is always a danger that goods will be stolen or accidentally destroyed or damaged, either during their production or while they are in transit to the consumer. Such events could be extremely expensive to producers, but in many cases the insurance companies will arrange to offer compensation if need be, in return for the payment of relatively small sums of money known as *premiums*. Few businesses would be prepared to send their goods by air or sea if the goods were not covered by insurance. Thus insurance helps to overcome another obstacle to trade (see Unit 19).

### 1.3.4   *Warehousing*

At various stages of their journey to the consumer, goods need to be stored, either because transport is not immediately available or because the demand for them is uneven or seasonal. Here warehousing is necessary, and this is yet another essential function of commerce.

### 1.3.5   *Communications*

Businesses have to be able to communicate with their suppliers and their customers. We can identify three distinct channels of communications (other than transport, which has already been mentioned).

**Advertising**   More goods are sold if potential customers are told about them by advertising. Many people feel that advertising adds to the cost of goods and is an unjustifiable expense but, as we shall see in Unit 17, it has a very important, even a cost-reducing, role to play in commercial life.

**The Post Office** is important in providing businesses with the means of written communication with others so they can maintain a permanent record of their transactions. We shall see in Unit 15 that the services it provides have become increasingly sophisticated in recent years.

**Telecommunications** allow businesses to keep even more closely in touch. These services are provided mainly by BT which was formerly run by the State. In 1984 it became, as British Telecom, a public limited company, changing to its shorter name in 1991 (although its registered name is British Telecommunications plc). A wide variety of services is provided to commerce and industry, as we shall see in Unit 16.

We thus have a system of production in which there is a great deal of inter-dependence. Manufacturers depend on commercial services to provide them with raw materials and components and to distribute their finished products. Without manufacturers, on the other hand, commercial workers would have nothing to do.

## 1.4   Specialization and division of labour

Within each of the sectors we have identified, a large number of different activities take place. In the secondary sector we can identify, for example, the motor vehicle manufacturing industry, the fashion industry and hundreds of others. (An *industry* is a group of independent businesses producing similar articles.) In the tertiary sector we can identify the banking industry or the insurance industry, for instance. Within each industry there is further special-ization as different firms concentrate on different aspects of the work of the industry. Thus in the banking industry we find not only the familiar high-street banks such as Barclays and Lloyds but also the less widely known merchant banks, such as N. M. Rothschild & Sons Ltd and S. G. Warburg and Co. Ltd, offering a variety of services to industry rather than to individuals.

Within each firm there are further subdivisions, for most firms are divided into departments and within the departments individual workers have their own specialized jobs. For example, in a bank some staff may deal directly with customers, receiving and paying out cash, while others deal with cheques or other documents behind the scenes, and yet others are responsible for programming the bank's computers. This is the principle of the *division of labour* or specialization, which is the basis of our modern economy. The alternative to this division of labour would be for each family to produce its own goods, not relying at all on the efforts of outsiders. Adam Smith, the eighteenth-century British economist, first explained the advantages of the division of labour in his book *The Wealth of Nations*, published in 1776.

### 1.4.1   Advantages of specialization

(a) Individual workers can concentrate on those jobs to which they are most suited. Thus accountants can develop their skills without needing to worry about producing food or clothes. These can be produced by others, who themselves do not have to worry about the problems of accountancy.

(b) Practice makes perfect. Once people have learned a job, their skill at it increases. For example, the experienced full-time checkout assistant at a supermarket can deal with a trolley-load of goods more efficiently than a novice can.

(c) Division of labour normally allows a great saving on tools and equipment. Instead of each worker having a complete set of tools, which would be necessary if there were no division of labour, one set can be shared out among the team.

(d) As the work is broken down into individual tasks, it is likely that new and more efficient techniques will be developed.

The result of all these advantages, and the real purpose of the division of labour, is increased efficiency and hence increased output.

### 1.4.2   Disadvantages of specialization

We should not lose sight of the disadvantages that accompany this kind of specialization.

(a) Each part of a factory or an industry depends on the performance of the others. This interdependence means that if there is a breakdown in one section it can quickly spread to other sections, causing delays and sometimes unemployment. A strike by typists processing orders might soon lead to a whole factory temporarily closing down. A fire at a factory making electrical components for cars might bring a large part of the motor industry to a temporary halt.

(b) There is a danger of boredom when a worker is performing a simple continuous routine, often hundreds of times a day.
(c) As machinery becomes more elaborate it replaces labour, causing unemployment.
(d) The spread of division of labour normally leads to a decline in craftsmanship.
(e) As machinery takes over, output is standardized and the choice of goods available to consumers is reduced.

## 1.5 Production

We can now summarize what we mean by production: it is the process by which raw materials are transformed into finished goods to satisfy the requirements of consumers or other organizations. In addition to being in the right *form*, the goods must be in the right *place* at the right *time* before the process of production is complete. It is wrong, therefore, to think that producers are only those who *make* goods, and that those who do not make anything are unproductive. Workers in each sector are increasingly dependent upon each other, and each sector is dependent on the others. Without the people who provide commercial services, the flow of goods to consumers would be very much reduced.

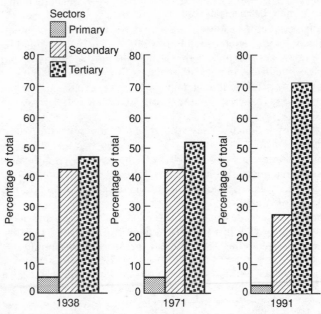

**Fig. 1.3** The changing structure of employment in the United Kingdom

Labour is one of the resources which economists refer to as the *factors of production* required to produce goods and services. These are classified as

(a) *land* – which is understood to include agricultural and building land, mines and quarries, rivers, oceans and the atmosphere and everything in them;
(b) *labour* – both physical and mental, whether undertaken for payment or within the family or household;
(c) *capital* – which includes not only wealth and finance but also physical assets (buildings, machinery, etc.) that can be used to produce goods and services; and
(d) *enterprise* – the actual taking of a risk in setting up a business (although many economists regard this as an aspect of labour). The person who takes this risk is known as an *entrepreneur*.

As economies become more specialized, a larger proportion of workers is employed in the tertiary sectory, producing services. This tendency is illustrated in fig. 1.3.

In the next three Units we shall examine the role of commerce in detail.

## 1.6  Questions

1. Name five occupations found in each of the three sectors of the economy.
2. What is the main purpose of economic and commercial activity?
3. Define *trade*.
4. What are the main branches of trade?
5. What are the main aids to trade?
6. What is meant by the phrase *division of labour*?
7. What is the main advantage of a system of division of labour?
8. Make a list of the disadvantages associated with division of labour.
9. What is meant by *production* in commerce?
10. Select a commodity and show how the division of labour assists its production.
11. What is meant by production? How do commercial occupations contribute to production?
12. Banking and insurance are two branches of commerce. What difficulties would arise for manufacturers and traders if these services did not exist?
13. What are commercial occupations? Outline the functions and importance of each branch of commerce.
14. Watch out for a major industrial dispute, and keep newspaper and magazine cuttings dealing with it. Once the dispute is over, write its history, showing how it affected the work of other sectors of the economy.

# The distribution of goods from the producer to the consumer

## 2.1 Introduction

The chief effect of the division of labour is that people working in an industry produce more goods than they themselves either need or can consume or use. For example, in 1990 the average output in the UK car industry was 15 vehicles per worker. This is not only more than the individual could produce without the division of labour but more than would be needed by one person.

It is the function of commerce to ensure that these surplus cars reach the people who want them. (Commerce will have already played an important part in their production by providing transport for raw materials and finance for machinery.) There are several different routes which goods can follow from the producer to the consumer, and they are summarized in fig. 2.1.

## 2.2 The pattern of distribution

### 2.2.1 Route one

This is the traditional route. Once a manufacturer has produced the goods he sells them in large quantities to the wholesaler, who redistributes them in smaller quantities to a large number of retailers. Small retail grocers obtain the bulk of their supplies in this way. The wholesaler provides a service to the manufacturing company by buying in large quantities and relieving it of storage problems, and to the retailer by obtaining goods from a number of different manufacturers and supplying them when required.

This method of distribution is especially important where the demand for the product is seasonal but production takes place throughout the year, as with fireworks or Christmas cards, or where the demand for the product is fairly even throughout the year but, as with many farm crops, output is concentrated into a few weeks. In each case the wholesaler has the important function of balancing supply and demand.

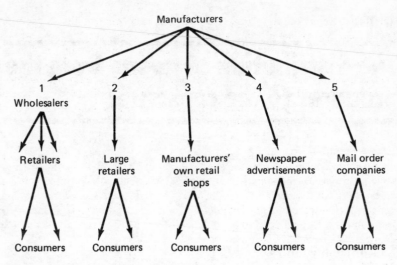

**Fig. 2.1** Routes from producer to consumer

### 2.2.2   Route two
Great changes have taken place in the structure of the retail trade, with the rapid development of transport and communications. Retail shops are generally larger than they were twenty-five years ago, when the manufacturer–wholesaler–retailer–consumer pattern of trade prevailed. This increase in size has in turn led to changes in the pattern of distribution. Route two is probably now more important than Route one in terms of the value of the goods involved. Retailers can frequently afford to buy direct from the manufacturer. This is particularly true where the retail shop belongs to a large group. Thus Marks & Spencer, Halfords, Richard Shops and many others obtain their stocks directly from the manufacturer, not from the wholesaler.

The size of the order that the retailer can place is the factor that determines whether this route is possible. Manufacturers produce in bulk and like to sell in bulk. Small retailers have neither the space nor the money to buy in large quantities, so they must deal with manufacturers indirectly through wholesalers. But even where retailers buy direct from the manufacturer, the essential functions of the wholesaler remain: buying in bulk, holding stocks and redistributing in smaller quantities. The only difference is that now they are performed by the retailers themselves.

### 2.2.3   Route three
Some manufacturers carry this process further still by combining the functions of manufacturer and wholesaler with that of the retailer, and selling their

products to the consumer through their own retail shops. This is useful to producers of perishable commodities, where the delay in selling to a wholesaler would spoil the product. Bread, for example, is often sold through retail shops owned by the baker. But many other goods also follow this pattern: Shell petrol is usually sold through filling stations owned by the company, and most beer produced in the UK is sold in public houses owned by the brewers. In each of these instances the manufacturer acts as the wholesaler, holding stocks until they are required by the retail branches.

### 2.2.4   Route four

A further way of eliminating the wholesaler and the retailer from the distributive process is for the manufacturer to sell directly to the consumer through newspaper advertisements or catalogues. While this method gives the producer access to a large number of potential customers it may be less satisfactory to consumers, who are deprived of personal contact with the seller and who may have difficulty in obtaining after-sales service.

### 2.2.5   Route five

Another variation is mail order selling, where goods are ordered from an expensively produced catalogue. Here the catalogue, which is carried by an agent or representative of the mail order company, acts as a permanent advertisement. In this case the company combines the roles of wholesaler and retailer.

A refinement of this kind of selling is the marketing of goods through agents who demonstrate them at 'parties' in the homes of potential customers. Cosmetics and kitchen equipment are notable examples of such goods, but clothes, jewellery and pottery are among the products sold in this way.

## 2.3   The distribution of primary products

Most manufactured goods reach the consumer by means of one of the routes we have just outlined. There are often special difficulties with primary products or raw materials, and several variations of the basic pattern have had to evolve. This is partly because most of these materials are very localized, and often occur far from the factories or consumers who need them. The difficulties of marketing certain industrial raw materials have resulted in the establishment of specialized *commodity markets* where the materials can be obtained, and often ordered in advance of requirements. (These markets are discussed in Unit 4.6.)

Agricultural produce also requires special disposal facilities because of its perishable nature. Most of it is sold in one of the ways shown in fig. 2.2.

(a) A small amount can be sold in the locality where it is produced. You are probably familiar with the stalls and small shops at farm gates, where farmers dispose of some of their produce.

**Fig. 2.2** The disposal of agricultural produce

(b) A substantial proportion is taken by road to local or regional markets, where it is sold either to wholesalers or direct to retailers.

(c) Some farmers send their produce to national markets, the most important of which is New Covent Garden Market in London, for fruit and vegetables. Goods from all over the United Kingdom and indeed from abroad are sent to New Covent Garden Market for redistribution. Other notable markets in London are Smithfield, for meat, and Billingsgate, for fish.

(d) It is now quite common for farm crops to be sold direct to supermarkets themselves, or to manufacturers for processing, for we buy an increasing amount of our food in a frozen or dehydrated state.

(e) Sometimes farmers may be compelled by law to sell their crops or produce direct to a *marketing board*. These are organizations set up to control the output and sale of a particular product. Such boards are really performing the function of wholesalers.

Having made this preliminary survey of the ways in which finished products reach the consumer, we shall examine the processes involved more closely in the following Units.

## 2.4   Questions

1. What are the distributive trades?
2. What is the traditional pattern of distribution of goods from producers to consumers?

3. By what route do most groceries now reach the consumers? Why has this route replaced the traditional route?
4. Name four goods whose production is seasonal but for which demand is steady throughout the year.
5. Name four goods for which the demand is seasonal but whose production may be steady throughout the year.
6. How can the problems caused by (a) seasonal demand and (b) seasonal production be overcome?
7. Describe two types of mail order selling.
8. By what route is it likely that fresh fish reaches the consumer?
9. What effect is the growth of large 'superstores' likely to have on wholesalers of grocery products?
10. Explain and comment upon the ways in which finished goods may reach the consumer.
11. What difficulties arise when manufacturers dispense with the services of wholesalers and sell direct to retailers?
12. In what respects has the growth of large firms affected the traditional pattern of distribution?
13. List eight or ten household goods that you or your family buy regularly. Compare the prices over several weeks in (a) two supermarkets, and (b) a small retail shop. What differences do you notice? Why do you think such differences exist?

# The retail trade

## 3.1 The definition of the retailer

To many of us the most familiar business units are the retail shops from which we normally buy the things we need. The word *retail* originally meant *to cut a piece off*, and a retailer is still someone who sells things in small quantities. Retailers may *buy* packets of detergent in their hundreds or thousands, but they will *sell* them to us one at a time.

## 3.2 The functions of the retailer

Retailers are *middlemen*, and perform functions for two groups of people. The first group are the manufacturers and wholesalers who provide them with goods; the second are the consumers who buy the goods from them. In fact, retailers exist to provide a link between the consumers and the producers of goods. As we shall see in the rest of this Unit, in providing services for consumers the retailer necessarily relieves manufacturers and other producers of several problems.

### 3.2.1 Providing local supplies

Procter & Gamble, the producer of a large proportion of our household soaps and detergents, has factories in Essex, Lancashire and Northumberland. It would be impossible for consumers to go to one of these factories every time they wanted to buy a bar of soap, nor would the firm be pleased to see them. Wholesalers would not welcome such customers either, for they like to sell in large quantities. Retailers, however, by establishing their shops in towns and villages and in housing estates and shopping centres throughout the country, provide consumers with a local and easily accessible supply of goods. As well as performing this important service for us, they are important to producers. This is because a wide network of shops enables producers to reach as many consumers as possible.

### 3.2.2 The breaking of bulk

Manufacturers and wholesalers – and many retailers as well – deal in very large quantities. But however many compact disc players Dixons buys, it will sell them to its customers one at a time. Retailers thus provide goods in convenient quantities.

### 3.2.3 Providing a variety of goods

Each manufacturer of, for example, wrist watches, makes a particular range of goods. The retail jeweller obtains supplies of watches from several manufacturers, and thus provides a variety of models for consumers to choose from.

### 3.2.4 Advice and information

In many fields of the retail trade this is less important than it used to be. Most of us don't need advice when buying our weekly groceries and household goods. But if we are decorating the house, the local supplier of paints and other materials may be able to give us some useful tips about new products that are available. Similarly, we may receive helpful advice from the chemist about medicines, while photographic dealers spend much of their time discussing the suitability of equipment for various purposes. Then, in the other direction, the retailer may well be able to give information to the manufacturers' representatives who call at the shop, especially with regard to how well certain products are selling. This could affect the manufacturers' future production plans.

### 3.2.5 Dealing with complaints

It sometimes happens that retailers sell goods that are in some way unsatisfactory. Even if the defect is not their fault, they have a legal duty to deal with the problem. For example, if you buy a can of lemonade that turns out to contain orangeade the retailer must replace the can or refund your money, and must not leave it to you to sort out with the manufacturer.

### 3.2.6 Other services

Retailers may provide a *pre-delivery service* for some goods: motor cars, bicycles and many kinds of electrical equipment should not be sold without the retailer checking over them to ensure that they are in good condition.

Some retailers provide *credit* for their customers. This may be on an informal basis such as the purchase of groceries at small shops or formally in the case of consumer durable goods (goods intended to last a long time, such as television sets or cars). Formal credit arrangements are discussed in Unit 6.

Retailers provide a *delivery service* in respect of most consumer durables. It would be very inconvenient if furniture stores, for example, did not deliver our purchases to us.

Many retailers provide an *after-sales service* for their customers. This again applies particularly to the sale of consumer durables. In the event of the television set breaking down, your retailer should be able to send an engineer to repair it.

Finally, some shops open very early or close very late as a service to their customers. Many newsagents, for instance, open at 7 a.m. or even earlier, and may not close until 7 p.m. Some general stores open all day on Sundays, although there may be restrictions on what they can sell. Supermarkets often work longer hours on Fridays and Saturdays. While the general purpose is to increase profits, the effect is also to provide a convenient service to customers.

Not *all* retailers provide *all* the services listed here, of course, but they do all try to provide goods for sale at a time, in a form, and in quantities convenient to consumers.

---

1. Provides goods in convenient quantities.

2. Provides goods in convenient locations.

3. Provides goods at convenient times.

4. May provide pre-sales and after-sales service.

5. Provides a variety of goods.

6. Provides a delivery service for some goods.

7. May provide credit to customers.

8. Provides advice to customers.

9. Deals with customers' complaints.

10. May act as a channel of information between customers and the manufacturers of goods.

---

**Fig. 3.1** A summary of the functions of the retailer

## 3.3   Types of retailer

You only have to think about the shops that you visit to appreciate that there are many kinds of retail outlet. The majority of these forms can be found in most major shopping areas.

### 3.3.1   Street markets

Many towns have street markets, but very few of them are open every day. Three kinds of retailers sell in these markets:

(a) the owners of shops who hope to increase their sales by renting a stall at a market in a neighbouring town;

**Fig. 3.2** Traditional street markets are a source of competitively priced goods, including vegetables and clothing

(b) the producers of agricultural goods who prefer to market their goods in this way rather than through the other possible channels discussed in Unit 4 – a choice which is much less popular than it used to be, however;

(c) traders who rent stalls at a number of different markets on different days.

The main advantage of market trading is that the *overheads* are low. (Overheads are expenses that have to be met whether goods are being sold or not, such as rent and heating.) In the market, heating and lighting are not usually needed. Since overheads are low, the market trader often sells goods at low prices. Frequently market traders will go out of their way to obtain goods direct from manufacturers, which also helps them to sell cheaply. The disadvantage to the customer is that the stallholders do not normally provide the kind of after-sales service you expect from other retailers.

### 3.3.2   The independent retailer

Independent retailers are people who own (or rent) and run their own shops. Such retailers are not commonly found in the town centre these days, for the expense of maintaining a shop there is considerable. Large profits can be made in high streets, because thousands of consumers do their shopping there, but the owners of shop sites can charge high rents, which only large firms can

**Fig. 3.3** Small shops often provide a variety of goods in a convenient location

afford. But as you move out of town towards the suburbs you will normally find a number of independent traders, including newsagents, butchers, tailors and florists. These small retailers may enjoy any or all of the following advantages.

**Independent management**    They have complete control of the business, so any decisions can be made quickly.

**Personal service**    Outside the town centre, the proprietor often knows the customers personally and can retain their custom by taking trouble to help them.

**Convenient opening hours**    In some trades, independent retailers can also offer convenience to the customer. Small newsagents, confectioners and general stores are frequently found open either early in the morning or late at night, or both. The same shops also tend to open on Sundays, as do independent motor car accessory dealers. Not only is this convenient for the customer, but it also enables the proprietor to compete with larger businesses which may have shorter opening hours (though many now stay open till late in the evening).

It would be a mistake to think that *all* small retailers open at these unusual times, however. Only in important tourist centres are you likely to find clothes shops, for example, open on a Sunday, and they are unlikely to open unusually early on other days. At the time of writing it is in many cases illegal for some shops to open on Sundays, though there have been many attempts to change the law.

**Credit services**   It was once common practice for the proprietor of a small general shop on a housing estate to allow informal credit to trustworthy customers, which meant that they could pay at the end of the week. While this practice undoubtedly continues here and there, it does not seem to be widespread nowadays. It certainly cannot be said to give small retailers, as a group, any real advantage over their competitors.

**Specialization**   Some small retailers are highly specialized, concentrating on a narrow range of goods but offering their customers a wide choice within that range. For example, while the average supermarket may stock ten or a dozen varieties of cheese, the specialist delicatessen can offer many more. The local ironmonger or do-it-yourself shop has traditionally offered a wider range of woodworking tools than the high-street multiple store.

This 'advantage' of the independent retailer should not be overstated, however, since many much larger organizations are following the same trend: some hypermarkets stock a vast range of cheeses and there are very large firms, such as B & Q, specializing in do-it-yourself equipment.

**Delivery services**   Some small retailers give a free delivery service. We cannot regard this as a special advantage, however, because it is also available from many larger retailers.

Thus there are certain advantages available to the independent retailer: the most important are those of convenience and specialization. Gradually, however, even these are becoming less significant as larger firms exert their influence. The result is that small retailers are increasingly confined to the small general-store part of the retail trade, or specialized areas such as health foods or high fashion.

### 3.3.3   Voluntary chains
One area in which the independents have been particularly affected has been the grocery trade, where supermarkets now predominate. Many of the independents have tried to compete by joining one of the voluntary groups such as Spar or Wavy Line. These groups are normally organized via wholesalers, and they allow independent retailers to enjoy some of the advantages of the large-scale retailers, which we shall discuss later. There are four main advantages to joining a voluntary chain.

(a) Individual retailers place their orders with wholesalers within the group, who can then place very large orders with manufacturers and secure important discounts (a *discount* is a reduction in price), which are passed on to the retailers. In this way the retailers buy more cheaply than they could from an ordinary wholesaler.

(b) National advertising can be undertaken by the group as a whole. Of course, for this to be effective the shops have to be recognizable as members of the group. This inevitably leads to a loss of individuality, but the group symbol does become a kind of guarantee to the public.

(c) The group may make loans for the renovation and decoration of members' premises.

(d) The groups often lay down minimum standards for members, thereby making them more attractive to consumers. For example, the group may insist that members carry a certain level and range of stock.

In return for these advantages the retailer has to sacrifice a degree of independence, for many policy decisions are taken by representatives elected to the management committee of the organization. The retailer may have little say in decisions about local advertising, window displays and even what goods are sold.

While voluntary chains are found mainly in the grocery trade, many independent photographic retailers now combine in a similar way to compete with large multiple firms.

### 3.3.4  Multiple shops

The tendency today is towards large-scale retailing, and there are a number of large-scale retailers which are known as multiple shops. Some of them specialize in a narrow range of goods; others sell a large variety of goods under one roof.

Among the specialist multiples are Halfords (motoring, cycling and camping accessories), Richard Shops (women's clothes) and W. H. Smith (magazines, books and stationery). Although each of these shops will have a branch manager responsible for the performance of the individual unit, the general policy of the shop (and that of all others in the group) is laid down by head office. These are centralized organizations: branch managers do not have the power to negotiate with manufacturers or wholesalers, and they are not responsible for the decor of their shops. These matters are all left to head office. (You will notice that multiple shops are recognizable by their uniformity.) In this way the business makes many savings. It can afford to employ specialists whose greater efficiency reduces costs, while individual units within the multiple chain need not advertise – this is normally done on a national scale by head office.

Other multiples offer a much wider range of goods. In shops like Tesco you can obtain the bulk of your weekly shopping: food, household goods, hardware, clothes, some electrical goods and many other things. Like the specialist

**Fig. 3.4** Multiple shops are among those to be found in any large shopping centre

multiples they enjoy very large discounts from the manufacturers and can frequently sell at lower prices than smaller organizations can.

Some shops, for long regarded as specialist multiples, have in recent years begun to diversify by selling a broader range of products, in order to increase their profits. Boots the Chemists sells far more lines of goods than the traditional pharmacist does. Marks & Spencer, which for many years sold only clothing, has established itself as a food retailer and wine merchant and now sells soft furnishings as well.

### 3.3.5 Department stores

These are generally regarded as being like several shops under one roof (and the same ownership) and they are traditionally found in town centres. The most famous British examples are Harrods and Selfridges in London. In many provincial cities and towns Debenhams is the main department store. Since there is a large number of department stores, they obviously overlap the multiple stores. In fact there is a further problem here, in that some stores such as Boots which were once specialist multiples have taken on some of the characteristics of department stores: they now offer a much wider range of goods in their major branches and they do operate on a clear departmental basis. But the distinction between the true department store and the enlarged multiple will become clear to you if you visit one of each.

Within the traditional department stores, separate departments cater for consumers' wants: electrical goods, furniture, clothing, glassware, china, books, toys and many other things will be found. Each department is under the control of a *buyer* or manager responsible for making the department profitable. The department store is said to offer luxury shopping, because many facilities are provided for customers: there is often a car park for customers only, and a coffee lounge or restaurant.

Many department stores are owned by very large firms, even where they retain their original names. The result has been a reduction in the independence of the stores and of individual departmental buyers, in the interests of centralization.

### 3.3.6   Supermarkets

A supermarket is generally defined as a self-service shop with over 186 square metres of floor space. Many supermarkets may be regarded as multiples as well, for they operate on a wide scale. They concentrate on food and household goods, and only stock goods which they know they can buy in bulk and sell quickly. Since they rely on rapid sales, they need to be in busy shopping centres. Their goods are normally pre-packed and frequently advertised nationally by manufacturers, but sometimes the supermarket chains buy in such bulk that manufacturers are prepared to produce foods specially for them under the supermarkets' own labels (see Unit 3.4). Supermarket prices are usually very competitive, because of their high rate of sales, but this is only one of the factors that has led to their rapid growth, as we shall see in Unit 3.5.

### 3.3.7   Superstores and hypermarkets

There are two kinds of outlet bigger than supermarkets, operated by companies such as Asda, Tesco and Sainsbury:

(a) *superstores*, which have at least 2500 square metres of selling space, and
(b) *hypermarkets*, which normally have over 5000 square metres of selling space.

Both tend to be single-storey buildings, rely on self-service and sell a wide range of food and non-food merchandise. These shops are mainly near urban areas and rely heavily on car-users for their business, normally providing large areas of free car parking space. To encourage non-car-owners, however, many of the firms offer a free bus service to and from their stores.

Stores of this size did not appear in the UK until the mid-1960s, and have enjoyed a steady expansion since this date. Both types provide competitive and convenient shopping. There is frequently opposition to their introduction because of fears that in the long run they may have a harmful effect on more conventional shops in town centres. In some areas high-street *shopping precincts* have been developed partly in response to the growth of out-of-town superstores. These precincts usually have good parking facilities and a wide range of shops, with access only for pedestrians.

**Fig. 3.5** Modern superstores attract thousands of customers each day and must provide ample parking space

### 3.3.8 Retail co-operative societies

The retail co-operative movement began in Rochdale in 1844 to protect working people from exploitation, and the movement developed rapidly. Today's societies still retain many features of the original co-operatives.

(a) Membership is open to anyone prepared to buy a share in the society. This normally costs £1. Each member may subscribe up to £5000 and receive interest on this capital. (It is not, of course, necessary to be a member to buy goods from the co-operative shops.)

(b) The society exists to serve the members. Members each have one vote in the election of the management committee, however much capital they have contributed and however much they purchase from the society.

(c) The profits of the societies used to be divided between members half-yearly, in proportion to their purchases from the society. This led to a considerable amount of book-keeping, and in many societies it is now the practice to give dividend stamps, exchangeable for cash, with purchases instead. Other societies arrange in-store special offers for members or provide shoppers' cards giving discounts on various services.

The co-operatives resemble department stores in that they embrace the whole field of retail trade within one organization. Indeed, since many provide milk, bread and coal as well as a laundry service and frequently a funeral service as well, they are even more comprehensive than most department stores. (They do not normally provide the same luxurious facilities, however.) In other respects they resemble the multiple stores, because they have the benefit of centralized purchasing and other services provided through the Co-operative Wholesale Society, which is owned and controlled by the retail societies.

The co-operative societies have objectives which are broader than those of other retail units we have discussed. While they need to make a surplus to pay out interest to their shareholders and to finance expansion and the building of new shops, they also finance a range of educational, political and social activities.

Originally, the main strength of the co-operatives was that they were local societies serving local communities. However, a process of amalgamation reduced the number of societies from 1015 in 1958 to 88 in 1989, causing them to lose their local identity. As a result, local control has been lost as well. Originally the management committees were known to members, who could make their views known and have a feeling of identity with the society. This is impossible in the very large societies which exist today. In addition, the policy of issuing dividend stamps, in imitation of some supermarkets, has caused the co-operatives to be regarded as just another retail outlet.

### 3.3.9   Discount stores
A comparatively recent development in distribution has been the establishment of *discount stores*. These are like wholesalers who buy in large quantities from manufacturers and sell direct to the public. They are especially common in the electrical goods industry, selling stereo equipment, freezers and television sets. They advertise widely in the national and local press. Discount stores are able to sell at very competitive prices by reducing staff and overheads, and by cutting out some of the retailer's profit. This is their chief advantage to consumers. While the goods they sell are subject to the same consumer legislation as other goods, you should not expect the same services from the discount stores that you obtain from the independent retailer. One of the ways they cut their prices is by eliminating the services they provide with the goods; for example, less trouble is taken over displays of goods and they may make a charge for the delivery of even very large items.

### 3.3.10   Franchising
Some retail outlets which look like multiples are, in fact, *franchises*. Franchising is the process whereby the owners of a business allow others to run branches in return for certain payments. The Wimpy, Kentucky Fried Chicken and Body Shop chains are examples. The people who operate the retail outlets (the franchisees) pay the owners (the franchisors) a substantial sum for the privilege of using the name, and have to buy or rent the premises. There is an

agreement that the franchisee makes payments either by purchasing all materials from the franchisor or by paying a royalty (a fixed percentage of sales).

The parent firm has the advantage of attracting capital from enterprising individuals and in effect receives a share of their profits. The franchisee has the advantages of being able to use a well-known and widely advertised name without having to build up a personal reputation, and of receiving other assistance from the parent company, for example in the form of cheap supplies.

### 3.3.11  Mail order firms
The term *mail order* covers several different forms of selling. The best known is that used by the nationwide firms who sell via catalogue and local part-time agents. The attractive catalogues, which are expensive to produce, offer a wide range of consumer goods which a customer may purchase on *credit* (see Unit 6) over a period of twenty weeks. This is the principal advantage to the shopper, especially as the credit is automatic and involves no formality. Normally the holders of catalogues show them to their families, friends and neighbours and place orders for goods on their behalf, receiving a commission of (usually) 10 per cent from the mail order firm for their trouble. The customers have the additional advantage of having the goods delivered to their door.

The mail order firm itself enjoys several advantages.

(a) It does not need expensive high-street premises – large buildings tucked away on industrial estates are perfectly adequate.
(b) The catalogues provide it with a permanent and enticing shop window in many homes, though the quality of the goods may be difficult to assess.
(c) The availability of instant credit persuades many people to buy goods on impulse which they would ignore in an orthodox shop window, even though prices are normally raised by the credit charge. In addition, a customer who gets used to paying perhaps 50 pence per week is often quite happy to buy further goods at the end of twenty weeks.
(d) The firm enjoys the usual economies associated with bulk buying and the profits of both wholesaler and retailer.

Against these advantages must be set the disadvantages of having to meet heavy packaging and postal charges, as goods are sent off in single units, and of frequently having to pay the postage on goods returned as unsatisfactory, especially in the case of clothing.

In another kind of mail order selling, manufacturers or wholesalers advertise in the national press, inviting orders by post. Most weekend newspapers carry advertisements of this kind. It is ostensibly a very convenient method of shopping, and frequently goods are offered at bargain prices. There is, however, the usual difficulty of not being able to inspect the goods in advance. Also, although you may have the right to return them if they are not suitable, there have been cases where customers have had difficulty in getting their money refunded. Such advertisements are now covered by the Fair Trading

Act 1975, and the national newspapers operate their own Mail Order Protection Scheme.

## 3.4    The changing structure of the retail trade

Although we have now identified a number of different types of retailer, you should realize that there are no hard and fast boundaries between them. We have seen that many multiple stores are similar to department stores; similarly, the Comet shops are sometimes regarded as discount stores, but it is difficult to define the difference between them and shops such as Rumbelows and Currys.

The real point is that the retail trade is changing all the time and we must not regard it as a rigid structure. In fact over the last thirty years there have been many changes in retailing. Most important has been the trend towards large-scale retailing, originally most noticeable in the food trade with the development of supermarkets but gradually spreading to other goods including furniture, carpets and electrical equipment.

Three principal factors have permitted and indeed encouraged the growth of large-scale retailing.

### 3.4.1    The end of price-fixing

Until 1964, any manufacturing firm was allowed to stipulate the retail price at which its goods must be sold, a practice known as *resale price maintenance* (RPM). The effect of this was to eliminate price competition between retailers and to force some retailers to charge higher prices than they thought necessary. Some early supermarket proprietors found themselves in court because they had sold goods for 30 pence rather than the 35 pence laid down by the manufacturer!

Following the Resale Prices Act 1964, the practice of RPM rapidly collapsed (although it still remains for books and pharmaceutical products). Its disappearance was important since it resulted in the growth of large retail outlets attracting customers by selling more cheaply than more traditional shops could do.

### 3.4.2    Growth of self-service

The ending of RPM facilitated the growth of self-service shops. These can be time-saving to customers and are convenient in that goods are well displayed and individually priced. There is, of course, a loss of personal service. For retailers the self-service system can be labour-saving (smaller wage bills). Moreover, the use of clever display techniques may increase sales through impulse buying, when shoppers buy goods over and above those they originally intended to purchase – for example, sweets are often strategically placed near checkouts where customers in the queue may be tempted. A disadvantage to retailers is the increase in shoplifting and pilfering that accompanies the growth of self-service.

### 3.4.3 Branding and packaging

The traditional function of the retailer was to buy fairly large quantities of sugar, cheese or vegetables from a wholesaler and weigh them off as consumers demanded them. Today almost anything we buy from the grocer or green-grocer can be pre-packed and pre-weighed. The packaging may be done by the manufacturer, the wholesaler or the retail firm itself, but, whichever is the case, the retailer can display the goods on fixtures from which the customers can help themselves.

The pre-packaging of goods has been accompanied by the *branding* of goods so that they are readily identifiable. There are two kinds of brands:

(a) *manufacturers' brands*, where the goods bear the manufacturer's name, and
(b) *retailers' brands*, where the goods bear a name that is readily associated with a particular retailer. Large-scale retailers are able to order in such bulk that manufacturers will produce goods and label them specially for individual firms.

In each case national advertising will periodically remind consumers of the brand names or of the trade marks of the producers.

**Fig. 3.6** Large retailers sell goods under their own brand label. Bulk orders often mean that prices are lower than manufacturers' brands

Branding and packaging have the advantage of making goods readily identifiable and ideal for self-service retailing. They do not necessarily benefit the large retailer at the expense of the small, for many small retailers are now using the self-service system.

While the end of price-fixing and the growth of self-service and branding and packaging were important in allowing the development of large-scale retailing, there are also various advantages which large retailers enjoy which have contributed to their growth.

## 3.5    Advantages of large-scale retailing

### 3.5.1    Economies of scale
An *economy of scale* occurs when the output of a firm increases faster than some cost – for example, if a hospital laundry discovered how to wash 20 per cent more linen with the use of only 5 per cent more detergent – and its effect is to reduce the cost per unit processed. The most important economies for retailers are the discounts obtained by buying in bulk, especially where retailers have their own brands. There are also considerable savings in labour for those large retailers who use self-service, though even with this system there is still much work to be done behind the scenes.

### 3.5.2    Specialization
The small retailer is responsible for all the decisions that have to be taken: what to sell, where to sell, whether to advertise, where to obtain goods and so on. The large firm can afford to employ specialists to cover each of these functions and many more. Each specialist works on only one aspect of the business: efficiency increases, profits rise and expansion continues.

In addition to these two economic advantages, several other factors have contributed to the large retailers' success.

### 3.5.3    Growth of private transport
The week's groceries for an average family constitute a fairly hefty load. The small grocer may be prepared to deliver such a load for you, but if you have your own transport you no longer need assistance. You can drive a short distance to the supermarket, place your purchases in a large box – which is usually available – and transport the goods yourself. There are 20 million private cars on the roads in the UK now, compared to 5 million in 1960; this indicates that many more families – about 76 per cent of households – are now able to shop in this way. This is very much to the benefit of the large-scale retailer.

### 3.5.4    Promotions
Retailers today find themselves in a very competitive situation. As a result, they place great emphasis on 'special offers' and price-cutting to promote sales. Until the mid-1970s much of this price-cutting took the form of the issue of trading stamps which consumers saved until they were ready to exchange them for goods or cash. They constituted, in effect, a delayed price reduction. Today there is more direct price-cutting. Large retailers are more likely than small ones to be able to afford this.

### 3.5.5    New technology
Retailing, like most industries, has been affected by the growth of new technology. Electronic cash tills are now widely used by all types of retailer. The

more sophisticated tills are really computer terminals and they are able to perform a variety of functions for their users. Initially they are expensive, and if full advantage is to be taken of them they need to be linked to a company's head office. It is only large retailers that can take full advantage of such equipment. Among the things this type of till can be used for are the following.

(a) The prices of goods can be read directly from the package, either through numerical codes or through special bar codes printed on the goods. This eliminates the possibility of transferring price tags to obtain goods at low prices.
(b) The system normally allows for the recording of each individual movement of stock, and by linking with a central warehouse computer enables stocks to be replaced automatically without staff at the retail end having to count their stock and then re-order.
(c) Sales achieved by individual staff can easily be recorded, and any commission due to them calculated.

Such systems result in a further saving of labour for large retailers, still further increasing their efficiency and their advantages over more traditional outlets.

## 3.6 Disadvantages of large-scale retailing

As you would expect from the rapid development of large retailers, their advantages heavily outweigh their disadvantages. It is important not to lose sight of the latter, however. There are three main disadvantages.

### 3.6.1 Decline in personal service
The nature of large-scale retailing means that the customer cannot normally deal directly with the proprietor or indeed the manager. Supermarket managers are seldom prepared to accept special orders: they are only interested in buying goods that they can sell very rapidly to a large number of people. Likewise delivery and after-sales service are not usually provided by supermarkets. Generally, the customer has to work harder in the supermarket than in other stores!

### 3.6.2 Staffing problems
Although the supermarket may require fewer staff in relation to its sales, many of the jobs that it can offer are routine and involve little contact with the general public.

### 3.6.3 Pilfering
Pilfering is a distinct problem in the supermarkets, and for most of the large retailers. Convictions for shoplifting are frequent, and the temptation is much greater in large self-service stores than elsewhere. The large retailer has the choice of either accepting heavy losses through shoplifting or installing

cameras and other security equipment and employing extra staff. Both alternatives are very expensive. In 1990 it was estimated that over £130 000 million of goods were stolen from retailers in the UK.

There are some trades, such as jewellery and bespoke tailoring, for which the very large outlet is not entirely suitable, and in these areas the small retailer still prevails. But elsewhere it is probable that the trend towards the large store will continue. The emergence of hypermarkets covering several acres shows this.

## 3.7   Questions

1. Make a list of the functions of retailers.
2. Make a list of the main kinds of retailer.
3. For each kind of retailer, state which functions – if any – are not provided.
4. Why are there so many different kinds of retailer?
5. Name two voluntary groups of retailers. What advantages do they have for their members?
6. Give five reasons why the number of multiple stores has increased in recent years.
7. Why do you think there are fewer retail co-operative societies than there were twenty years ago?
8. Explain what is meant by (a) branded goods, (b) pre-packaging. How are these concepts related to the growth of self-service shops?
9. Why has the development of hypermarkets and superstores increased in recent years?
10. (a)  Why have large retailers grown rapidly in the last twenty years?
    (b)  How do small retailers still survive?
11. Select some goods from mail order catalogues or the colour supplements of Sunday newspapers. Compare their prices with those of similar goods available in your locality. What explanations are there for the differences?

**Table 3.1**  Retail trade in the United Kingdom

|  | Number of businesses | | Number of outlets | | Value of sales (£m) | |
| --- | --- | --- | --- | --- | --- | --- |
|  | 1982 | 1989 | 1982 | 1989 | 1982 | 1989 |
| Single-outlet retailers | 203 160 | 215 613 | 203 160 | 215 613 | 21 090 | 32 702 |
| Small multiple retailers | 28 660 | 25 779 | 76 350 | 67 878 | 9 610 | 13 976 |
| Large multiple retailers | 1 140 | 895 | 70 160 | 66 522 | 39 080 | 71 892 |
| Total | 232 960 | 242 287 | 349 670 | 350 013 | 69 780 | 118 570 |

12. Table 3.1 summarizes aspects of the UK retail trade in 1982 and 1989.
    (a) Draw bar charts to show the changes that occurred in the number of businesses, the number of outlets and the value of sales for each type of retailer between 1982 and 1989.
    (b) Describe the main trends that are revealed by the statistics given in the table.
    (c) Explain why these trends have developed.
    (d) What evidence is there in the table to suggest that retail firms are growing in size?
    (e) Explain carefully the term *multiple retailer*.
    (f) Give three examples of multiple retailers in different parts of the retail trade.

# UNIT 4

# The wholesale trade

## 4.1  Introduction

Specialization and division of labour are the main characteristics of the industrial and commercial systems of the advanced countries. These two factors have
led to mass production and the standardization of output. Firms and factories
turn out their goods in vast quantities and may spend thousands of pounds on
both materials and labour to produce the goods. The firm may have used its
own money, which could otherwise be earning interest at the bank; alternatively, it may have borrowed money from the bank, in which case interest is
being paid. It is thus important that the goods are sold rapidly, so that the firm
does not have too much capital tied up in stocks of finished goods.

On the other hand, final consumers only want to buy small quantities of
goods at any one time. For consumers this problem is overcome by the
existence of retailers who hold stocks of goods ready to sell in small quantities
to individual customers. Producers are helped over the problem in many
industries by the existence of *wholesalers*, who buy in very large quantities
from manufacturers and sell in smaller amounts to retailers. The wholesaler
thus acts as a kind of reservoir, which is kept topped up by large inflows of
goods from a limited number of manufacturers and emptied by smaller out-
flows of goods to a large number of retailers.

There are, however, several variations on this pattern of distribution, as we
saw in Unit 2.2. As retail units get larger they may deal directly with the
manufacturer, buying in large quantities and redistributing the goods to their
branches in smaller amounts. Some manufacturers sell direct to the consumer,
cutting out both wholesaler and retailer. But whether there is a separate
wholesaler or not, the job of holding stocks and releasing them in small
quantities still has to be done. It is important, therefore, that we examine the
role of wholesalers in detail – the more so as they are frequently accused of
being unproductive.

First let us identify the different kinds of wholesaler.

## 4.2 Types of wholesaler

The channel of distribution for any given product depends on several influences.

(a) *The nature of the product* Perishable goods have to be treated differently from durable ones; some goods are mass-produced, while others are made to order by craftsmen.

(b) *The conditions of production* Manufactured goods are normally produced on a steady, continuous basis with some goods being completed every day, but agricultural produce may be harvested in only one month of the year. Some goods are home-produced, while others are only obtainable from overseas.

(c) *The demand for the product* Demand is continuous for many goods, but for others, such as Christmas cards or swimming costumes, it is seasonal.

As you can see, many combinations are possible and it would be surprising if all goods could be treated alike on their way from the producer to the retailer or consumer. We can, in fact, identify three types of wholesaler: general, specialist, and cash-and-carry.

**General wholesalers** may operate on a national or regional basis; some serve a strictly local market. General wholesalers normally stock a wide range of goods and need a substantial amount of capital to finance their large warehouses, stock and advertising, and to pay the salaries of the salesmen they send round to obtain orders from retailers.

**Specialist wholesalers** or merchants restrict their activities to a particular trade and to a particular area. There is almost certainly a builders' merchant in your home town who carries a wide range of materials for resale to local builders or do-it-yourself shops. In large cities there are often wholesale fruit and vegetable markets selling to retailers over a fairly wide area.

**Cash-and-carry wholesalers** have developed rapidly in recent years, especially in the grocery business, where they have about two-thirds of the wholesale trade. Their name indicates their method of trading: they do not allow credit purchases and they do not usually offer transport facilities. Since customers have to transport their own goods, cash-and-carry wholesalers usually have local markets. Sometimes they deal with the general public as well as with retailers.

In the electrical goods and household furniture trade this has led to the rise of *discount stores* (see Unit 3.3.9), which are a mixture of wholesaler and retailer. Like orthodox wholesalers, they operate from large, often sparsely decorated premises and they buy in large quantities. Like retailers, they sell to the public in small quantities.

## 4.3   The functions of the wholesaler

We know that the general purpose of wholesalers is to facilitate the flow of goods from the producer to the consumer. In fulfilling this role they provide a range of services both to producers and to retailers.

### 4.3.1   *Warehousing*

We have seen that manufacturers produce goods in large quantities and need to sell them quickly. Wholesalers enable them to do this, by undertaking to buy the manufacturers' output in bulk and store it in warehouses until it is required by retailers. If the wholesalers did not exist, either the manufacturers would incur the expense of warehousing the goods or retailers would have to buy in much larger quantities. The provision of warehousing by wholesalers brings many incidental benefits for both producers and retailers – and, indeed, for consumers.

### 4.3.2   *Marketing*

To some extent the wholesaler relieves producers of the task of finding a market for their goods. Retailers may visit the wholesaler's warehouse or

**Fig. 4.1** In a wholesale warehouse, large quantities of goods and convenient access for trucks and trollies are more important than attractive displays

showrooms, which gives the wholesaler the opportunity of promoting the sale of goods by means of effective displays. Wholesalers may also undertake other kinds of advertising on behalf of manufacturers, thereby helping their sales. Nevertheless, most producers do maintain their own representatives and sales force to visit shops and promote their products. They need to keep a close eye on market trends.

### 4.3.3  A reservoir

The wholesaler's services include providing a market for the manufacturer and, in just the same way, a source of supply to retailers. Since they are offered a wide selection of goods from many different manufacturers, they are saved a lot of effort: they do not have to visit each individual manufacturer to choose their goods. Without wholesalers the distribution of goods from manufacturers to retailers would require a far greater number of separate journeys and transactions, as fig. 4.2 shows. Wholesalers reduce not only the number of transactions and journeys, but also the clerical work that goes with them. Some of the benefits of this should accrue to the consumer, in the form of lower prices.

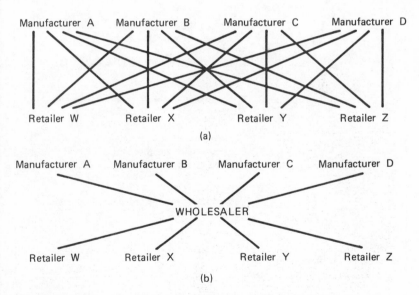

**Fig. 4.2** The importance of the wholesaler: (a) wholesaler omitted; (b) wholesaler included

### 4.3.4  Breaking bulk

One of the essential functions of the wholesaler is that of *breaking bulk* – that is, buying large quantities of goods and dividing them into smaller quantities for the retailer. In the past the wholesaler was often responsible for the packaging and branding of goods as well, but today this is more commonly undertaken by the manufacturer. In the tea trade, however, wholesalers are still responsible for *blending*: teas are bought in bulk from various sources and mixed by the wholesaler to produce the correct blend. It is at this stage, too, that the grading of goods sometimes take place. This is especially important in the commodity markets where, as we shall see in Unit 4.6, dealers may be buying or selling materials which have not yet been produced.

### 4.3.5    Price stability

In Unit 4.3.1 we saw that warehousing is important to the smooth marketing of those goods where production or demand is seasonal. An incidental role of the wholesaler in carrying large stocks of such goods is as a controller of the price movements that would otherwise occur. If no one were prepared to hold stocks of, say, seasonal agricultural produce, we could expect their price to be very low when they were being harvested and exceptionally high at other times of

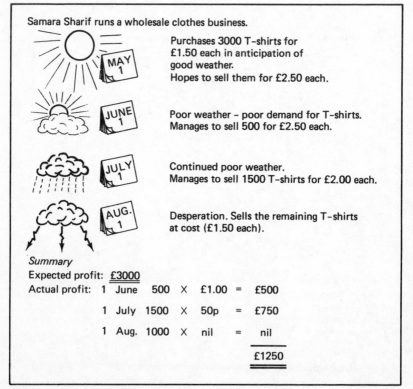

Samara Sharif runs a wholesale clothes business.

MAY 1 — Purchases 3000 T-shirts for £1.50 each in anticipation of good weather. Hopes to sell them for £2.50 each.

JUNE 1 — Poor weather – poor demand for T-shirts. Manages to sell 500 for £2.50 each.

JULY 1 — Continued poor weather. Manages to sell 1500 T-shirts for £2.00 each.

AUG. 1 — Desperation. Sells the remaining T-shirts at cost (£1.50 each).

*Summary*
Expected profit:  £3000

| Actual profit: | | | | | |
|---|---|---|---|---|---|
| 1 June | 500 | X | £1.00 | = | £500 |
| 1 July | 1500 | X | 50p | = | £750 |
| 1 Aug. | 1000 | X | nil | = | nil |
| | | | | | £1250 |

**Fig. 4.3**  Risk-bearing in the fashion trade

the year. By buying the produce at harvest time and releasing it gradually over the year, the wholesaler can eliminate the wilder price fluctuations. On the other hand it is still possible for unscrupulous dealers to hold stocks of goods and wait for market prices to rise, so that they can then sell at an unusually high profit.

### 4.3.6 Risk-bearing

In holding large stocks of goods or materials, the wholesaler also removes a number of risks from the shoulders of producers and retailers.

First, the goods bought in bulk by the wholesaler – giving a ready market for the manufacturer's output – may fall in price or go out of fashion before they can be passed on to the retailer. Heavy losses may be incurred. (This is a problem for the retailer too, but a less important one, since retail stocks are smaller.) The wholesaler also bears the risk that goods will deteriorate or be damaged while stored, and must take appropriate steps to prevent this from happening.

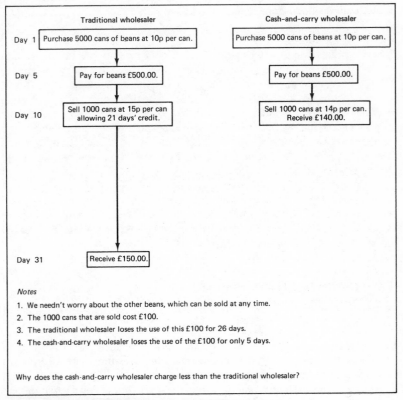

| | Traditional wholesaler | Cash-and-carry wholesaler |
|---|---|---|
| Day 1 | Purchase 5000 cans of beans at 10p per can. | Purchase 5000 cans of beans at 10p per can. |
| Day 5 | Pay for beans £500.00. | Pay for beans £500.00. |
| Day 10 | Sell 1000 cans at 15p per can allowing 21 days' credit. | Sell 1000 cans at 14p per can. Receive £140.00. |
| Day 31 | Receive £150.00. | |

*Notes*
1. We needn't worry about the other beans, which can be sold at any time.
2. The 1000 cans that are sold cost £100.
3. The traditional wholesaler loses the use of this £100 for 26 days.
4. The cash-and-carry wholesaler loses the use of the £100 for only 5 days.

Why does the cash-and-carry wholesaler charge less than the traditional wholesaler?

**Fig. 4.4** Wholesaler finance

Many of the risks that the wholesaler takes are related to financial arrangements. The manufacturer spends large sums of money on raw materials,
components and wages in order to produce goods. Once they have been
delivered to the wholesaler, payment is expected fairly promptly – in commercial terms, the wholesaler is allowed a short period of credit. The manufacturer
needs prompt payment so that the production of the next batch of goods can be
financed. On the other hand, small retailers cannot usually afford to pay cash
for their supplies from the wholesaler until they have sold the goods to the
consumers. They therefore need a longer period of credit, which is normally
allowed by the wholesaler, who thus takes the risk of a retailer defaulting on a
debt. You can see, therefore, that the wholesaler needs a large amount of
capital in order to engage in this kind of arrangement with suppliers and
customers.

### 4.3.7  Delivery
Wholesalers generally deliver goods to retailers, thereby saving them the
expense of running their own van or lorry. In addition they often make it their
job to collect goods from suppliers.

### 4.3.8  Information
It is sometimes said that the wholesalers are a useful source of information to
producers and retailers, and to some extent this is true. They can, for example,
tell retailers about new products that are becoming available, although this is
more likely to be done either through the trade press or by representatives
making direct contact with the retailers. Wholesalers might also let producers
know which of their goods are selling well and which are less acceptable to the
public, but the producers can make their own assessment of this from the
orders they receive, so the importance of the wholesaler in this respect should
not be exaggerated.


We can now see that the wholesaler provides a wide range of services to
producers, retailers and, indirectly, to consumers. Without these services the
distribution of goods would be far less efficient than it is.


## 4.4  The decline of the wholesaler
Although small retailers still need their services, wholesalers are declining in
importance. There are four main reasons for this:

(a) the growth of large retailers who can undertake their own wholesaling,
    and who buy direct from manufacturers (over two-thirds of groceries are
    now traded in this way, avoiding the wholesaler);
(b) the tendency of some manufacturers to establish their own retail outlets
    and to sell direct to the consumer;

(c) the growth of goods which have been pre-packed and branded by the manufacturer;
(d) the decision by many manufacturers to sell direct to retailers so that they can push their own products more than the wholesaler would.

Even if the wholesaler is eliminated, however, his functions remain and either the producer or the retailer must undertake them. So we cannot expect his decline to result in spectacular price reductions.

## 4.5   Other kinds of middleman

Wholesalers are the best-known example of *middlemen*, traders who provide links between other traders. In some trades there are specialists who are not really wholesalers but perform some of the services of wholesalers. Three of these – brokers, factors and *del credere* agents – are important in certain circumstances.

**Brokers** are also middlemen. They are *agents* who work on behalf of a *principal*: their job is to find buyers for the seller's goods. They are not responsible for the delivery of the goods, for they do not normally have them in their possession; the buyer and seller make their own arrangements over this. Brokers, like all agents, receive a commission for their services.

**Factors** are a special kind of agent in that they do not merely bring buyer and seller into contact with each other, but actually have the goods in their possession. They are especially important in the export trade (see Unit 20.5.1).

**Del credere** agents guarantee a sale for their principals. They charge a higher commission for their services because they run the risk of being left with goods on their hands. The ordinary broker does not carry this risk.

## 4.6   The commodity markets

So far we have seen wholesalers as a link between manufacturers and retailers. Other organizations that deal in large quantities of goods, but which are not normally regarded as wholesalers, are the firms which operate in the commodity markets, buying and selling large quantities of agricultural produce, raw materials and metals, using a variety of different systems. It is appropriate that we should deal with them at this point.

A *market* is any arrangement which allows buyers and sellers to get in touch with each other. Commodity markets are found in many international trading centres but the oldest are those established in London, mainly in the nineteenth century when large amounts of raw materials began to be imported to sustain manufacturing industries. They are complex organizations dealing in valuable consignments. The people who work in them – frequently the agents or brokers described above – develop a high degree of skill in buying and selling a narrow range of items. We will consider briefly a few of the main markets.

### 4.6.1    The London Commodity Exchange

The Exchange provides facilities for the marketing of a wide range of commodities such as coffee, cocoa, vegetable oils and rubber. The methods of dealing vary: sometimes the goods are sold by auction, sometimes brokers and dealers make private arrangements. The goods themselves do not actually pass through the Exchange – they are sold by description or by sample. For example, a coffee blender in The Netherlands who needs a supply of coffee from Kenya may well instruct a broker in London to buy the coffee, which will then be delivered direct from Kenya to The Netherlands without going near the Commodity Exchange.

### 4.6.2    The London Metal Exchange

A variety of metals are bought and sold here, where the method of dealing is known as *ring trading*. The members assemble around a ring painted on the floor. Each metal is traded for five minutes, and during that time dealers call out their bids or the prices they want for the metal in question. Clerks keep a record of the deals made in this rather unusual and often noisy way. The process is repeated for each metal several times a day. Between these sessions a great deal of private trading occurs between members. Ring trading, which is not confined to the Metal Exchange, ensures that prevailing prices are well known to all interested parties.

Not all metal is obtained through the Exchange. A company manufacturing copper pipes probably obtains most of its raw material direct from smelters. But if extra supplies are suddenly needed, or if there is a surplus of copper to dispose of, the company will probably deal through the Exchange.

### 4.6.3    The London Corn Exchange

Established in the middle of the eighteenth century, the London Corn Exchange provides a centralized market for all kinds of cereals produced in the United Kingdom.

### 4.6.4    The Baltic Exchange

The main business of the Baltic Exchange is the chartering (hiring) of ships and aircraft (or space on them) but there is also a long-established trade in grain, seeds and oils. Trade is by description only: there are not even any samples for dealers to inspect. Wheat, for example, can be graded according to its type and quality. All the dealers know what is implied by the various gradings, and business proceeds on this basis. This itself means that only approved persons can deal: the public – in this case the industrialists who need raw materials – always deal through agents or brokers.

There are many other specialized markets – we can mention only these few here. One more problem remains to be examined, however: the time-scale involved in purchasing goods in the commodity markets.

## 4.7   Futures

If you were running a manufacturing firm needing materials for immediate use – to meet an unexpected order, for example – you could instruct a broker to obtain the material required, agreeing to pay the going price in the market for immediate delivery – the 'spot' price, as it is called.

On the other hand, suppose you are a manufacturer wanting to buy metal for machinery that you are going to produce in three months' time. You need to be sure that you can buy that metal at a fixed price. During the next three months its price may rise, however, causing you a loss if you have agreed to sell the machine at a fixed price. You could overcome this problem by buying the metal now and storing it until you need it, but this would tie up your capital unnecessarily.

The alternative policy would be for you to buy *futures* – that is, arrange to buy the metal from a dealer at an agreed price in three months' time. If the price rises in the interval, you are safeguarded by your *future* agreement; if the price falls you need not worry, for you will have based the cost of the machine on the agreed *future* price.

This system also benefits the sellers of metals. By arranging future contracts they can safeguard themselves against a fall in price, for their client will have to buy at the agreed price, even if it is higher than the prevailing market price. Of course, if the price rises after the future contract has been made, the seller will be bound to sell at the lower price. On the other hand, other uncommitted supplies will probably be available for sale at the new market price.

The buying or selling of futures is a form of 'hedging' – the practice whereby a buyer guards against a future rise in price, or a seller guards against a possible fall in price.

It is an important feature of the commodity markets that these extra facilities are available to help traders.

## 4.8   Questions

1. Why are wholesalers sometimes called 'middlemen'?
2. Why is the wholesaler sometimes referred to as a 'reservoir'?
3. What factors account for the increase in business of cash-and-carry wholesalers?
4. What services not provided by cash-and-carry wholesalers are provided by general wholesalers?
5. Most business activities involve risks. What are the main risks undertaken by wholesalers?

6. Why are wholesalers becoming less important in the distribution of general groceries?

7. (a) In what respects are wholesalers' functions being taken over by manufacturers?

   (b) In what respects are wholesalers' functions being taken over by retailers?

8. Explain how a wholesaler might help to stabilize the price of a good which can only be produced in June and July but for which there is a constant monthly demand.

9. Outline the main factors which have led to a decline in the number of wholesalers.

10. It is sometimes said that the wholesaler simplifies the process of distributing manufactured goods. Give examples to show how this may be true in relation to (a) transport, (b) the amount of paperwork involved.

# The documentation of trade

## 5.1 Introduction

Millions of business transactions take place every day. Most of them consist of
the straightforward sale of goods by a retailer for cash, and there is no need to
keep a specific record of such a transaction. But other transactions are more
complex, and the completion of a deal may be spread over several months. In
such a case it becomes important to keep a clear record of each stage of the
transaction. This can be achieved by each party concerned keeping a kind of
diary in which all deals are recorded. In some markets, such as Lloyd's
insurance market (discussed in Unit 19.5.2), this is exactly what happens; but
in most branches of commerce a more formal record is needed, so that
reference can easily be made to a particular transaction.

There are two types of record. One is the books of account kept by every
firm, showing all its income and expenditure, money owed and money owing.
The study of these belongs to book-keeping and accounting and does not
concern us here. The other type consists of the documents that pass between
buyers and sellers: each side retains copies of the documents it sends, as well as
those it receives, so that it can keep track of the transaction.

The best way to learn about these documents is to examine a hypothetical
transaction between two businesses. Suppose that Mr Smith, who owns and
manages a sports shop, wants to ensure that he has an adequate supply of
equipment for the beginning of the summer season. This is not an industry in
which wholesalers are very active, so he has to contact the suppliers of
equipment direct. He will do this as early as November, to ensure delivery of
the goods he wants at the right time. (Retailers have to look ahead: it is no
good waiting until the end of November to order Christmas cards, or until
April to order Easter eggs.) We will go through the transaction step by step.

## 5.2 The inquiry

Smith is probably in contact with a number of suppliers. If he is not, he will be able to get their names from *trade journals* relating to the industry or from *trade directories*, which list businesses according to the goods or services they supply.

Having obtained the name and address of the supplier, the retailer will make an inquiry as to whether the supplier can let him have the goods he needs, and on what terms the goods would be delivered. It is quite likely that the inquiry would take the form of a letter, as shown in fig. 5.1, but some retailers have specially printed forms on which to make their inquiries. In some cases a telephone call will be enough to obtain the necessary information. Smith will

---

# Thurays Sports Ltd

Telephone Graybury 12345

*10 High Street*
*Graybury*
*Essex WV21 3AB*
*(registered office)*

*Our ref.*  WL/PG/35

The Sales Manager                                    5.11.19..
Sports Supplies Ltd
Willow Road
Haston
Cambridgeshire   XY31 3RR

Dear Sir

We are anxious to increase our range of tennis and cricket
equipment for the forthcoming season.

I would be grateful if you would advise us of the prices at
which you could supply us with the following:

                30 junior tennis racquets
                25 size six cricket bats
                20 boxes of leather cricket balls
                50 boxes of tennis balls

I would be grateful for an early reply.

Yours truly

*T. Smith*

T. Smith
Director

**Directors** T. Smith, J. Thuray
Registered in England: No.987654

---

**Fig. 5.1** An inquiry

probably send the same inquiries to two or three suppliers to be sure that he is buying on the most favourable terms. Of course, if Sports Supplies of Haston has a representative who calls on Thurays Sports, the information on prices will be immediately available.

## 5.3   The quotation

The supplier will reply by sending a *quotation*, which is a statement of

(a) the prices at which he can supply the goods,
(b) the terms on which he can supply them, including any discounts available,
(c) the costs of carriage of the goods, and
(d) the amount of time needed for delivery.

Smith can compare the quotations provided by different suppliers and place his order with the firm that offers the best terms.

In practice, there is often no need for such an inquiry followed by a quotation, because many suppliers circulate *price lists* to their established customers, incorporating the terms on which they do business in the list. Larger firms issue illustrated catalogues, both to their regular customers and to potential customers making inquiries. The catalogue is frequently accompanied by an order form, on which retailers can make their orders. Alternatively, the retailer may have his own order forms printed; this will make his filing tidier, for all the carbon copies will be of the same size.

## 5.4   The order

An order should always contain the following items (compare fig. 5.2):

(a) the names and addresses of the two parties,
(b) a description of each item as well as its catalogue number (to prevent mistakes),
(c) the delivery date required, and
(d) the address to which the consignment is to be sent.

The total cost of the order is not shown, in case the supplier cannot provide all the items listed.

If Sports Supplies already has the goods in stock, it can begin to process the order; if not it will deal with it as soon as possible. In the meantime it may send Thurays an *acknowledgment of the order*, so that Thurays knows it has arrived. If it is the first time that it has dealt with Thurays Sports, Sports Supplies will probably require a *banker's reference* (see Unit 11.12.10) before it will supply goods on credit. A favourable reference will reassure the supplier that a customer has the means of payment.

# Thurays Sports Ltd

Telephone Graybury 12345

VAT reg. 987654321

*10 High Street*
*Graybury*
*Essex WV21 3AB*
*(registered office)*

Order no. 7631

To: Sports Supplies Ltd
    Willow Road
    Haston
    Cambridgeshire XY31 3RR

| Item | Catalogue Number | Quantity | Unit Price |
|---|---|---|---|
| | | | £ |
| Junior tennis racquets | T241 | Thirty | 15.00 |
| Size six cricket bats | C106 | Twenty-five | 20.00 |
| Cricket balls | C193 | 20 boxes (6 per box) | 48.00 |
| Tennis balls | T109 | 50 boxes (6 per box) | 6.00 |

Delivery: March 19..  to this address

Signed:  *T. Smith*
Date:   1.12.19..

Directors T. Smith, J. Thuray
Registered in England: No. 987654

**Fig. 5.2** An order

## 5.5    The invoice

Perhaps the single most important document in the transaction is the invoice, which is the bill for the goods sent by the supplier to his customer. A typical invoice is shown in fig. 5.3.

There are several important points to notice about the invoice.

(a)  An invoice is prepared for each delivery by the company, and is sent to the customer. It can accompany the goods, but is often sent separately.

(b)  When the invoice is prepared, several copies are made. One copy, identical with that shown in fig. 5.3, is retained by the supplier's accounts department, so that it can keep track of money owed. The other copies (which we deal with in Unit 5.6) have the prices and terms of business omitted.

# INVOICE

43011

## Sports Supplies Ltd

Willow Road
Haston
Cambridgeshire XY31 3RR
(registered office)

*Telephone Haston 31111*
*Telex 0011 2345*

VAT reg. 831765123

To: Thurays Sports Ltd
    10 High Street
    Graybury
    Essex  WV21 3AB

*Date:* 5.3.19..

*Your order no:* 7631

| Quantity | Description | Unit Price | Total | VAT | Total |
|---|---|---|---|---|---|
| | | £ | £ | £ | £ |
| 30 | T241 Racquets | 15.00 | 450.00 | 78.75 | 528.75 |
| 25 | C106 Bats | 20.00 | 600.00 | 105.00 | 705.00 |
| 20 | C193 Cricket balls | 48.00 | 960.00 | 168.00 | 1128.00 |
| 50 | T109 Tennis balls | 6.00 | 300.00 | 52.50 | 352.50 |
| | | | | Invoice total | 2714.25 |

Terms of trading:     7 days settlement:     5%
                      28 days settlement:    2½%

E. & O. E.

*Directors* F. Ball, C. Batt
Registered in England: No. 876543

**Fig. 5.3** An invoice

(c)  The invoice contains:
   (i)   The appropriate names and addresses.
   (ii)  A reference to the customer's order number, so that Thurays Sports
         can check the invoice against the goods ordered. Similarly, Sports
         Supplies gives a reference number of its own, in case Thurays has a
         query to raise.
   (iii) The supplier's registration number for Value Added Tax (VAT). This
         tax is levied on almost all transactions, but most businesses that pay it

are entitled to claim it back from the Government. For example, if a retailer collects VAT amounting to £500 from his customers but has himself paid £200 VAT to his suppliers, he will send only £300 to the authorities. The VAT invoice enables traders to prove that they have paid the tax (see Unit 22.3).

(iv) A description of the goods, their unit price, the VAT payable and their total price. The total amount due for the order is given at the bottom.

(v) The terms of business. In this example, if the account is settled within seven days, a 5 per cent discount will be allowed (that is, 5 per cent can be deducted from the bill). Payment after seven days but within 28 days entitles Thurays Sports to a 2½ per cent discount. The function of this discount is to encourage early payment. It is called a *cash discount* even though the payment will normally be made by cheque, not cash.

(d) For convenience we have assumed that the prices shown on the invoice are the trade prices, that is, the prices that the buyer has to pay. In this case, Smith will subsequently add on a percentage to cover his expenses and to make a profit. Frequently, however, the invoice will show the *retail* price of the goods being supplied. Clearly, the retailer would be unable to buy and sell at the same price and still make a profit! There would therefore be another entry on the invoice – *trade discount*, perhaps of 30 per cent. In other words the retailer, being in the trade and not a final consumer, can buy the goods at a discount of 30 per cent of the price stated.

(e) Many firms have the letters 'E. & O.E.' printed on their invoices. This is an abbreviation for *errors and omissions excepted* and safeguards the supplier against any clerical errors that may have occurred during the compilation of the invoice. (In fact the invoice in fig. 5.3 does contain a clerical error, which will be dealt with in Unit 5.8. Can you spot the error?)

(f) The invoice is not normally a request for immediate payment. Many retailers will receive several deliveries each month from the same suppliers and will probably settle their account on a monthly basis.

Now we must see what happens to the other copies of the invoice.

## 5.6   Advice note, delivery note, consignment note

These terms are often used in different ways by different people (there is no legal definition of them).

### 5.6.1   *Advice note*

This contains details of the goods being sent. It is sometimes sent before the goods, to advise the buyer to expect delivery of the order shortly. If the goods do not arrive within a few days, it would be sensible to begin to make inquiries about them. Sometimes, on the other hand, the advice note is enclosed with the goods, enabling the recipient to check that the right goods have been sent.

### 5.6.2 Delivery note
This accompanies the goods, and once they have been delivered it is signed by the buyer or the buyer's representative and handed back to the van driver as proof of delivery. Frequently the driver brings both the advice note and the delivery note and asks the buyer to sign one copy.

### 5.6.3 Consignment note
This note is different from the other two, in that it is used when the supplier firm uses transport other than its own to deliver the goods. The consignment note is a formal instruction to the transport firm to accept the goods and deliver them to the customer. The driver usually wants the customer to sign a copy of the consignment note to prove that the goods have been delivered.

## 5.7 The debit note
We saw that invoices often carry the proviso 'E. & O.E.', which entitles the supplier of the goods to correct any errors that have crept into the invoice. The *debit note* is a document sent to a customer who has been undercharged on an invoice.

Suppose, for example, the typist preparing the invoice types £2451.00 instead of £2541.00. The matter can be corrected, once the mistake has been discovered, by sending the customer a debit note for £90.00. But many firms do not bother to draw up a separate debit note. They find it more convenient to send another invoice to rectify the mistake.

## 5.8 The credit note
The mistake on the invoice may be in the opposite direction: in fact Thurays Sports has been overcharged. The cricket bats should have cost £500 plus £87.50 VAT. To correct this, Sports Supplies issues a *credit note* (fig. 5.4) reducing the price by £100 and the VAT by £17.50. The credit note is normally printed in red to distinguish it from other documents (for it represents a flow of money in the opposite direction to the usual one). There are several possible reasons for issuing a credit note.

(a) There has been an overcharge, as above.
(b) Damaged goods have been returned by the retailer.
(c) Packing cases or crates have been returned by the retailer, who would have been charged a deposit on these on the invoice.
(d) The retailer has returned gift vouchers or coupons to the supplier. The retailer has allowed customers a cash discount on these and is entitled to claim payment from the producer. Rather than insisting on cash, a retailer

# CREDIT NOTE

## Sports Supplies Ltd

*Telephone Haston 31111*
*Telex 0011 2345*

*Willow Road*
*Haston*
*Cambridgeshire XY31 3RR*
*(registered office)*

*VAT reg. 831765123*

*Date:* 13.3.19..

Credit:  Thurays Sports Ltd
         10 High Street
         Graybury
         Essex   WV21 3AB

|  |  | VAT |
|---|---|---|
| Overcharge on invoice 43011 | £100 | £17.50 |

Signed:  *F. Ball.*

*Directors F. Ball, C. Batt*
*Registered in England: No.876543*

**Fig. 5.4** A credit note

is normally prepared to accept a credit note, which will appear in the credit column of the monthly statement, reducing the total payable.

It is important to understand that the *invoice* must never be altered. This is to avoid giving rise to the suspicion that someone is trying to defraud the company. Errors are always adjusted by the issue of another document – another invoice or a debit note when customers have been undercharged, a credit note when they have been overcharged.

## 5.9   The statement

At the end of each month Sports Supplies will send a statement to Thurays Sports, summarizing the transactions that have taken place between them and showing the amount owed by Thurays.

# STATEMENT OF ACCOUNT

## Sports Supplies Ltd

*Telephone Haston 31111*
*Telex 0011 2345*

Willow Road
Haston
Cambridgeshire XY31 3RR
(registered office)

VAT reg. 831765123

Issued:  8.4.19..

Thurays Sports Ltd
10 High Street
Graybury
Essex   WV21 3AB

| Date | Details | Debit | Credit | Balance |
|------|---------|-------|--------|---------|
| 1.3.19.. | Balance b/f | | | 121.07 |
| 3.3 | Cheque | | 121.07 | |
| 5.3 | Invoice 43011 | 2714.25 | | 2714.25 |
| 10.3 | Credit note | | 117.50 | 2596.75 |
| 27.3 | Cheque | | 2541.50 | 55.25 |
| 27.3 | Discount | | 55.25 | |
| 30.3 | Goods | 1811.25 | | 1811.25 |

This statement does not include items dispatched or payments received after **31.3.19..**

*Directors F. Ball, C. Batt*
*Registered in England: No. 876543*

**Fig. 5.5** A statement of account

Like the other documents, the statement contains the names of the two parties and any relevant reference numbers. The statement in fig. 5.5 shows that at the beginning of March, Thurays Sports owed Sports Supplies £121.07. It paid this off by cheque on 3 March. On 5 March the invoice for the goods we dealt with appears. Then someone has realized that there has been an overcharge of £117.50 in respect of the cricket bats. Deducting this £117.50 from the balance we arrive at £2596.75 owing.

On 27 March Thurays Sports decides to settle the balance so that it can qualify for the 2½ per cent discount. We need to be careful here, because Thurays cannot earn a discount on the Value Added Tax (the Government wants all of that). If we refer back to the invoice and allow for the credit note, we find that the outstanding amount of £2596.75 can be broken down into £2210 for the goods plus £386.75 VAT. The discount has to be calculated on the £2210 so we get

$$£2210 \times \frac{2\frac{1}{2}}{100} = £55.25$$

So Thurays has to send a cheque for £2596.75 minus £55.25, that is £2541.50. (This is £2154.75 for Sports Supplies plus £386.75 VAT.) This leaves a balance of £55.25, and when Sports Supplies enters this on the statement the balance disappears.

Finally, on 30 March Thurays Sports is invoiced for goods worth £1811.25 including VAT. This remained outstanding at the end of the month.

The accountant at Thurays Sports should of course check the statement against the invoices and other relevant documents, including the company's cheque book, to ensure that the balance is correct.

## 5.10   Payment and receipt

Normally the customer settles his account through the banking system, paying by cheque or bank giro (see Units 11.4 and 11.7). If payment is by cheque Thurays probably does not want a receipt, as the cleared cheque would be accepted as proof of payment should a dispute arise. If payment is by credit transfer, the bank itself issues a receipt. In the unlikely event of Thurays paying by cash, it would want a receipt from Sports Supplies as proof of payment. Even if it pays by cheque it may insist on a receipt, so as to complete its records.

We have now looked at all the main documents used in business. Every stage of a transaction between two parties can be traced by these documents, and each party to the transaction is careful to keep the documents it receives as well as copies of those it sends. They are useful at the end of the trading year when firms make up their books to determine their profits.

These days, much of this documentation is dealt with by computers. The basic processes are the same, however, and the need for a permanent record is just as important.

## 5.11   Questions

1. Why are business documents necessary?
2. As a retailer, how might you discover the goods and terms offered by a wholesaler or manufacturer?
3. What are the essential features of an invoice?
4. Distinguish between cash discount and trade discount.

5. Distinguish between a credit note and a debit note, showing when each is used.
6. What is the purpose of the statement sent by a supplier to his customer? Why should the customer check the statement carefully?
7. Why do some business documents contain the letters 'E. & O.E.'?
8. 'If you pay by cheque, a receipt is not necessary.' Why?
9. Find out the meaning of the term *banker's reference*. Why is it important to a trader dealing with a new customer?
10. Explain the purpose of each of the documents used when A. Trader buys goods for the first time from A. Wholesaler on credit.
11. A. Vernon regularly buys goods on credit from T. Littlewood. On 5 July 1992 he orders the following goods:

> 3 dozen video tapes at £3.00 each + VAT
> 100 audio cassettes at 60 pence each + VAT
> 10 personal stereos at £15 each + VAT

The goods and invoice arrive together on 10 July. VAT is charged at 17.5 per cent. A. Vernon receives a trade discount of 40 per cent, and a cash discount of 5 per cent if he pays his bill by 19 July, which he does.

Draw up all the documents involved in this transaction, including the statement of account dated 31 July 1992, assuming that no other transactions took place in that month and allowing for the fact that the original invoice, by mistake, charged for only 8 personal stereos.

(Assume that the balance owed by Vernon on 5 July was £110 including VAT, and that this was paid in full by cheque on 7 July.)

# UNIT 6

# Consumer credit

## 6.1  Introduction

We saw in Unit 5 that transactions between manufacturers, wholesalers and retailers are often conducted on a credit basis: payment is made some time after the goods are delivered. This is known as *trade credit* and is very widespread.

Most consumer transactions are on a cash basis, the customer paying by cash or cheque as soon as the goods are received. But the purchase of consumer durable goods such as washing machines or microwave ovens may require more money than the consumer has available. Rather than waiting to save up the necessary money, the consumer may choose to buy the goods on credit. Of course some consumers are able to pay cash for the goods they want but simply prefer to delay payment for a few weeks or months.

## 6.2  Types of credit

A consumer may be able to borrow the money required from a bank by means of a loan or overdraft, and these are discussed in Unit 11.11. There are many other ways of obtaining credit, however, and they may be divided into short-term credit (usually arranged fairly informally) and medium- or long-term credit, which often involves more formalities.

## 6.3  Short-term credit

### 6.3.1  Credit accounts and budget accounts

Regular customers may be allowed to take delivery of goods at any time and pay for them all at the end of the month. This is clearly similar to trade credit. Many filling-stations offer this arrangement to their customers. The customers sign for the petrol as they buy it and pay for it when they receive the account at the end of the month. They have the assurance that they can obtain petrol without immediate cash, and the proprietor is assured of regular custom from account-holders.

Larger stores sometimes operate *budget accounts* whereby, in return for set monthly payments, the customer can take delivery of goods up to a certain value and further goods whenever the amount owed falls below that value.

### 6.3.2   Credit cards

An extremely popular way of obtaining credit from retailers is by means of a credit card. These cards fall into two broad groups: those that can be used in all kinds of retail outlets – Barclaycard and Access are probably the best known – and those issued by particular retailers for use only in their own stores – Dixons and Marks & Spencer, for example. Both types operate in basically the same way (fig. 6.1).

A credit company enrols on the one hand retailers, garages, hotels and others prepared to accept its card in payment for goods or services, and on the other hand individual people who want to use the card. Cardholders have a credit limit, which is the maximum they can have outstanding on their account. They sign for goods or services supplied to them, and for each purchase they are given a copy of the bill. Another copy bearing the signature and card number is kept by the firm and paid into its bank with the usual cash and cheques. A third copy is sent to the credit card company. The company charges the firm a commission on sales which varies according to the type of business concerned.

Each month every cardholder receives a statement from the credit card company, setting out a record of the purchases made and of the amount owed. Within 25 days of the date of the statement either the whole amount must be paid or, if preferred, only part of it – for example, £5 per month or 5 per cent of the total owing, whichever is greater. Interest accumulates daily and is charged on a monthly basis on any balance on the account that is still outstanding after the 25-day period has expired.

Cards such as Access may also be used to obtain a cash advance from any of the banks operating the scheme, up to the cardholder's credit limit. In this case interest is charged from the day the cash is withdrawn.

The advantages of credit cards to the holders are that there are no formalities involved in obtaining goods on credit, that it is safer to carry the credit card than a large amount of money and that, used properly, the card can provide its holder with up to eight weeks of free credit (fig. 6.2).

The disadvantages are that the rate of interest is high compared with that charged for bank loans, and that consumers tend to spend more when using their cards than when paying by other means, so incurring the high interest rates. It is this that makes the operation profitable for the card companies.

As for retailers, they have the benefit of extra business from people using the cards but the disadvantage of the commission that they have to pay to the credit card company. (Incidentally, the need to pay this commission can result in all consumers paying slightly higher prices for their purchases.)

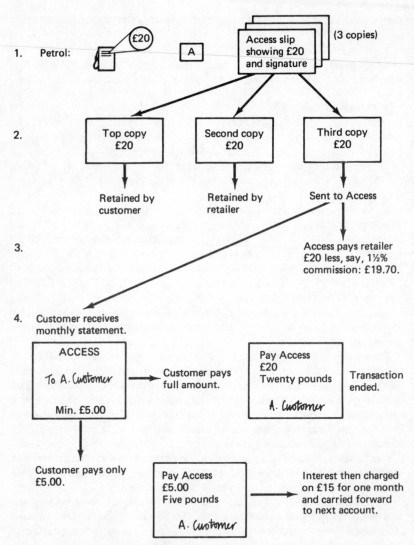

**Fig. 6.1** A transaction using an Access card

### 6.3.3   *Charge cards*

These are very similar to credit cards, but there are two differences. First, there is an initial entrance fee as well as the annual subscription. Secondly, the account must be settled in full each month, so these cards offer only very short-term credit. Perhaps the best known are American Express and Diners Club.

1. Each customer's monthly statement is compiled on a specific day each month – say the first of each month.

2. Payment has to be made within 25 days.

3. Suppose our customer buys a video recorder on 1 January 1992, for £300, paying by Access.

> *Statement*
> Compiled 1.2.92
>
> Payment to arrive by 26.2.92

4. This will appear on the customer's statement of 1 February. This has allowed 31 days' free credit.

5. The statement asks for payment by 26 February.

6. If the £300 is paid on, say, 25 February the customer pays no interest: 56 days' interest-free credit.

7. Meanwhile the £300 could be earning interest in a building society!

**Fig. 6.2** Interest-free credit

### 6.3.4 Check trading

This is a useful type of informal credit for small purchases. The *checks* are available, in various denominations, from agents who have a regular round and who call to collect repayments. The customer can, for example, buy a check for £20, making an initial payment of 5 pence for each £1 borrowed and twenty subsequent payments of the same amount, making £21 in all. The checks can be used to buy goods at a large number of shops participating in the scheme. The cost to the customers is not exorbitant, and the scheme allows them to buy the goods they want at their cash price, without the trouble of filling in documents for more formal credit.

The retailer returns the collected checks to the issuing company, which redeems the face value of the checks less a discount of perhaps 2½ per cent. The retailer who joins the scheme must therefore aim to increase sales sufficiently to offset this fall in profits.

The biggest of the check-issuing companies is Provident Personal Credit Ltd, and so the checks are often known as 'Provident checks'.

## 6.4 Longer-term credit

Sometimes the informal types of credit discussed above are not available to a particular individual for a particular purchase. The customer may be unaware of their existence, or the supplier may not participate in the appropriate schemes. The consumer will then have to arrange more formal credit. The term *hire purchase* is commonly used to describe this kind of credit, but this expression covers several different arrangements, only one of which is, legally, hire purchase.

### 6.4.1 Conditional sale agreement
Under this type of agreement, the goods remain the property of the seller until the purchase price has been paid by instalments, or until other stated conditions have been fulfilled. It is not normally relevant to individual consumers, being used mainly for the sale of plant and equipment to industry. As far as consumers are concerned, so long as the amount of credit involved is not more than £15000, the Consumer Credit Act 1974 has removed any distinction between hire purchase and conditional sales.

### 6.4.2 Hire purchase agreement
The goods are *hired* to the user, who is given the option to purchase them for a token sum at the end of the hire period. The consumer is not obliged to buy them, but it would be most unusual not to do so. Consumer durable goods such as freezers and stereo equipment are sold in this way, and the finance may be provided either by finance houses (see Unit 12.5) or by retailers themselves. The fundamental point is that the goods do not become the property of the purchaser until the last payment has been made.

| Particulars of Goods | | Cash Price Incl. VAT | |
|---|---|---|---|
| Qty. | Description | £ | p |
| | | | |
| | | | |
| | | | |
| | | | |
| | | | |
| | | | |
| | | | |
| | | | |
| | Identification Nos: | | |
| | Total Cash Price (incl. VAT) | | |

| Financial Details and Payments | | £ | p |
|---|---|---|---|
| Total Cash Price | | | |
| Less: Deposit | (a) | | |
|     = Credit Extended | | | |
| Add: Charges | | | |
|     = Balance Payable | (b) | | |
| Total Amount Payable | (a) + (b) | | |
| A.P.R. | | | % |
| Number of monthly payments | | | |
| Date of first payment | | | |
| Subsequent payments on same day of each succeeding month | | | |
| Amount of each payment | | | |
| Amount of final payment (if different) | | | |

**TERMINATION: YOUR RIGHTS**
You have a right to end this agreement. If you wish to do so, you should write to the person authorized to receive your payments. We will then be entitled to the return of the goods and to half the total amount payable under this agreement, that is £ .[1] If you have already paid at least this amount plus any overdue instalments, you will not have to pay any more, provided you have taken reasonable care of the goods.

[1] Insert one-half of the total amount payable.

**REPOSSESSION: YOUR RIGHTS**
If you fail to keep to your side of this agreement but you have paid at least one-third of the total amount payable under this agreement, that is £ ,[2] we may not take back the goods against your wishes unless we get a court order. (In Scotland, we may need to get a court order at any time.) If we do take them without your consent or a court order, you have the right to get back all the money you have paid under the agreement.

[2] Insert one-third of the total amount payable

**Fig. 6.3** Part of a hire purchase agreement

### 6.4.3 Credit sale agreement

On payment of the deposit or first instalment the goods become the property of the buyer, who undertakes to buy them through five or more instalments. Since the seller has no security for the goods this kind of agreement is not normally used for expensive items, but it is commonly employed where goods have very little second-hand value and where there would be little point in the seller repossessing the goods should the buyer default. This kind of sale is widely used by the mail order companies, for example.

In the rest of this Unit we shall for convenience use the term *hire purchase* to cover all these three types of agreement. In all such agreements the consumer undertakes to pay the purchase price plus interest, where charged. (In very competitive situations it is not uncommon to see offers of interest-free credit, particularly during special sales promotions.) The total purchase price is normally payable by equal instalments. On most agreements the seller will insist on the payment of an initial deposit of perhaps 25 or 30 per cent of the selling price, this sometimes being a legal requirement laid down by the Government.

The retail firm may choose to finance the sale itself, but it is more likely that it will act as the agent of a finance house. In this case the retailer actually sells the product to the consumer on behalf of the finance house, which pays the retailer the full value of the goods covered. Thereafter the consumer's payments are either passed on by the retailer to the finance house or paid direct to the finance house by the consumer. The process is illustrated in fig. 6.4.

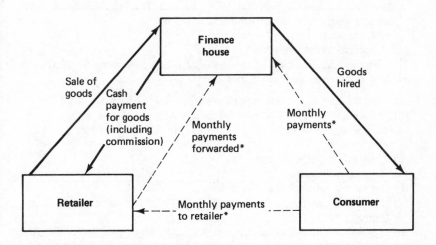

*Payments may follow either route to the finance house.

**Fig. 6.4** Financing a hire purchase agreement

**1 Payment**
Before signing this agreement you must have paid the deposit shown overleaf. By signing this agreement you agree to pay the Balance Payable by making the payments set out overleaf, by their specified dates, to us at the address given overleaf or to any person or address notified by us in writing. Punctual payment is essential. If you pay by post you do so at your own risk.

**2 Failure to pay on time**
We have the right to charge interest at the annual percentage rate shown overleaf on all overdue amounts. This interest will be calculated on a daily basis from the date the amount falls due until it is received and will run both before and after any judgment.

**3 Ownership of the goods**
You will become the owner of the goods only after we have received all amounts payable under this agreement including under Clauses 2 and 11. Until then the goods remain our property and your rights are solely those of a hirer.

**4 Selling or disposing of the goods**
You must keep the goods safely at your address and you may not sell or dispose of them or transfer your rights under this agreement. You may only part with the goods to have them repaired. You may not use the goods as security for any of your obligations.

**5 Repair of the goods**
You must keep the goods in good condition and repair at your own expense. You are responsible for all loss of or damage to them (except fair wear and tear) even if caused by acts or events outside your control. You must not allow a repairer or any other person to obtain a lien on or a right to retain the goods.

**6 Change of address**
You must immediately notify us in writing of any change of your address.

**7 Inspection**
You must allow us or our representative to inspect and test the goods at all reasonable times.

**8 Insurance**
You must keep the goods insured under a fully comprehensive policy of insurance at your own expense. You must notify us of loss of or damage to the goods and hold any monies payable under the policy in trust for us. You irrevocably authorize us to collect the monies from the insurers. If a claim is made against the insurers we may at our absolute discretion conduct any negotiations and effect any settlement with the insurers and you agree to abide by such settlement.

**Fig. 6.5** Part of the conditions attached to a hire purchase agreement

## 6.5    The Consumer Credit Act 1974

You can judge from the documents reproduced in fig. 6.5 that credit agreements are fairly complicated. Most of us are not very good at reading and understanding this kind of thing. To make sure that we are not exploited, all such agreements are subject to the Consumer Credit Act 1974. The Act, whose provisions are supervised by the Office of Fair Trading, seeks to protect consumers under four broad headings, as follows.

### 6.5.1    Right to information

The most important aspect of this relates to the financial particulars which must be given to the customer, notably:

(a) a description of the goods together with their cash price,
(b) the amount of any deposit or advance payment,
(c) the amount of credit to be provided (or, in the case of a credit card, the credit limit),
(d) the total charge for credit,
(e) the rate of interest,
(f) the timing and amount of repayments,
(g) the Annual Percentage Rate (APR) of the total charge for credit (see below),
(h) a summary of the consumer's rights and obligations under the Act, together with a warning such as that shown in fig. 6.6.

The annual percentage interest rate is important, for interest rates can be quoted in misleading ways. Suppose you buy a refrigerator on hire purchase,

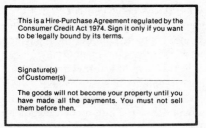

This is a Hire-Purchase Agreement regulated by the Consumer Credit Act 1974. Sign it only if you want to be legally bound by its terms.

Signature(s)
of Customer(s) _____

The goods will not become your property until you have made all the payments. You must not sell them before then.

**Fig. 6.6** The warning that must be read before a hire purchase agreement is signed

and when you have paid the deposit you borrow £100 from the finance company for one year at a quoted rate of interest of 16 per cent. This is the *nominal rate*. You agree to repay your total debt of £116 in twelve equal instalments of £9.67. Each month you repay one-twelfth of the interest (£1.33) and one-twelfth of the sum borrowed (£8.34). So at the end of the first month you pay £1.33 interest for borrowing £100 for one-twelfth of a year. At the end of the second month you pay £1.33 interest again, but you have not borrowed £100 for two months. Since you repaid £8.34 at the end of the first month you have borrowed only £91.66 for two months. The interest rate is therefore higher than the quoted rate. In the last month you owe only £8.34 (one-twelfth of £100), and yet you still pay £1.33 interest. If you average out the rate of interest paid on each monthly instalment, you find that the true rate of interest (Annual Percentage Rate) is approximately double the quoted rate. If you bear in mind that on the opening day you owe £100, after 6 months £50 and after 12 months nothing you will realize that *on average* you owe £50 – this explains why the nominal and true rates are so different.

The customer must be given a copy of the agreement within seven days of its being signed. If it is signed at any place other than the business premises of the seller the customer must receive two copies, one upon signature and one by post within seven days.

### 6.5.2 Right to withdraw
If you go to the business premises of a firm and sign a hire purchase agreement, you are totally bound by the agreement. But if you sign the agreement anywhere other than at the business premises of the firm, you have the right to withdraw from the agreement within five days of receiving your second copy of the agreement (which comes by post). Any deposit that you have paid becomes repayable and the supplier is under an obligation to collect the goods from you. Your only obligation is to keep the goods safely for three weeks.

The reason for this provision was that unscrupulous door-to-door salesmen often persuaded people to sign agreements for goods that they didn't really want by presenting them in a very favourable light in the comfort of the consumer's own home.

### 6.5.3   Right to terminate the agreement

Despite the safeguards we have already discussed, there are still occasions where the hirer becomes unable to continue the repayments. The Act gives the hirer the right to terminate the agreement at any time, once any installation charges plus half of the total purchase price have been paid. If half the price has not yet been paid the agreement can be terminated if the hirer pays the balance up to 50 per cent and returns the goods, paying for any damage done to them. This right exists only under a true hire purchase agreement. If the goods are subject to a credit sale agreement the full amount must be paid.

Under the Consumer Credit Act, hirers who settle their accounts early are entitled to a rebate of a proportion of the credit charges that are otherwise payable for the transaction.

### 6.5.4   Right to retain possession of goods

It has happened in the past that impatient finance companies have taken repossession of goods when hirers have fallen slightly in arrears with their payments. Now, once one-third of the total purchase price has been paid by the hirer, the owner cannot repossess the goods without a court order (again this applies only to true hire purchase agreements, not to credit sale agreements). If the owner applies for a court order, the court has certain extra powers:

(a) it may order that the goods be returned to the owner, and
(b) it may vary the terms of the agreement to enable the hirer to fulfil his obligations more easily.

Thus the Consumer Credit Act protects hirers, not only from the suppliers of goods but from themselves. Further protection is given by the Act's provision that all organizations offering consumer credit must be licensed by the Office of Fair Trading, which ensures that appropriate standards are maintained.

The Act makes quite clear to suppliers their rights and obligations, as we have seen, but it also offers them some protection, described in Unit 6.9.

## 6.6   The advantages of buying on credit

The level of credit purchases of various kinds (see fig. 6.7) implies that despite the extra costs, it is an extremely popular way of buying. Its popularity stems largely from the following advantages:

(a) Without hire purchase many people would be unable to obtain consumer durable goods. It is true that they could save up for the goods for a number of years, but the self-discipline needed for this is too great for many. Hire purchase enables people to do their saving retrospectively: once they are committed to their repayments, most people will honour them.
(b) If hire purchase were unavailable it would be the poor who would suffer.

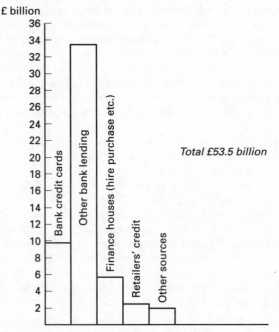

**Fig. 6.7** Outstanding consumer credit, December 1991

The wealthy would be able to pay cash anyway. Refrigerators, freezers and modern heating equipment all raise the material standard of living, and credit purchases enable more people to obtain them.

(c) Mass production needs a mass market. If you are mass-producing packets of detergent your customers can afford to pay cash, but if you are mass-producing kitchen furniture many of them cannot. For consumer durable industries, hire purchase is essential to maintain an adequate turnover. This is true for retailers too: by offering hire purchase facilities, they can attract more customers and increase their profits.

(d) In some industries hire purchase helps to maintain employment. If no one can afford to buy automatic dishwashers, there is no point in employing people to make them. When people buy dishwashers on hire purchase, they are helping to maintain employment in the industry.

## 6.7 Problems linked to credit purchases

We have seen that the Consumer Credit Act was designed to prevent the exploitation of consumers. Even so, a number of problems surround hire purchase and similar transactions.

(a) For reasons which do not concern us here, rates of interest payable on hire purchase and credit charge transactions tend to be higher than those incurred with other forms of borrowing. It would normally be preferable to borrow the money from a bank.

(b) Some consumers overburden themselves with hire purchase repayments. What sounds like a modest repayment when you are buying goods worth £300 or £400 may prove to be difficult to maintain for two or three years. Similarly it is quite common for credit card users to build up debts which are difficult to pay off.

(c) Selling on hire purchase leads to more work for the retailer: records have to be kept, and reminders sent to slow payers.

(d) Ultimately there is the risk of the adverse publicity involved in taking a customer to court. (Even though it is the customer who is at fault, the trader can often be made to appear in a bad light.)

(e) Retailers who operate their own hire purchase schemes have more of their capital tied up in debts. They will have paid their supplier for the goods, but will not yet have received full payment from their customer. On the other hand, of course, the retailer will ultimately receive more money for the goods.

(f) Some goods may be returned to dealers by defaulting customers, and they may have trouble finding a market for such second-hand goods.

## 6.8   Hire agreements

While the objective of credit agreements is the eventual purchase of the goods, many people prefer to hire some goods from their owner. In this case the ownership of the goods never passes to the hirer. Although, strictly speaking, no credit is given, most consumer hire agreements (mainly for television sets and video equipment) are governed by the Consumer Credit Act. The hirer is afforded broadly the same protection as that given to the purchaser under a credit agreement.

## 6.9   Protection for the seller

The 1974 Act includes some clauses which restrict the consumer and thus provide some protection to the seller of goods. For example:

(a) there are limits on the freedom of consumers to withdraw from an agreement once they have signed it;

(b) a consumer who wishes to end the agreement and return the goods must have paid at least half of the total amount due;

(c) in the event of early settlement of the account, the rebate due is rather less than proportional to the period of time saved, to cover any extra expenses incurred by the seller;

(d) the consumer must not dispose of the goods before making all the payments due under the agreement.

## 6.10 Questions

1. What do you understand by the term *buying on credit*?
2. In what way might 'trade credit' be regarded as informal credit?
3. What is the main advantage to a retailer of selling goods on credit?
4. Identify two sources of income for a credit card company such as Barclaycard.
5. Distinguish carefully between a hire purchase agreement and a credit sales agreement.
6. Make a list of the 'rights' of the consumer contained in the Consumer Credit Act 1974.
7. What are the main differences between the operation of a credit card system such as Access and a charge card system such as American Express?
8. State, with reasons, which form of credit would be most appropriate for purchasing each of the following:
   (a) a microwave oven;
   (b) a tank full of petrol at a motorway service station;
   (c) curtains specially made to fit your windows.
9. J. Smith is about to purchase a television set. List the advantages and disadvantages for J. Smith of paying by (a) cash, (b) through hire purchase, (c) by using a credit card.
10. When buying a stereo system you take out a hire purchase loan of £200 at an interest rate of 12 per cent per year. You agree to pay the total debt in twelve monthly instalments.
    (a) Calculate the monthly payments.
    (b) Show how much of the monthly payments is interest and how much is repayment of the original £200.
    (c) Explain why the Annual Percentage Rate of interest (APR) is greater than 12 per cent.
    (d) How would it affect the APR if you repaid the whole debt in one payment after twelve months?
11. Read the following article and answer the questions on page 68.

   *Who Takes the Credit?*
   Go into almost any department store and you are likely to be approached by a lady asking if you are interested in having an in-store credit card. Say 'Yes' and the likelihood is that at least £200 worth of goodies will be yours, instantly. Not to mention the prospect of free gifts and special offers, discounts and sale previews.

   The growth of in-store credit cards has been *the* retail success story of the 1980s. Virtually every high street chain now has its own plastic, and the number of retail credit cards issued is reckoned to be a staggering 9 million. Even Marks & Spencer succumbed to the fever eighteen months ago and launched their charge card, probably now the single biggest, with 1.3 million takers at the last count. (However, it is one of the few places where you can't get *instant* credit.) Like many retailers, Marks & Spencer have a card which is operated by an outside finance house. Others, like Next, have their own credit card companies. Debenhams' finance subsidiary, Welbeck, runs cards for Debenhams *and* for dozens of rival retailers.

One measure of the importance of the in-store credit card is the fact that according to Department of Trade figures, £2.6 billion of the £7 billion spent in the shops in August 1986 was financed by consumer credit and one-third of all retail spending is currently financed through credit.

Maggie Drummond
*The Telegraph Sunday Magazine*

(a) What is an in-store credit card? How does it differ from a card such as Access?
(b) Why do the stores issue such cards?
(c) Are there any disadvantages for card-holders?
(d) Explain what is meant by 'free gifts and special offers, discounts and sale previews'.
(e) (i) Explain the term 'finance house'.
 (ii) What other activities are undertaken by finance houses?
(f) (i) What is meant by 'instant credit'?
 (ii) Why do some companies not allow instant credit?

# Consumer protection

## 7.1 Why do consumers need protection?

In a free enterprise system, firms can only stay in business if they sell their products to the public at a profit. Firms need to keep their costs as low and their revenue as high as possible. There are many ways of doing this, and if firms were left entirely to themselves consumers might easily be exploited. The following possibilities come readily to mind.

(a) Prices might be fixed artificially high either by one firm or, worse still, by a group of firms acting together.
(b) Misleading price reductions might be offered: recommended prices might be unnecessarily high so that retailers can offer 'attractive' reductions.
(c) Customers might not receive the correct weight or quantity of goods.
(d) Advertisements might make false claims for goods.
(e) Inferior and even dangerous ingredients and components might be used in production to keep costs down.

In these examples it is clear why the consumer may need protection, and laws have been introduced to control the worst abuses. In other situations, however, the consumer finds it difficult to tell whether a fair deal is being offered, or it is difficult to obtain a satisfactory answer to a complaint.

It is now the practice to sell many goods in standard quantities so that consumers do not have the problem of comparing, for example, two bottles of shampoo containing 50 centilitres and 8 fluid ounces. The shopper may need to be more watchful with some goods, however. For example, if cauliflowers are sold at 60 pence each, value for money will depend on the size and the quality of the cauliflowers.

Do you want to buy a microwave oven? The price of any given model varies from shop to shop, which is one problem. But even if you are trying to choose between two similarly priced machines, how do you go about it? You could take the retailer's advice, but the staff might be tempted to recommend the model that gives them the best profit, irrespective of the actual merits of the machines. If this is true of a relatively inexpensive item such as a microwave oven, you can see that the difficulty of making a rational choice between two or three new motor cars is far greater.

Even if legislation were completely comprehensive in controlling abuses, consumers would still face difficult choices. To help them there are now a number of official and unofficial bodies which examine various goods and assess their merits objectively. We shall be looking at some of these bodies later in this Unit.

We may summarize by saying that there are two broad reasons why consumers need protection. First, some producers may be less than honest, and Parliament has a responsibility to protect the public against them. Secondly, it is impossible for consumers to make a proper assessment of many of the goods they wish to buy.

## 7.2   How the Government helps

We have already seen how the Consumer Credit Act helps consumers by establishing a clear set of rules for hire purchase and credit purchases. Consumers are protected from other abuses, too, by a whole range of legislation, and this is the main way in which Parliament helps them. It has also established official bodies to cater for consumer interests in particular fields. First we deal with the legislation.

## 7.3   Consumer legislation

The starting point must be the legitimate right of traders to make as good a profit as possible. This often leaves consumers in a weak position – they might not have the technical knowledge needed to secure a fair deal. For this reason they are given a general protection by the Sale of Goods Act.

### 7.3.1   The Sale of Goods Act 1979

For many years the 1893 Sale of Goods Act formed the basis of consumer protection, but from about 1960 onwards it became apparent that it was not equal to the task of dealing with the sale and distribution of highly sophisticated products and modern selling techniques. The Sale of Goods Act 1979 updated and replaced the 1893 Act and now regulates most day-to-day buying and selling. The basic provisions are:

(a)  goods must suit the purpose for which they are sold,
(b)  goods sold by description must fit the description,
(c)  goods sold by sample must correspond with the sample, and
(d)  goods must be of merchantable quality – that is, safe and in good condition.

In the event of any of these conditions not being fulfilled buyers are normally entitled to choose whether the retailer refunds their money, replaces the unsatisfactory item or repairs it. (Retailers cannot escape this obligation even if they are unaware of the defect, though they might themselves be able to make a claim against the manufacturer of the goods.) Incidentally, the Act generally applies only to business transactions: if you buy a car from your neighbour it is your responsibility to ensure that it is in good condition.

Some producers and suppliers of goods used to try to avoid their obligations to customers by getting them to sign guarantees that effectively took away their rights under the Sale of Goods Act. Now this cannot be done: any guarantee or warranty offered by producers can only be additional to their obligation to supply goods which are of merchantable quality and fit for their purpose. This is embodied in the Unfair Contract Terms Act 1977.

The 1979 Act did not specifically cover services. This was remedied by the 1982 Supply of Goods and Services Act so that services now have to be of adequate standard.

The greatest difficulty for consumers is the fact that they are unorganized, whereas groups of manufacturers and traders often form tightly knit groups to serve their own interests. To overcome this imbalance, various Acts of Parliament have been passed as different problems have become apparent.

### 7.3.2   The Trade Descriptions Act 1968
This Act lays down heavy penalties for traders who deceive the public by making false claims for their goods or services, or who make inaccurate price comparisons. Before the Act came into force it was quite common for shops to offer apparently large price cuts at sale times, when in fact the reductions were minimal. It is now an offence to claim that the price of an article has been cut – for example, from £10 to £7 – unless the article has actually been offered at £10 for a continuous period of 28 days during the previous six months. This is obviously helpful to consumers, but you will now find shops that publish a disclaimer to the effect that a price reduction does *not* indicate that the goods have been on offer at the higher price for 28 days in the previous six months!

But the Act, which is enforced by the trading standards officers, is concerned with the descriptions of goods, as well as with their prices. The producer or trader must not describe goods as waterproof or unbreakable unless they really are proof against water, or really cannot be broken.

### 7.3.3   The Unsolicited Goods and Services Act 1971
This gives consumers extra protection. If goods are delivered to a person who has not ordered them, the sender is given six months from the delivery date within which to collect them. After that the recipient is allowed to keep the goods, unless he or she has undertaken to return them.

### 7.3.4   The Fair Trading Act 1973
Consumers were given further protection by this Act, which established the Office of Fair Trading, controlled by a Director-General who has wide-

ranging powers to control trading practices that are considered unfair to consumers. The Director-General is assisted by the Consumer Protection Advisory Committee. The Office of Fair Trading has investigated and made recommendations on a range of matters affecting consumers.

(a) Comparative pricing is the practice of advertising goods at '20 pence off' the recommended price, when it is virtually impossible for the consumer to discover the recommended price. Retailers of consumer durable goods are no longer allowed to quote manufacturers' recommended prices.

(b) Shopkeepers may not deny consumers the right to obtain their money back if they have been supplied with unsatisfactory goods. Notices such as 'No cash refunded' mislead consumers as to their rights. This practice is forbidden under the Unfair Contract Terms Act 1977.

(c) Traders who are selling goods must not pretend to sell them as private citizens, since consumers might then believe that their legal rights are less than they are.

(d) The Office of Fair Trading has been an important influence in establishing codes of practice for traders in many industries, so that customers get a fair deal. A code sets down clear requirements: for example, in the motor repair business the Code of the Motor Agents Association says that repairs must be guaranteed against bad workmanship for a specific mileage or period of time. Procedures for dealing with complaints are usually established. While these codes do not have the force of law, they do help to adjust the balance between traders and customers.

### 7.3.5    The Consumer Protection Act 1987

As well as possibly being misled or defrauded, consumers may also be endangered by goods they buy. This 1987 Act replaces the Consumer Safety Act 1978, giving the Government power to make regulations governing goods which may injure or kill their users. For example, household fires (gas, electric or oil) must be fitted with a guard which prevents clothing touching the flame or element. The 1987 Act also strengthens some of the provisions of the Trade Descriptions Act relating to the misleading pricing of goods and services, but, most important, for the first time it specifically imposes on manufacturers a duty to supply safe products. Failure to do so may render firms liable to pay unlimited compensation.

There are two further groups of legislation which pre-date the rash of consumer legislation that characterized the 1970s: on food and drugs and on weights and measures.

### 7.3.6    The Food and Drugs Act 1955

This Act is of the utmost importance to consumers. It controls the contents of food products, their labelling, and the conditions under which they are manufactured and sold. The more obvious requirements are that there should be no smoking where food is handled, and that running hot water and hand basins must be provided for washing, but if you consult the Act itself you will find an enormous range of detailed regulations. The Act is enforced by the local environmental health department, and people believing themselves to be victims of breaches of the Act should report the matter to that department.

The Food and Drugs Act is also concerned with the amounts of various ingredients found in food products. In this respect it is reinforced by the *Labelling of Food Regulations*. A few examples out of their many provisions will show you the effects.

(a) Jam must contain a minimum proportion of the named fruit: blackcurrant jam must contain 25 per cent of blackcurrants, for instance, and strawberry jam 38 per cent of strawberries.
(b) Meat pies must contain at least 25 per cent meat, but sausage rolls need contain only 10½ per cent.
(c) At least 50 per cent by weight of sausages must be meat (65 per cent for pork sausages).

Furthermore, pre-packed food must be labelled with the common name of the food and carry a list of the ingredients.

Separate regulations of 1976 control the premises from which food is sold and give the local authority power to close down those considered dangerous to the public.

The powers of the authorities were increased by the Food Safety Act 1990 which established new standards of hygiene and treatment throughout the food chain. The new powers are further enhanced by European Community laws which make it a criminal offence to supply unsafe consumer products.

### 7.3.7   Weights and Measures Acts 1963 and 1979
The 1963 Act lays down the standard measures by which goods can be sold, and there is a trading standards officer in each area to enforce the regulations. You can imagine the difficulties that might arise if there were no precise definitions of terms like *pint* or *ounce*, *litre* or *kilogram*.

The main effect of the 1979 Act was to remove the necessity for each packet of goods to be exactly a prescribed weight. So long as the weight of a batch of the packet averages out at the prescribed amount, no offence has been committed by the producer or seller.

An important requirement of the Weights and Measures Acts is that certain pre-packed goods be sold in packets which indicate the weight of the contents.

## 7.4   Consumer protection agencies

It is impossible for Parliament to legislate for every likely example of consumer exploitation or difficulty. Instead, a number of organizations have been established to keep a day-to-day watch on consumer affairs. Some have been established by the Government; some by independent groups. Some are concerned with only one industry; others have a more general role. We can get some idea of their scope by looking at a few examples.

### 7.4.1  The National Consumer Council
The National Consumer Council was established in 1975 by the Government, from whom it receives an annual grant. Members of the Council are drawn from trade unions, Parliament, industry, commerce and independent consumer organizations. The general role of the Council is to make the consumers' view known to the Government, and it has involved itself in a wide range of activities: for example, a Government campaign to encourage and subsidize loft insulation followed pressure from the organization.

The Council has a special role to play in speaking up on behalf of inarticulate and disadvantaged consumers, and it concerns itself with public services as well as those provided by the private sector. It has, for example, made strong representations to the Government about bus services and the Social Security system, as well as optical services and shop opening hours.

The Council is concerned with general policy and does not take up individual consumers' complaints.

### 7.4.2  Citizens Advice Bureaux
The role of the Citizens Advice Bureaux is much wider than that of consumer protection but, in areas where there is no local consumer protection organization, the CAB often acts as a mediator between consumers and traders, with considerable success. In this respect the CAB has the advantage of an up-to-date knowledge of the law and is also probably in regular contact with retail trade organizations in its area.

### 7.4.3  The British Standards Institution
This Institution is another non-profit-making body which receives a Government grant. It lays down minimum standards for the manufacture of consumer and other goods. But while it can specify the desirable quality, performance and dimensions of certain goods it has no authority to enforce its recommendations, as it is independent of the Government.

The influence of the BSI is often demonstrated, however, when the Government compels manufacturers to produce goods to the Institution's standards. Electric cookers and motor-cycle crash helmets are notable examples.

The kite-mark of the BSI is now well known, and regarded as a sign of quality (fig. 7.1). Consumers know that any product bearing the kite-mark has been the subject of extensive tests by BSI inspectors.

**Fig. 7.1** BSI's kite-mark

### 7.4.4 The nationalized industries

The nationalized industries (see Unit 9) are very large organizations and many consumers have no alternative but to deal with them. To help in cases of dissatisfaction, a consumer protection or consultative council is attached to each of them. The Post Office Users National Council, for example, will assist with individual problems as well as taking a general view of the policies and activities of the Post Office.

### 7.4.5 Other industries

While the nationalized industries have consumer bodies established by law, many other industries establish voluntary codes of practice for the guidance of their members and the protection of consumers.

*The Advertising Standards Authority* is an example. Although the consumer is already protected by the Trade Descriptions Act, the ASA tries to maintain high standards in advertising. Its *Code of Advertising Practice* is described in Unit 17.8. The *Retail Trading Standards Association*, and the *British Electrotechnical Approvals Board for Household Equipment* are other examples, and there are many others associated with different industries.

### 7.4.6 The media

Some newspapers have been running their own consumer protection service for many years. An individual consumer will find it far from easy to make a complaint to the head office of a national company, and even more difficult to get satisfaction. But a telephone call from the consumer adviser on a national newspaper or a television programme, and the threat of adverse publicity that it carries, will very often produce results.

The press, television and radio are important not only in dealing with individual complaints. They also play a vital educational role, making consumers aware of their rights and of the sharp practices to which they might be subjected.

### 7.4.7 The Consumers' Association

The most important and comprehensive protection is provided by the Consumers' Association, an independent and non-profit-making organization financed through its membership of over 800 000. It operates mainly by conducting comparative tests on goods and publishing the results of them in its monthly magazine *Which?*. When a particular product is going to be tested it is bought from an ordinary retailer, who is not told about the purpose of the purchase. Different brands of the product are bought, and all are subjected to the same detailed and controlled tests. In its report, *Which?* lists the good points and the bad, and often suggests which products offer good value for money.

The Consumers' Association goes a long way towards redressing the imbalance between producers and consumers, for it provides consumers with an objective assessment of a range of goods. It is not unusual for producers to modify their products after adverse criticisms from *Which?*. Where a particular injustice to consumers becomes apparent, the Consumers' Association may adopt a campaigning attitude, exerting pressure on the Government to put things right. The Association also provides a personal service for its members, enabling them to obtain advice on consumer problems.

While *Which?* deals with almost any product, the Consumers' Association also publishes two more specialized magazines, *Gardening from Which?* and *Holiday Which?*, and a variety of publications offering guidance to consumers on topics ranging from pregnancy, through housebuying and letting, restaurants, cars, health, stress, divorce and taxes to wills and probate.

## 7.5   Self-protection

Initially you should consider the prices and compare the quality of any goods and services which are being offered and the terms on which they are being sold. If subsequently you have a cause for complaint about goods or services supplied to you, you should first raise the matter with the supplier, who will normally recognize the legal position. You will probably be able to come to an agreement if your complaint is genuine and provided you adopt a reasonable approach.

Most retailers are prepared to correct genuine mistakes, even if the consumer is partly to blame, for two reasons. First, they are jealous of their reputation and it is good for them to be known as fair traders. Secondly, it is a cheaper way of dealing with the problem than becoming entangled in a lengthy dispute that could finish up in court. Further, where genuinely faulty goods are concerned, the retailer will probably have little trouble in obtaining a refund from the manufacturer.

## 7.6   Questions

1. A producer of audio cassette tapes wants to increase his profits. Since it is difficult to increase sales, he decides to do this by deceiving consumers. How might he do this?
2. What are the main ways in which the Trade Descriptions Act protects consumers?
3. You have bought a pair of shoes and one heel has fallen off the second time you wore them. What is the legal position if the retailer refuses to return your money?
4. A book club that you do not belong to sends you some books. It later writes and asks you to send them back. Explain your legal position.
5. Why is it important that full details of the contents of pre-packed and processed food should be stated on the packs?
6. What is meant by the phrase *code of practice*? How might a code of practice for the manufacturing of gardening tools be of benefit to consumers?

7. Obtain a copy of *Which?* and use it to show how the Consumers' Association can help consumers in choosing between different brands of goods.
8. Explain the differences between the work of the Consumers' Association and that of the National Consumer Council.
9. State what protection exists for consumers in respect of the following:
   (a) dangerous electrical goods;
   (b) the purchase from a dealer of a second-hand car whose mileage has been falsely stated;
   (c) a meat pie that contains a spider.
10. Distinguish between
    (a) the Sale of Goods Act and the Unsolicited Goods and Services Act;
    (b) the Trade Descriptions Act and the Fair Trading Act;
    (c) the Consumer Credit Act and the Consumer Safety Act.
    Explain carefully what each piece of legislation does.

# Business units: the private sector

## 8.1 Introduction

The production and distribution of goods are in the hands of a very large number of business enterprises, which vary immensely in their scale and organization. The reason for this variety of business organizations is that some activities can only be carried out by large firms, while others are best conducted by small ones. For example it needs a large firm to build fifty miles of motorway, but a quite small business could make a garden path. Whether a firm is large or small, however, three problems have to be resolved: capital, control and objectives.

### 8.1.1 Capital

First, the owners must obtain the capital necessary to run their business. The *initial capital* is the money set aside for the use of the business, and the amount needed varies enormously. On the one hand the business might be a very small enterprise, with the owner buying skirts at a wholesale market and selling them on a casual basis to her friends and workmates: the capital needed for this is very small and easily accumulated. If, on the other hand, the object of the business is to generate and distribute electricity to a community of 800000 people, far more capital is needed – probably more than one person can raise. Between these two extremes lies a whole range of possibilities, explaining to some extent why so many different kinds of business exist.

### 8.1.2 Control

The second problem is the control of the business. The woman dealing in skirts has few problems of control: she knows her source of supply, she probably has a very limited stock and she knows her customers. The same is true of many small retailers. But consider the manufacture of steel. The manufacturing plant probably occupies a site of several square miles. Raw materials have to be gathered from all over the world and arrangements must be made for them to arrive at the site at the correct time and in the right condition. Several thousand people are employed in the process of turning the raw materials into finished steel sheets or tubes. Finally, arrangements have to be made for storing the finished products and distributing them to customers. An operation of this sort is highly complex and much more difficult to control, partly because there is more to go wrong.

Again, between these extremes there is a wide range of possibilities: you only have to consider the variety of retail outlets to realize this.

So the combined influences of capital and control are reflected in the development of many different types of business. These fall into two broad categories, the *private sector* and the *public sector*. The main difference between the sectors concerns the ownership of the businesses.

Firms in the private sector have identifiable owners. Sometimes there is only one owner – this might be true of your local hairdresser, for instance. Sometimes there may be thousands of owners, as in the case of a business such as British Airways.

Businesses in the public sector are best regarded as being owned by the community in general. There is no particular group of individuals that can be called the owners; instead, the Government looks after them on behalf of us all.

Countries, such as the UK, which have both active public and private sectors are said to have a *mixed economy*.

### 8.1.3   Objectives
It is possible to draw a distinction between the aims of business organizations in the two sectors. The main aim of those in the private sector is to make a profit: if they cannot make a profit they will eventually have to close down (fig. 8.1). You can probably see this in your local shopping area. It is likely that some of the shops are disused. You can certainly see evidence of the process in the newspapers where bankruptcies and closures are often reported. Businesses in the public sector are also usually required to make a profit, or *surplus* as it is sometimes called. They may have other more important objectives, however. For example, a Government may require a publicly owned electricity board to supply electricity to outlying areas as a matter of public service, even though it may be unprofitable. Similarly, off-peak railway services may be provided even though they may make a loss.

In this Unit we confine our attention to the firms in the private sector, leaving the public sector organizations to Unit 9.

## 8.2   The private sector
There are five forms of enterprise to be identified in the private sector:

(a)  sole traders – one owner;
(b)  partnerships – from two to twenty owners;

**Fig. 8.1** Closing down. Small businesses or branches may find themselves in difficulty as their customers are attracted to larger suppliers

(c)  private limited companies – at least two owners;
(d)  public limited companies – at least two owners and £90 000 of capital;
(e)  co-operatives – any number of members.

(It is important to remember that *public* limited companies are found in the *private* sector – see Unit 8.8.)

## 8.3   The sole trader

The simplest and most common form of business organization is that of the sole trader. Sole traders start business with their own capital and labour, assisted perhaps by one or two employees, and take the profits as their reward. Such enterprise is not confined to the retail trade, although it is very widespread there. In any local newspaper you will see advertisements from builders, plumbers, hairdressers, printers and others in business on their own account (fig. 8.2), while in the public announcements column of the same paper you will probably read notices of the bankruptcy hearings of other similar sole traders.

It is easy to establish such a business, for there are few formal procedures, and there are two other great advantages:

(a)  the owner makes independent decisions, and
(b)  the owner has personal contact with employees and customers.

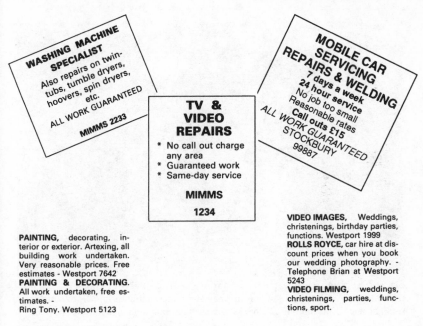

**WASHING MACHINE SPECIALIST**
Also repairs on twin-tubs, tumble dryers, spin dryers, hoovers, etc.
ALL WORK GUARANTEED
MIMMS 2233

**TV & VIDEO REPAIRS**
* No call out charge any area
* Guaranteed work
* Same-day service

**MIMMS 1234**

**MOBILE CAR SERVICING REPAIRS & WELDING**
7 days a week
24 hour service
No job too small
Reasonable rates
Call outs £15
ALL WORK GUARANTEED
STOCKBURY 99887

PAINTING, decorating, interior or exterior. Artexing, all building work undertaken. Very reasonable prices. Free estimates - Westport 7642
PAINTING & DECORATING. All work undertaken, free estimates. -
Ring Tony. Westport 5123

VIDEO IMAGES, Weddings, christenings, birthday parties, functions. Westport 1999
ROLLS ROYCE, car hire at discount prices when you book our wedding photography. - Telephone Brian at Westport 5243
VIDEO FILMING, weddings, christenings, parties, functions, sport.

**Fig. 8.2** Examples of sole traders

There are many difficulties for the sole proprietor, however.

(a) Sole traders do not have the advantage of *limited liability*: they are liable for the debts of the business to the full extent of their private assets. Thus, if a business fails, the owner could be forced to sell his or her home to pay creditors. (In other forms of business, except partnership trading, the owners are liable only to the extent of the capital they have committed to the business.)

(b) Legally no distinction is made between the owner and the business, so not only is there the problem of unlimited liability, but also there is often a lack of continuity in the event of the owner's death. The business may have to be sold to meet inheritance tax liabilities.

(c) Sole traders have difficulty in raising capital. Initially they will probably use their own savings and later, if they do well, they can expand by ploughing back profits. They may also be able to borrow from a bank, but in times of economic difficulty small businesses often find overdraft facilities withdrawn. In addition sole proprietors may have to pay a higher rate of interest than larger firms do. Private loans are possible, but sole traders are not allowed to advertise to the public for capital.

(d) Business is very competitive nowadays, and success demands hard work, long hours and not inconsiderable worry. In other forms of business these burdens can be shared, but the sole trader must bear them alone.

**Fig. 8.3** Although few sole traders can afford a heavy capital outlay on new technology, the advent of relatively inexpensive microcomputers has allowed many small businesses to computerize operations such as book-keeping and stock control

(e) Technological progress is often difficult for the sole trader because few such businesses can afford the heavy capital outlay. But it is often this progress that increases efficiency, so the gap between small and large firms widens, and the small trader's market shrinks as customers patronize the more efficient larger firms where goods and services are cheaper.

(f) A further problem is that some state Social Security payments which are available to employees while they are in work and afterwards are not automatically available in full to self-employed people. This means that sole proprietors may have to make independent arrangements about things such as sick pay and pensions. This can be expensive.

If the sole trader can overcome these difficulties and the business becomes established, expansion may become desirable. This will need the following:

(a) more capital, which may be obtained by setting aside the profits of the business for reinvestment;

(b) more employees, who are not usually difficult to find;

(c) more expertise in various aspects of the work;

(d) assistance with the management of the business.

A convenient way of overcoming these problems is to form a *partnership* with another interested party.

## 8.4 Partnerships

Partnerships do not necessarily grow out of sole proprietorships. Sometimes a business begins life as a partnership, when two or three employees of one firm decide that they would rather work for themselves than for their employer. Many partnerships in accountancy and the building trade begin in this way.

The main features of a partnership are as follows.

(a) There may be between two and twenty partners, except in a professional partnership (solicitors, for example) where there is no upper limit.
(b) Profits or losses are shared between the partners. It is best to have a written partnership agreement stating how they will be divided. If there is no written agreement the Partnership Act 1890 states that:

    (i) profits and losses must be divided equally,
    (ii) no interest is payable on capital contributed to the firm,
    (iii) partners cannot claim a salary for work they do, and
    (iv) any loans that a partner makes to the partnership carry interest of 5 per cent per year.

Some of these terms are unlikely to be acceptable to businesses today (for example, interest of 5 per cent is far lower than the rate obtainable elsewhere, and also people expect to be paid for work that they do!). As a result many partnerships find it desirable to draw up an agreement which is rather more generous.

(c) All partners are entitled to be involved in the management of the business. For example, they should all be consulted before a new branch or office is opened.
(d) An agreement made by one partner on behalf of the partnership is binding and has to be accepted by all the partners. So if you are in a hairdressing partnership and one of your colleagues agrees to buy 100 cases of hair spray at £50 per case, you have to accept this even though you know that the same product is available elsewhere at £25 per case. You need to be careful in the selection of your business partners!
(e) The partners, like the sole proprietor, have unlimited liability.

The risk of unlimited liability used to deter many people from entrusting their capital to a partnership. But in 1907 Parliament passed the Limited Partnership Act, which allows partners to assume limited liability on the following conditions:

(a) they take no part in the running of the business (though they do share in the profits, of course);
(b) there must be at least one ordinary partner who has unlimited liability for the debts of the business;
(c) the partnership must be registered with the Registrar of Companies (this is because normally only companies have limited liability).

### 8.4.1   Advantages of partnerships

Clearly there are more formalities involved in establishing a partnership than a sole proprietorship. Why do people go to this bother? There are three main advantages.

(a) More capital is available, because more people are involved.

(b) The introduction of new partners allows specialization, and can add a new dimension to a business. A general builder who trained as a bricklayer may improve the business and offer a better service by going into partnership with a plumber and a carpenter. Of course they could simply be taken on as employees, but if they become partners their interest is identified with that of the firm, and they may contribute to the capital of the business – though it is not a legal requirement for a partner to do so. A firm may take someone into partnership simply to benefit from his or her particular expertise.

(c) Unlike a company, a partnership can keep its affairs to itself. Its annual accounts do not have to be submitted to anyone other than the Inland Revenue.

### 8.4.2   Disadvantages of partnerships

Despite the benefits of forming a partnership, there are several drawbacks that need to be considered.

(a) As with the sole proprietor, there is no distinction between the owners and the business. They too face unlimited liability. (There are very few limited partnerships, for it is usually better to form a limited company.)

(b) Because the business is identified with its owners, a partnership also suffers from a lack of continuity. If one of the owners dies or leaves the partnership for some reason, the partnership is at an end, and a new one has to be formed. This is not an especially difficult operation, but it is an irritating necessity.

(c) Since any undertaking of one partner binds the others, it is important not to enter a partnership with someone whose business judgement is suspect.

(d) Since each partner is entitled to a say in the management of the firm, there may well be disagreements. This may cause delays damaging to the business.

(e) As the business grows, the partnership may well face the same shortage of capital as the sole proprietor. There is a limit to the amount of capital that can be obtained from the partners or by ploughing back profits. Further expansion may require the establishment of a limited company. Nevertheless, partnerships do not have to remain small – some of the largest accountancy firms are partnerships.

## 8.5 Limited companies

Not all businesses begin life as a sole proprietorship or a partnership. Many people establishing a business for the first time immediately set up a limited company. The principal attraction of this is that the owners' liability is limited to the nominal value of the shares held. This facility was originally conferred by Act of Parliament in 1856. Limited liability allows a large number of people to contribute funds to a business without risking all their personal possessions. Furthermore, the company has its own legal existence quite separate from that

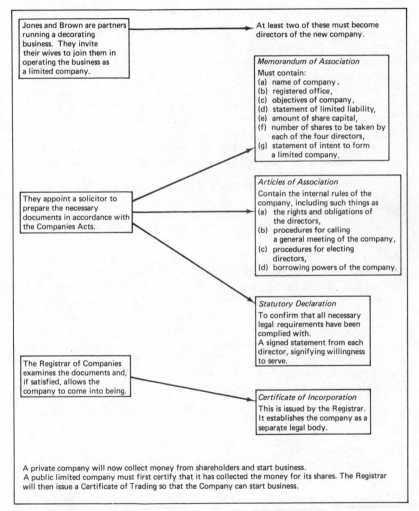

Jones and Brown are partners running a decorating business. They invite their wives to join them in operating the business as a limited company.

At least two of these must become directors of the new company.

*Memorandum of Association*

Must contain:
(a) name of company,
(b) registered office,
(c) objectives of company,
(d) statement of limited liability,
(e) amount of share capital,
(f) number of shares to be taken by each of the four directors,
(g) statement of intent to form a limited company.

They appoint a solicitor to prepare the necessary documents in accordance with the Companies Acts.

*Articles of Association*

Contain the internal rules of the company, including such things as
(a) the rights and obligations of the directors,
(b) procedures for calling a general meeting of the company,
(c) procedures for electing directors,
(d) borrowing powers of the company.

*Statutory Declaration*

To confirm that all necessary legal requirements have been complied with.
A signed statement from each director, signifying willingness to serve.

The Registrar of Companies examines the documents and, if satisfied, allows the company to come into being.

*Certificate of Incorporation*

This is issued by the Registrar. It establishes the company as a separate legal body.

A private company will now collect money from shareholders and start business.
A public limited company must first certify that it has collected the money for its shares. The Registrar will then issue a Certificate of Trading so that the Company can start business.

**Fig. 8.4** Setting up a limited company

of the shareholders, so its continuity is not threatened by the death of one of them.

There are many formalities involved in forming a company and we can only look at them in outline.

Limited companies must be registered with the Registrar of Companies. To comply with the Registrar's requirements, which are laid down by the Companies Acts 1948–85, the promoters of the company must conform to the procedure shown in fig. 8.4.

## 8.6    The capital of limited companies

The promoters of a limited company can raise capital in several different ways. They try to attract contributions from all kinds of people and institutions, by offering them *shares* in the business. Some shares carry a guarantee of repayment and a fixed income, while most have no offer of repayment and the income from them is not fixed. Every person who buys a share becomes a part-owner of the company, and is entitled to a share of the company's profits. The income received from shares is called a *dividend*. The way in which dividends are calculated is illustrated in fig. 8.5.

The term *capital* can be a confusing one, and we shall return to it in Unit 13. For the time being you should distinguish between the following:

(a) The *nominal* or *authorized capital* of a company is the maximum amount of money the company is allowed to raise by issuing shares.
(b) *The issued capital*   The company may not wish to issue the maximum amount of shares at the outset. The issued capital is simply the amount that it does issue.
(c) *The paid-up capital*   When the shares are issued, the company does not always need the full amount to be paid immediately; the paid-up capital of the firm is that part of issued capital which is actually paid for. If the company fails, the holders of shares which are not paid-up are required to pay the difference between the nominal value and the paid-up value of their shares. For example, if a company has an authorized capital of £800000 in £1 shares, it may decide to issue them all. If it does not need all the money immediately, it may call for payment of 75 pence on each share, giving it a paid-up capital of £600000. The shareholders would then eventually have to pay a further 25 pence for each share held.

Companies may issue two types of share: ordinary shares and preference shares.

### 8.6.1   Ordinary shares

All companies issue ordinary shares, which are sometimes referred to as the *risk capital* of the business. This is because the owner of the shares receives a dividend on them only if there is sufficient profit. If profits are too low (or if there is a loss), the company may not pay a dividend. When profits permit,

---

Bardag Co. Ltd: Issued share capital

| | | | |
|---|---|---|---|
| Ordinary shares: | 20000 @ 50 pence | = | £10000 |
| 5% preference shares: | 5000 @ £1.00 | = | £5000 |

Let us assume that after meeting all its costs, including interest on debentures and taxation, Bardag Ltd has £1400 remaining.

1. We know that the dividend of 5 per cent must be paid to the preference shareholders. They have to be given

$$£5000 \times \frac{5}{100} = £250 \text{ between them}$$

   This leaves £1150.
2. Bardag Ltd could divide all this between the ordinary shareholders. It is more likely that the company will keep some of it in reserve for possible future use. Suppose that it keeps £350 for this purpose.
3. The rest of the money (£1150 less £350 = £800) is now available to be divided between the ordinary shareholders. So, the payment of each ordinary share is

$$\frac{£800.00}{20000} = 4 \text{ pence per share}$$

4. An alternative way of expressing this is as a percentage dividend:

$$\frac{\text{amount of dividend}}{\text{nominal price of share}} \times 100\% = \frac{4p}{50p} \times 100\% = 8\%$$

**Fig. 8.5** The distribution of company profits: an example

each shareholder will receive an equal amount for each ordinary share held (which is why ordinary shares are sometimes called *equities*). A further risk faced by ordinary shareholders is that should the company fail altogether they will be repaid, if at all, only after all other debts have been paid.

In exchange for the risk, the ordinary shareholders have ultimate control of the company, in that they have one vote for each share when it comes to electing the board of directors who are responsible for the general policy of the company (see Unit 8.9.2).

### 8.6.2 Preference shares
While ordinary shares provide an attractive investment for those who do not mind the risk of getting no reward in some years, others find that preference shares offer a safer investment. Preference shares fall into several groups. There are *basic preference shares*, the holders of which receive a fixed dividend out of profits before anything is paid to ordinary shareholders. With *cumula-*

*tive preference shares*, a dividend missed in one year is carried forward to the next. *Participating preference shares* not only carry a fixed rate of dividend, but also entitle their holders to a further share of the profits once they reach a certain level. Most preference shareholders have no say in the control of the company, as they have a privileged position with respect to dividends.

### 8.6.3 Debentures

A company can also issue *debentures*. These are not shares, since debenture-holders do not share in the ownership of the company. Debentures are simply loans to the company on which a fixed rate of interest is paid before preference or ordinary shareholders receive anything. They are normally secured against some property owned by the firm. That is to say, if the company fails, the agreed property must be sold and the proceeds used to repay the debenture-holders. If debenture-holders do not receive their annual interest, they can force the company into liquidation.

## 8.7    The private limited company

As we have seen, when a small business expands there is a need for extra capital. The partners or sole proprietor may decide to turn the business into a limited company to raise this capital. Sometimes, however, the proprietors may start the business as a limited company just to obtain the benefits of limited liability. The main points to note about private companies are:

(a)  their name must end with the word 'Limited';
(b)  they are not allowed to issue shares or debentures to the general public;
(c)  there is no longer any limit to the number of shareholders.

### 8.7.1 Advantages of private companies

Let us look at the advantages of forming a private company.

(a)  The main advantage of a limited company is its independent legal status, and hence the limited liability enjoyed by its shareholders.
(b)  With limited liability the company is able to attract capital from people who would not otherwise be prepared to invest.
(c)  In a private company, the founders of the business can usually keep control of it, by holding a majority of the shares.

These advantages have led to the creation of many private companies, most of them operating on a purely local basis, but many of them nationally or internationally known. Indeed the publishers of this book are formed into a private limited company.

### 8.7.2 Disadvantages of private companies

Like all business units, however, the private company also has its disadvantages. There are three main drawbacks.

(a) The shareholder in a private limited company may be able to transfer his or her shares to someone else only with the consent of the other shareholders.
(b) The company is not allowed to appeal to the public for extra capital, so it may find it difficult to raise money for expansion.
(c) The accounts of the company must be filed annually with the Registrar of Companies. They are then available to anyone on payment of a nominal fee.

## 8.8 The public limited company

The largest and most important business units are the public limited companies. Some of these are very large – some examples are shown in fig. 8.6.

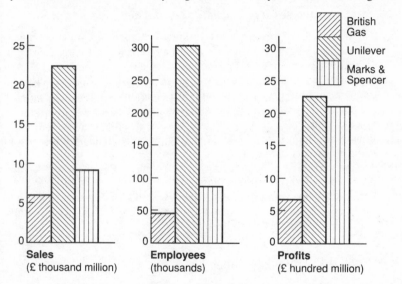

**Fig. 8.6** Some large limited companies (1992)

Unilever, for instance, employs over 300 000 people, and its sales average over £60 million every day of the year.

The great majority of companies are private companies, and in order to become a public company the business must meet the following conditions:

(a) It must be stated in the Memorandum of Association that the company is public.
(b) The name of the company must end with the words 'public limited company' (plc).
(c) The issued capital of the company must be at least £50 000.

### 8.8.1    Advantages of public limited companies

(a) Like the private company, the public limited company has independent legal existence, limited liability for shareholders and continuity of the business.
(b) It is allowed to appeal to the public for funds, whereas the promoters of a private company have to rely on friends and relations for capital.
(c) There is no restriction on the transfer of shares.
(d) Public companies are normally larger than most other businesses. As such they often benefit from *economies of scale*. These result in the cost per unit of output falling as the level of output rises. For example, the cost of operating a 30-tonne lorry is not double the cost of a 15-tonne lorry.

### 8.8.2    Disadvantages of public limited companies

(a) The formalities of forming a public limited company are quite complex.
(b) Raising capital can be expensive. Normally a merchant bank (see Unit 11.1.3) will organize a share issue and charge on a commission basis.
(c) Sometimes a public limited company grows so big that it becomes difficult to manage (this problem can also occur in other forms of business organization, however, and is an example of a *diseconomy of scale*).
(d) Once established, public companies have to comply with many regulations. Extra requirements are frequently put upon them by the Government, to protect either shareholders or the general public.
(e) The accounts of a public company must be published, so there can be little secrecy or privacy about its affairs.
(f) Perhaps the most important disadvantage of this kind of business is that the owners can normally exercise little control over it. This is so important that it deserves a section to itself.

## 8.9    The control of companies

If a business is run by a sole proprietor, it is quite clear that he or she contributes the capital, takes the decisions and enjoys the profits. But in a limited company, and especially in a public limited company, these functions are divided between different groups of people.

### 8.9.1    Ownership

A public limited company is owned by its shareholders, and there may be many thousands of them in a large company. Their rights vary according to the kind of shares they own, but it is quite clear that they cannot all be consulted about every decision that needs to be made in the running of the business – if they were, nothing would ever get done. Therefore arrangements are made to delegate the control of the company to a small group of shareholders.

### 8.9.2 Control

Each year the company holds an Annual General Meeting to elect a *board of directors* to run the business. Each ordinary shareholder has one vote for each share held, so anyone who owns 51 per cent of the ordinary shares can control the business. This does not occur very often; in fact, most shareholders' meetings are sparsely attended, which to some extent reflects their lack of real power. (In many companies the lack of shareholder participation means that the holder of 25–30 per cent of the shares may have control.) The directors elect a managing director from their number, and together they are responsible for the general policy of the company. They must always act within the terms of the Memorandum of Association, and the Articles of Association.

Increasingly in recent years one company buys shares in another company. Such companies are often known as Holding Companies and this may be indicated in their names. Thus under the umbrella of United Biscuits (Holdings) Plc exist, among others, McVities Group (biscuit manufacturers), KP Foods Group (snack food manufacturers) and Terry's Group (chocolate and confectionery manufacturers). Some Holding Companies may control hundreds of apparently independent companies.

### 8.9.3 Management

When a company employs tens of thousands of people it is impossible for a board of directors of perhaps two dozen people to take all the necessary decisions. The directors therefore lay down the general policy of the firm, and each of them assumes a particular area of responsibility. One may be responsible for marketing the product, another for safety and so on. The firm also employs full-time managers to make the day-to-day decisions in running the firm. Each of these managers heads a team that runs a particular department, and many decisions are taken by quite junior people who have no financial interest in the company.

You can see, therefore, that there may be a great division between the owners of the business and those who control it: while it may be necessary for the directors to have shares in the company, there is nothing to say that the managers must. Some people argue that the aims of the managers do not always coincide with those of the owners, and that this is a serious weakness of the public limited company.

## 8.10 Co-operatives

In Unit 3.3.8 we examined the retail co-operative societies. In many countries, *producer* co-operatives are very popular, but it is only in recent years that they have begun to be significant in the UK. Encouraged by the Co-operative Development Agency – a Government-funded organization – there are now about 1500 such groups, mainly in the services sector. Some of these will be organized as partnerships, some as limited companies. By pooling their resources, the producers in a co-operative can afford to purchase equipment that they could not afford individually and so are better able to compete with larger organizations.

## 8.11   Chambers of commerce

In many areas, private sector firms join together to form a *chamber of commerce* which, among other things, represents the interests of the business community in relation to the local authority.

## 8.12   Questions

1. What is the main difference in ownership between firms in the private sector and those in the public sector?
2. Explain the main differences between the private limited company and the public limited company.
3. In which sector of the economy is the public limited company?
4. Explain carefully what is meant by the term *limited liability*.
5. How does limited liability benefit the individual shareholder?
6. How might limited liability enable a company to attract more shareholders?
7. Why might limited liability be a disadvantage for someone to whom the company owes money?
8. What are the main disadvantages associated with sole proprietorships and partnerships?
9. Trace the stages by which a small sole proprietorship might develop into a public limited company.
10. (a) Distinguish between the Memorandum of Association and the Articles of Association.
    (b) In what ways do the Articles protect the shareholders?
11. (a) What is meant by the word *capital*?
    (b) Distinguish between authorized, issued and paid-up capital.
12. A company has the following issued and fully paid-up capital:

    1000 × 50 pence ordinary shares
    2000 × £1.00 5% preference shares

    The profits available for distribution to shareholders were £300 in 1991 and £400 in 1992.
    (a) How much money is due to the preference shareholders in total each year?
    (b) How much money is paid in dividend on each ordinary share in 1991?
    (c) What is the percentage dividend on the ordinary shares in 1992?
13. Show how the functions of the sole proprietor are divided between different groups in a limited company.
14. Explain why it might be difficult for the owners of a public limited company to control the company.
15. Distinguish between partnerships and private limited companies under the following headings: (a) ownership, (b) formation, (c) distribution of profits, (d) liability.

# Business units: the public sector

## 9.1 Introduction

While most of the economic and commercial activity in the United Kingdom is conducted by the types of firm we examined in Unit 8, some goods and services are provided by the public sector – that is, by central or local government authorities, either directly or through specially appointed agencies. The reasons for this are discussed in Unit 9.5, but first we shall consider the various types of public enterprise.

### 9.1.1 Government trading

Sometimes central government carries out trading activities under the direct control of a Government department – Her Majesty's Stationery Office is under the control of the Treasury, for example. Some local government authorities provide transport services in their area and may undertake catering on a commercial basis.

### 9.1.2 The Government as shareholder

The Government holds shares in some public limited companies. These may have been acquired for a number of reasons. For example the Government had a long-standing interest in the development of the petroleum industry and until recently had a substantial shareholding in BP. Sometimes a company may receive Government finance to help it survive. The Rover Group in its earlier existence as British Leyland and Rolls Royce were both in this position in the 1970s. In each case the Government became a major shareholder. Occasionally the Government sets up a limited company under its sole ownership, where there is an important service to be performed but not much profit to be made – Remploy, the agency which finds employment for handicapped people, is such an example.

The British Technology Group, a public sector organization, among its other activities acts as a holding company for the Government and supervises the Government's investments in companies in general.

### 9.1.3 The public corporations

Public corporations are the most obvious form of public enterprise in the United Kingdom. Their development has been gradual. The establishment of the Port of London Authority in 1908 was an early example, but the peak of the movement came in the period 1945–51, with the nationalization of the transport, energy and iron and steel industries.

The public corporations may be divided into two groups.

(a) Those which sell a product or service directly to the public, charging each customer for what is used. The main examples that now fall into this group are British Rail, the Post Office and the coal industry. Until recently British Airways, British Steel and British Telecom could have been added to the list.

(b) Those which provide a service but do not charge for it directly. In this category are the British Broadcasting Corporation, the Independent Television Commission and the Radio Authority (which has the task of supervising the private sector firms that actually provide the broadcasting services).

This Unit is mainly concerned with the first group, which number the majority of UK households among their customers directly or indirectly.

## 9.2   What are public corporations?

First let us clear up one ambiguity. In the United States the term *public corporation* refers to what we in the United Kingdom call a public limited company, and it is therefore part of the *private* sector. In the UK, however, a public corporation is a separate legal form found only in the *public* sector. Each one is set up by an Act of Parliament to run the whole of, or most of, an industry. Each corporation has a legal identity separate from that of the Government and has its own management board selected by the Government. Like a limited company, it may sue and be sued in its own name.

The general policy of the corporation is laid down by the Act of Parliament that set it up, and may be revised from time to time by the Government.

The day-to-day management of a public corporation is theoretically free from Government interference. Matters such as the negotiation of wages with trade unions and the determination of prices are intended to be left to the corporation itself, though the Government sometimes intervenes in the public interest or for political reasons.

## 9.3   Who does the shareholders' job?

In a public limited company, individual members of the public and institutions such as insurance companies are the shareholders and therefore the owners of the business. The public corporation has no such group of identifiable owners.

The best view is that a public corporation is owned by the Government in trust for the community as a whole. This can lead to difficulties with regard to *control* and the subscribing of *capital*.

In a limited company these two important functions are the responsibility of the shareholders. They exercise control over the board of directors. If the company is not running effectively, the shareholders have the power to get rid of the directors and elect replacements, and it is to the shareholders, as owners, that the annual accounts and report of the company are presented. The shareholders also subscribe capital. Since the public corporations have no shareholders in the ordinary sense, alternative arrangements have had to be made. Over the years a system has been built up through which the public corporations are accountable to Parliament, which thus fulfils part of the shareholders' role.

### 9.3.1 Control
Control of the public corporations is exercised in several ways.

(a) Each corporation must publish its accounts annually. These may be the subject of close examination by the *Public Accounts Committee* of the House of Commons, a group of specialists who may well be more demanding than the shareholders of a limited company.

(b) Other Parliamentary committees, known as *Select Committees*, have the power to make more general investigations into the affairs of the corporations. Members of the boards of the nationalized industries are sometimes called before a Select Committee to report on their performance and policy. This again may provide a greater degree of control than that exercised by the shareholders of most companies.

(c) There is provision for an annual debate in Parliament on the affairs of each corporation. In practice, the pressure of Parliamentary business means that these are often cancelled in favour of other debates, but if a corporation is experiencing difficulties the debate is held. This is a useful way of examining problems, and provides another example of the way in which Parliament takes over the role of shareholders.

(d) A more continuous control is exercised by the appointment of a Government minister to have political responsibility for each industry.

(e) Since 1980 the corporations have also been subject to investigation by the *Monopolies and Mergers Commission*, a Government-appointed body which looks into the activities of business organizations that may be behaving in ways that are against the public interest.

### 9.3.2 Capital
The other important function of the shareholders in a limited company is to subscribe capital. In the case of the public corporation the capital has come or may come from a variety of sources.

(a) The corporations used to issue their own securities to the public. At one time, for example, before the privatization of the British gas industry (see Unit 9.8), the Gas Council issued British Gas Stock on which it paid a fixed rate of interest. All the proceeds from issuing the securities went to the gas industry. The holders of these securities were in no sense the owners of the industry, nor were they taking any risks: they received their interest whether the industry made a profit or not, because it was guaranteed by the Government.

(b) Since this was abandoned the corporations normally borrow from the Treasury to finance capital projects that cannot be met out of current income. If necessary the Treasury issues *gilt-edged securities* (see Unit 13.5.1) to raise the money required. (Sometimes, however, the Treasury may be unwilling or unable to lend the corporations the amounts they want at the time they want it. This is another way in which the activities of the nationalized industries are controlled.)

(c) More recently some of the corporations have been allowed to raise considerable sums of money from the UK's European trading partners, mainly Germany. One of the important side effects of this is to bring a temporary improvement to the balance of payments (see Unit 21). These loans are guaranteed by the British Government.

## 9.4   What happens to their profits?

There was once a large public service element in the work of the nationalized industries, which provided many services that were unprofitable but socially worthwhile. These days they are much more concerned with making a profit (see Unit 9.6) and this might amount to hundreds of millions of pounds per year for a single corporation. It can be used in several ways.

(a) It may be used to make interest payments on capital. All the nationalized industries began with enormous capital debts, because compensation had to be paid to the previous shareholders. Interest on all that capital has to be paid at a fixed rate. (This situation is quite different from that of the limited company, which may have some fixed-interest capital, but does not have to pay a dividend on the ordinary shares if it has a bad year.) Recently, however, some corporations have issued a new kind of security, on which interest is payable only if profits are above a certain level. At the moment these securities are held only by the Government, but they could well become available to the public in the future.

(b) It may be set aside for the future repayment of loans.

(c) It may be reinvested, to finance expansion in the industry.

(d) It may be used by the Government to meet its general expenditure commitments.

If the industry fails to make a surplus, so that it is unable to meet its interest payments, the stockholders do not suffer, for the Treasury will pay. In effect this means that the taxpayers will pay the interest, since it is from them that the Treasury obtains most of its revenue. These interest payments are added to the accumulated debt of the industry. If this debt itself goes on increasing, because the industry is unable to make a profit, it may eventually be *written off* (cancelled), to allow the corporation to make a fresh start, or to make it more attractive if it is privatized.

## 9.5  Why are industries nationalized?

There is no single answer to the question of why industries were taken into public ownership. Many influences have been at work, and we shall look at some of the more prominent reasons for nationalization.

### 9.5.1  Financial necessity
Sometimes an industry may have become so run down that only vast sums of money from the Government can save it. This was an important factor in the nationalization of both the coal industry and the railways after the Second World War.

### 9.5.2  Strategic necessity
Some industries are essential for national well-being and security. The coal industry and Rolls-Royce are good examples. In 1947 coal was the United Kingdom's only native source of power, so it was essential for the industry to be placed on a sound footing. Rolls-Royce makes an important contribution to the defence programme of the United Kingdom and other western countries, and likewise could not be allowed to go out of business when it ran into financial difficulties in 1971.

### 9.5.3  Basic industries
There are some industries on which the whole economy depends: the fuel, power, transport and steel industries are examples. If these are not working efficiently, all the other industries suffer. Some Governments have felt that the importance of these industries is so great that the decisions about their investment programmes and their rates of expansion should not be left to boards of directors who represent the interests of only a relatively small number of shareholders. They saw nationalization as the best way of protecting the interests of the community as a whole.

### 9.5.4  Natural monopolies
Although competition is appropriate to most industries, there are certain circumstances in which a *monopolist* may be more efficient. (A monopolist is someone who has exclusive control of the supply of a commodity or service.) At one period in the nineteenth century three different railway companies had separate lines between London and Brighton. Not one of them was profitable, for their trains were never full. In this situation it makes better economic sense

to have just one operator. The same applies to many public services: for example, we do not want two or three firms competing to sell us gas, each with its own elaborate system of pipelines. Industries like this *need* to be monopolized to avoid wasting capital.

Industries like gas and electricity were nationalized in the 1940s because it was felt that such large monopolies needed to be under the direct control of the Government. More recently the Government preferred to allow the businesses to be owned by private sector shareholders, but ensured that adequate controls over the level of service and the prices charged to consumers were in operation, through organizations such as OFTEL, the Office of Telecommunications, an independent body charged with protecting the interests of telephone users.

### 9.5.5  Economies of scale
Some industries need to be very large to take full advantage of economies of scale (see Unit 3.5.1). The generation of electricity is an example. Once again many people feel that, if very large units of production are going to be established, they should be publicly owned.

### 9.5.6  Political belief
Some people believe that the private ownership of the means of production is wrong in itself, and that nationalization is the only way of returning industry to the people who they see as its rightful owners – the community as a whole.

## 9.6  What are the aims of public corporations?

The aim of a private sector company is to make a profit for its shareholders. If it fails to make profits it eventually closes down. The objectives of the public corporations are not always so clear and they have changed over the years.

The original financial aim for the corporations was to break even, taking one year with another. Thus they were allowed to make a loss one year so long as there was a profit to offset it later. Subsequently each corporation was given a specific profit target to achieve over a number of years. In the 1980s the policy concentrated generally on maximizing profits and making the industries efficient. Many jobs were lost. This made the corporations more attractive when they were privatized.

The aims of the public corporations that remain have moved a long way from the original aims. For example, each has specific financial targets and performance aims; there are limits on the amounts they can borrow to finance their activities; and their investment policy and prices are subject to control.

## 9.7  How does the public benefit from public corporations?

There are four principal benefits of the public corporations.

(a) Industries that are essential to an economic system can be kept going as public corporations even if they are not profitable. This has been true of the railway system in the United Kingdom. If British Rail had been a private sector, profit-driven organization it would long ago have had to close down, or at least abandon many of its routes. Instead the Government for many years paid subsidies to the Railway Corporation to keep services in operation. Such a policy is widespread around the world since railways provide many benefits such as speedy travel between major towns and the reduction of traffic congestion on the roads. It can be argued that it is worth paying higher taxes for such benefits. However, the subsidies have been reduced in Britain in recent years as part of a general move towards the privatization of large public organizations.

(b) Factors other than profits can be taken into account when planning these industries. For example, it might be considered better to keep an uneconomic coal mine in operation rather than incur the high and perhaps continuing Social Security costs that would follow its closure.

(c) Nationalization can avoid the wasteful competition involved in having two or more firms competing to offer consumers a utility, such as electricity or water.

(d) Any profits that are made go to the Government and can be used for general purposes, rather than going to private individual shareholders.

## 9.8  Privatization

From 1979 the Government set out to reverse the process of nationalization. This policy is known as privatization and it originated in the belief that the efficiency of the industries would be improved by the greater financial disciplines imposed by the private sector and by the introduction, where possible, of competition. Perhaps the Government also wanted to keep the level of its own expenditure down: if it privatized the industries it would not have to subsidize them. By 1992, 46 businesses had been privatized.

Some believe that the main benefit to the Government was the revenue generated by the sales. The most profitable examples are shown in Table 9.1. Overall more than £35000m was raised from privatization between 1979 and 1991. One of the benefits of this was that the Government did not have to raise this amount through taxation.

**Table 9.1** Major privatizations

| Name of business | Year of sale | Amount raised (£m) |
| --- | --- | --- |
| Britoil | 1982–85 | 9619 |
| British Petroleum | 1979–87 | 6648 |
| British Gas | 1986 | 5293 |
| Regional Electricity Co. | 1990 | 5182 |
| British Telecom (BT) | 1984–91 | 3685 |
| Water Companies | 1989 | 3454 |

In the longer term the Government loses revenue through privatization since future profits will go not to the Treasury but to the shareholders, many of whom are employees of the industries who were able to buy shares on preferential terms. In terms of profitability the privatized industries have been successful. It has been calculated that BT makes a profit of over £5800 per minute! On the other hand, it invests over £7600 per minute in new equipment.

Privatization is not, of course, without its critics. In particular, there are doubts about the extent to which consumer interests are safeguarded. It has not always been possible to introduce even competition within privatized industries; perhaps only in telecommunications where Mercury Communications offer a challenge to BT is there clear domestic competition.

## 9.9   Municipal enterprise

Most local government authorities undertake some trading activities. Some of their services, such as education and street lighting, are provided free of direct charge to the actual user but are paid for indirectly by the whole community in the form of local taxes or government grants. For many other services the local authority makes a charge in order to cover costs: swimming pools, sauna baths, golf courses, football and cricket pitches, theatres, dance halls and bus services are just a few of these. It is felt that the users of these services should make some direct contribution to the costs. The income from these services is frequently insufficient to cover costs, however, and so they too have to be subsidized.

## 9.10   Questions

1. Explain the main difference between a public corporation and a public limited company.
2. Name four reasons why an industry may be nationalized.
3. In what respect may the aims of a nationalized industry differ from those of a public limited company?
4. What is meant by the term *privatization*?
5. For what reasons did the Government privatize some nationalized industries from 1979 onwards?
6. (a) Why is it that the railway industry is nationalized, but your local taxi service is privately owned?
   (b) How do the problems of the railway industry and your local taxi service differ?
7. (a) Describe the functions of the shareholders in a public limited company.
   (b) Show how these functions are carried out in a public corporation.
8. (a) What is meant by *municipal trading*?
   (b) What trading activities are undertaken by your local council?

# UNIT 10

# The monetary system

## 10.1 What is money?

Most people feel happier if they have some money in their pocket or in the bank or a building society. People go to work to earn money. They may spend it on goods and services or they may save it. We value goods in terms of money and we may measure a person's wealth in monetary terms. Few of us, however, pause to ask the question: what is money?

The answer is that money is a claim to goods and services. It is anything that is generally acceptable in exchange for goods and services. In itself, our money is practically worthless: if you are starving you cannot eat it, and if you are thirsty you cannot drink it, but you may use it to buy food or drink.

Another answer to the question 'what is money?' is contained in the saying 'money is as money does.' Let us consider more closely what it is that money does.

## 10.2 The functions of money

If our money ceased to exist tomorrow, we should soon discover the importance of the jobs it performs. It has four separate functions.

### 10.2.1 Money as a means of exchange

Without money a normal shopping expedition would be difficult. Consider what happens now: we decide what goods we wish to buy, go to the appropriate shops and hand over our money or write a cheque for the goods we want. This is money as a means of exchange, and we probably obtained the money in the first place by exchanging our services for it in the form of labour. Without money our employers would have to pay us in some other way for our services, perhaps by allowing us to take some of the goods we helped to produce. While this might solve their problems it would be only the beginning of ours, for we should now have to exchange our 'wages' – wheat or clothes or

A has fish
and wants bread.

B has potatoes
and wants fish.

C has bread
and wants potatoes.

**Fig. 10.1** Barter. Clearly it is impossible for A to satisfy his need simply by trading with B or C. A must exchange his fish for B's potatoes and then exchange the potatoes for C's bread. Obviously there could be further stages before A's requirements are satisfied

computers – for the goods we require. If we have been paid in computers we must find someone who not only wants a computer but who is anxious to get rid of food and books, say, in the quantities we wish to buy. This could be difficult, to say the least! In fact under a system of *barter* a modern industrial society such as ours could not exist, and the great advantage of money is that it does away with the need for barter.

### 10.2.2    Money as a measure of value
Even if the owner of the computer were successful in finding someone prepared to accept it in exchange for books, there would be the further problem of deciding how many books should be exchanged for one computer. And it would be the same with any other goods: the exchange rate between the two would have to be the subject of negotiation between the parties. Traders would need to bear in mind exchange rates between all kinds of commodities. If you were dealing with four kinds of goods you would have to remember six exchange rates; ten kinds of goods implies 45 exchange rates or prices, and twenty goods, 190 rates. Trade would be almost impossible.

In our present society the value of all goods is measured in terms of money so they can be compared easily. It thus becomes much easier to recognize a bargain and to avoid paying excessive prices.

### 10.2.3  Money as a store of wealth
We do not always wish to spend all of our income as we receive it. If we are paid in money we may keep it to spend in perhaps three or four years' time. Suppose we were paid in the form of fruit: it would quickly deteriorate and become worthless. Money is thus a convenient way of storing wealth. It is true that money kept in a tin for years on end may fall in value because the prices of everything rise, but this is not the same as fruit quickly going bad.

### 10.2.4  Money as a standard for deferred payments
All kinds of contracts and agreements are drawn up in monetary terms. When a trader obtains a bank loan, for example, the future repayments are fixed in terms of money. This is money being used as a standard for deferred payments, though once again the falling value of money may cause complications.

We can therefore say that the role of money is to facilitate trade, and that money is at the heart of our economic and commercial system. It is impossible to imagine modern society without it. We must now consider the characteristics of money and the way in which it has developed into its present forms.

## 10.3  The nature and characteristics of money

### 10.3.1  Acceptability
At one time money had *intrinsic value*, that is, it was wanted in its own right irrespective of its value as money. Thus in many societies over many centuries gold and silver were used as money. Today's money has no intrinsic value; it is valuable because shopkeepers and others accept it in exchange for goods. It is *legal tender* and authorized by Parliament. Thus the most important characteristic of money is that it should be generally *acceptable*. As long as the public have *confidence* in the money in circulation, it will be generally acceptable, but if that confidence does not exist then it will not. There have been isolated occasions when a nation has lost all confidence in its money because its value was falling daily – so that the price of a loaf of bread might double between breakfast and tea-time. This brings us to its second essential characteristic.

### 10.3.2  Stability of value
Money should have a stable value if it is to facilitate the production and distribution of goods. The tendency for prices to rise means that our money is correspondingly falling in value and cannot properly fulfil its role as a measure of value or indeed as a standard for deferred payments. Since the changes in prices are usually gradual, however, we need not let this worry us too much at

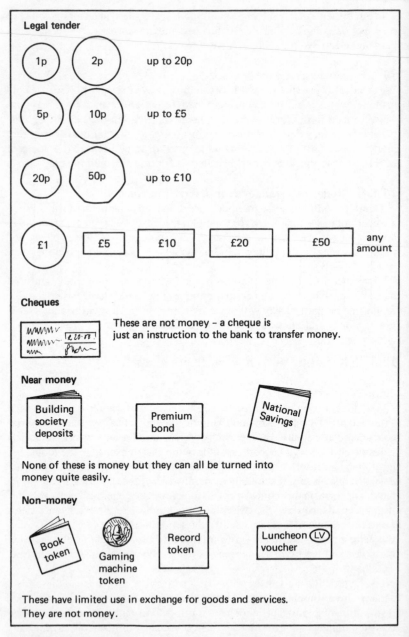

**Fig. 10.2** Money: legal tender, near-money, non-money. Money must be *generally* acceptable in exchange for goods and services

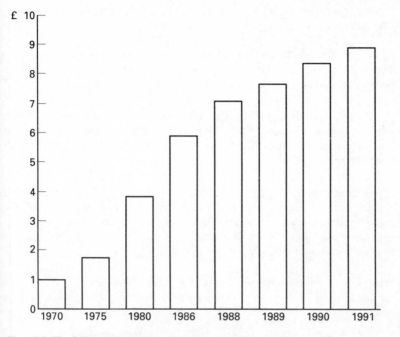

**Fig. 10.3** The falling value of money: the lengths of the columns are in proportion to the amounts of money required to purchase a given amount of goods

this stage, although it is worth looking at fig. 10.3 to see how the value of money has changed since 1970. If we assume that a given parcel of goods could be bought in 1970 for £1 we can read from the chart what the same parcel of goods would have cost in subsequent years. Thus in 1975 we could have bought the same parcel of goods for £1.68 and in 1988 for £7.12. By 1991, however, it would cost nine times as much as in 1970: £8.88. This tendency for prices to rise, which is known as *inflation*, is one respect in which our money does not have all the traditional characteristics that it should have.

In practice in the United Kingdom the fall in the value of money is often assessed from changes in the *retail prices index*. This index is constructed by calculating the cost of purchasing a wide range of goods and services at a certain time, allowing for the proportions in which they are purchased by representative households. Then each month the prices of the same goods and services are obtained again and the overall cost is expressed as a percentage of the original cost.

The index was revalued in January 1987 and the cost of buying the goods and services then was called 100. By December 1991 the index stood at 136, showing that on average prices had increased by over one-third in four years, with a corresponding fall in the value of money.

### 10.3.3    Other characteristics of money

There are several other characteristics that money should have, none of them perhaps as fundamental as the two we have already outlined.

**Portability**    It is obviously desirable that money should be portable, so that shopping can be done conveniently. In some societies huge boulders have been used as money. Imagine the difficulty of doing the weekly shopping in such circumstances!

**Divisibility**    It is also important that money should be divisible, so that small payments can be made. One of the reasons for the use of copper and other base metals in monetary systems was the impossibility of making small payments in gold or silver. Again, we would be faced with great difficulties if the smallest monetary unit in circulation was the £10 note.

**Durability**    If money is to act as a store of value it is necessary that it should not deteriorate. In those communities where livestock was used as money, people would find their wealth depreciating as it aged.

**Uniformity**    It is generally agreed that money should be uniform in quality. At one time British coins contained precious metals in varying proportions, and people tended to hoard those coins that contained the most gold or silver and thus had the highest intrinsic value.

## 10.4    Types of money

We have already mentioned some of the commodities that have been used as money in the past. Although a wide variety of commodities have been used as money, most societies have now settled on metallic coins. We conclude this Unit by looking at the kinds of money that have been used in the United Kingdom.

### 10.4.1    Gold and silver

For a long period gold and silver coins with a guaranteed metal content were in circulation. They thus had intrinsic value, and the public were eager to accept them.

### 10.4.2    Base metals

The relative shortage of gold and silver, and the difficulty of making small payments, led to the introduction of other metal coins, such as copper and nickel ones. Eventually the use of gold and silver was abandoned altogether. Now our coins are merely tokens which we accept because we know other people will accept them from us, not because of their intrinsic value.

### 10.4.3 Paper money

It was once the practice of wealthy merchants and traders to leave their gold and silver with a goldsmith for safekeeping. In exchange they received a note from the goldsmith, in which he promised to pay a fixed amount of gold or silver on demand. Such notes were often used to buy goods from local dealers, the dealer then claiming the gold from the goldsmith. These, in effect, were the first banknotes.

Most of the holders of such notes never bothered to cash them for gold, and the gold consequently lay idle in the goldsmith's vaults. Before long the goldsmiths realized that they could issue notes in excess of the amount of gold in their vaults: no difficulty would arise, provided that not everyone wanted to withdraw gold at the same time. These banknotes which were not fully covered by gold were known as *fractionally backed* notes (see Unit 11.2).

The proportion of gold to notes issued fell over the years, and we are now in a position where the entire note issue is unbacked by gold. We accept the notes only because we are confident that other people will accept them from us.

### 10.4.4 Bank money

Table 10.1 shows the total amount of money available in the United Kingdom in December 1991. You will notice that, while the volume of notes and coins is considerable, it is dwarfed by the second item, bank deposits. Nowadays, most money changes hands through the use of these bank deposits, which are transferred by means of cheques, as discussed in the next Unit.

**Table 10.1** The UK supply of money, December 1991

|                        | £m      |
| ---------------------- | ------- |
| Bank notes and coin    | 15728   |
| Bank deposits          | 260657  |
| Total                  | 276385  |

## 10.5 Questions

1. Define barter and invent an example to show the difficulties involved in a system based on barter.
2. Describe the four main functions of money.
3. What qualities does an item need if it is to fulfil the four functions of money?
4. How can the value of money be measured?

5. What would be the disadvantages of using each of the following as the only form of money in the UK: (a) chalk, (b) eggs, (c) cattle, (d) mercury, (e) five-pound notes.

6. State with reasons whether each of the following can be regarded as money: (a) a five-pound note, (b) a cheque for five pounds, (c) a five-pound postal order, (d) a five-pound record token, (e) a five-pound premium bond.

7. It is said that money enables trade to take place more easily.
   (a) Define money.
   (b) Define trade.
   (c) Give examples to show how trade would be more difficult without money.

8. In 1991 Emma Roberts was paid £140 per week, and she was due for a pay rise on 1 January 1992. During 1991 retail prices increased on average by 4 per cent. Also during 1991 Emma took on extra responsibilities. Draft a letter from Emma to her employer setting out her claim for a pay increase, showing how much she would need to cover the rise in prices and suggesting an amount for the extra responsibilities.

# The banking system: the retail banks

## 11.1 Introduction

No institutions are more important to business people than the banks. People may want to borrow money to help them start a business or to finance the purchase of stocks once the business is under way, or they may simply need to settle their debts with their suppliers or to collect money from their customers. The bank will help them in each situation. In this Unit we examine briefly the early development of the banks and the functions they perform for businesses and for the community in general.

First we must distinguish between the different kinds of bank.

### 11.1.1 The central bank

The central bank of the United Kingdom is the Bank of England. It is the Government's bank and its functions are explained in Unit 12.6.

### 11.1.2 The retail banks

The UK retail banks include Barclays, Lloyds, Midland, National Westminster, TSB, Abbey National, Bank of Scotland, the Royal Bank of Scotland, the Co-operative Bank, Yorkshire Bank and Girobank, which was established within the Post Office and is now owned by the Alliance and Leicester Building Society. Sometimes these banks are called 'clearing' banks since one function is to clear or process cheques.

### 11.1.3 Merchant banks

As their name suggests, these banks were originally merchants or traders. They began to take part in the finance of trade in the nineteenth century, and their interests have spread from there. Now they offer a range of services to commerce and industry, as we shall see in Unit 12.3.

### *11.1.4   Overseas banks*

Over 250 overseas banks have offices in London. Originally they went there to help people in their own country who were trading in the UK. If someone in Saudi Arabia has £500000 to collect from a British firm, it could be helpful to have an agent (a bank) established in London.

These days the foreign banks locate in London to take advantage of its position as a leading financial centre, and many of them make excellent profits by dealing on the foreign exchange market (see Unit 21.4).

## 11.2   The development of the retail banks

As we saw in Unit 10.4.3, the original bankers were goldsmiths and jewellers, whose vaults provided a place of safekeeping for the valuables of local people. Rather than carry large amounts of gold around with them or leave it at home, people would deposit it with the goldsmith, who would make a small charge for the service and issue a receipt to the depositor. The receipt could be exchanged for gold at any time if the depositor wanted to make purchases. Once the newly withdrawn money had been spent, the recipient would almost certainly redeposit it with the goldsmith. It eventually became the practice not to withdraw gold for every purchase but to pass on the receipt to traders from whom you bought goods. As long as the trader recognized the receipt and trusted the goldsmith who had issued it, this was a safer and much more convenient way of making payments, since the receipt represented a claim on an amount of deposited gold.

This benefited the goldsmiths too, in that only a small proportion of the gold deposited with them was ever withdrawn. The goldsmiths soon realized that they could turn this situation to their own advantage. Suppose, for example, they had £10000 deposited and knew from experience that a maximum of £2000 was withdrawn on any one day, and that this would be redeposited within a day or so. They deduced that if the ratio of gold in their vaults to the value of the receipts they had issued was greater than 20 per cent, they need never run out of gold. So they began tentatively to issue *receipts* or *promises to pay* to people who had not deposited any gold but who wanted to borrow instead. Naturally they made a charge for this service. Since these receipts were identical to those issued to the original depositors, they could be used for purchases in exactly the same way. The danger lay in the temptation to issue too many receipts unbacked by gold. When this happened and the ratio of gold to promises to pay fell to, say, 5 per cent, rumours would sometimes grow of the goldsmith's inability to meet his liabilities. The holders of his paper promises would then clamour for repayment, bringing about the collapse – bankruptcy – of the goldsmith.

The next development was the growth of what we now know as cheques. If you had a sum of money deposited with a goldsmith, or a bank as we may now say, you might instruct your bank to transfer money to someone else. Such orders would be individually written – there was no such thing as the printed

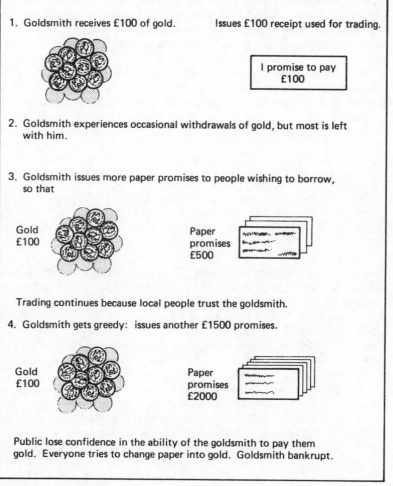

1. Goldsmith receives £100 of gold.　　Issues £100 receipt used for trading.

I promise to pay
£100

2. Goldsmith experiences occasional withdrawals of gold, but most is left with him.

3. Goldsmith issues more paper promises to people wishing to borrow, so that

Gold £100　　　　　　Paper promises £500

Trading continues because local people trust the goldsmith.

4. Goldsmith gets greedy: issues another £1500 promises.

Gold £100　　　　　　Paper promises £2000

Public lose confidence in the ability of the goldsmith to pay them gold. Everyone tries to change paper into gold. Goldsmith bankrupt.

**Fig. 11.1** Goldsmiths and money

cheque that we know today – but the role of these early banks was essentially the same as that of today's. We can now examine that role in detail.

## 11.3   The functions of the banks

### 11.3.1   The safeguarding of customers' money

As we have seen, this was the original function of the banks, and it remains important today. Bank accounts are divided into two groups: sight deposits which can be withdrawn on demand and time deposits which require notice of withdrawal.

**Sight deposits**  These are current accounts and are essential to all businesses. Money or cheques can be deposited into such an account at any time and, more important, withdrawals can be made at any time without giving notice to the bank. Payments can also be made to creditors by writing cheques in their favour.

The banks do not pay interest on most current accounts. Indeed they may make charges for running an account, though the policy on this varies from time to time. Prompted by competition from building societies, most banks have introduced current accounts on which they pay interest subject to certain conditions (for example, the maintenance of a minimum balance of, say, £2000).

**Time deposits**  These are sometimes known as deposit accounts or savings accounts. On most of them seven days' notice of withdrawal is required though in practice the money can normally be withdrawn on demand with the loss of seven days interest. The rate of interest on such accounts may be increased if the depositor agrees to a long period of notice.

Opening a bank account is not difficult. The current account is the most useful type for general purposes. At the bank you will be asked to provide a specimen signature, so that the bank can subsequently see that your cheques are properly signed, and to fill in a form giving the names and addresses of referees (probably two) who are able to vouch for your honesty. Provided that the references are favourable, the bank will accept an initial deposit to open your account. You will then be issued with a cheque book and a paying-in book, and will be able to use the services outlined in this Unit.

An important aspect of the safekeeping of deposits is that the banks must always make sure that they have enough money to meet likely withdrawals by customers or, in technical terms, that they retain sufficient *liquid assets* to meet anticipated withdrawals. 'Liquidity' in this context means *nearness to cash*, so liquid assets are those that can be turned into cash quickly. In Unit 11.11 we shall see how the banks arrange their assets in order to meet this requirement.

### 11.3.2  Supplying cash to customers
If we are going to entrust our money to the bank, we need to be sure that we can withdraw it when we want it. Thus the banks must always have money available for their customers. Since all branches of the banks receive deposits of cash from their customers, you might imagine that they will normally be able to meet their customers' requirements when they want to withdraw. In fact, it is unlikely that the deposits and withdrawals at any one bank will exactly balance. For example, in those branches located near industrial estates, withdrawals are likely to exceed deposits as firms draw money to pay wages. High-street branches, on the other hand, are likely to experience a net inflow of cash, as shops pay in their takings. There has to be a transfer of cash from the

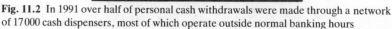

**Fig. 11.2** In 1991 over half of personal cash withdrawals were made through a network of 17 000 cash dispensers, most of which operate outside normal banking hours

high-street branches to the industrial estate branches. Similar transfers may need to be made between urban and rural branches. Other branches – seaside branches, for example – may experience seasonal fluctuations in their requirements. The banks therefore have to organize the physical transfer of money from place to place.

The banks are also the means of getting new notes and coins into circulation, although these originate at the Bank of England and the Royal Mint respectively. It is also the function of the banks to withdraw badly soiled or mutilated notes from circulation when they are deposited. These are returned to the Bank of England, where they are destroyed.

### 11.3.3 Operating the cheque system

A *cheque* is an order to your bank to pay a stated sum to the bearer of the cheque or a named person. We saw earlier that the original cheques were letters from customers to their banker or goldsmith, telling him to transfer money. Today it is usual to write cheques on printed forms issued by the banks, though there is nothing illegal in writing a cheque on blank paper. Indeed there are many examples of cheques being written on unusual materials: the friends of A. P. Herbert are said to have written a cheque on a cow as a means of demonstrating that there is no legal obligation to use printed cheques. However, the bank will probably close your account if you do not use the printed cheques which facilitate automatic processing.

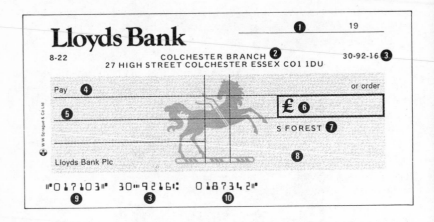

**Fig. 11.3** Specimen cheques: blank (*top*) and completed (*bottom*)

Figure 11.3 shows a specimen of a completed cheque.

**(1) The date**    All cheques should carry the date on which they are drawn (that is, written out). When you receive a cheque, you should pay it into your bank immediately. The drawee bank will refuse to honour a cheque after six months have elapsed from the date of issue. (An exception is made at the beginning of each year when many cheques appear to have been drawn the previous January or February, having been absent-mindedly dated with the wrong year.)

Sometimes cheques are *post-dated*, a practice which is frowned upon by the banks. Suppose you receive a bill on 15 March and know that you have insufficient funds in your bank account to cover the bill, but that your salary will be paid in on 28 March. You may be able to keep your creditor quiet by sending off a cheque dated 28 March, in which case you will have gained two weeks' delay. This is a post-dated cheque. The bank will not process the cheque until 28 March.

**(2) The drawee** The cheque is said to be *drawn* on the bank. Each cheque carries the name of the bank and the address of the branch on which it is drawn. This is the branch at which the account is held. The bank is known as the *drawee*. If there is a query about the cheque, reference can easily be made to the drawee bank.

**(3) The branch code number** This appears in the top right-hand corner of the cheque and again at the bottom, where it is printed in magnetic characters to facilitate the automatic handling of the cheque.

**(4) The payee's name** This must be written on the top line of the cheque. United Stores can then pay it into its account. If the cheque is an open cheque (see Unit 11.4.1) United Stores could cash the cheque over the counter at the bank on which it is drawn.

**(5) and (6) The amount** that is to be paid must appear both in words and in figures. It is important that these numbers agree. If there is a discrepancy between the sum in words and the sum in figures the cheque will not be honoured by the bank.

**(7) The drawer's name** is often printed beneath the box in which the figures are written.

**(8) The drawer's signature** The drawer must also *sign* the cheque, to authorize the bank to pay the money out. Again, if the cheque is not signed, or if the signature does not correspond with the specimen signature provided by the client when the account was opened, the bank will not honour the cheque.

**(9) The cheque number** appears in magnetic characters in the bottom left-hand corner of the cheque and also appears on the customer's bank statement, so that the details on the statement can be checked.

A further figure will appear at the bottom of the cheque once it has been paid into the bank. This will be the amount of the cheque, printed by the bank on the basis of the figures written in by the drawer.

**(10) The account number** appears at the bottom of the cheque, again in magnetic characters, to facilitate the automatic handling of the cheque. Every customer has a unique account number which appears on all his or her cheques and paying-in slips (see Unit 11.5).

## 11.4   Types of cheque

### 11.4.1   Open cheques

The cheque shown in fig. 11.4 is an open cheque. It would still be an open cheque if the payee's name was on it. Anyone who finds an open cheque can take it to the bank on which it is drawn, pretend to be the payee, and obtain cash by endorsing the cheque on the back with the payee's name. Obviously it is not normally safe to write such a cheque, but it may be necessary if you wish to pay someone who does not have a bank account.

### 11.4.2   Bearer cheques

These are very rarely used today. They are made out 'Pay Bearer', as in fig. 11.4, and anyone in possession of such a cheque can demand cash from the bank without any identification, since the name of the payee is immaterial.

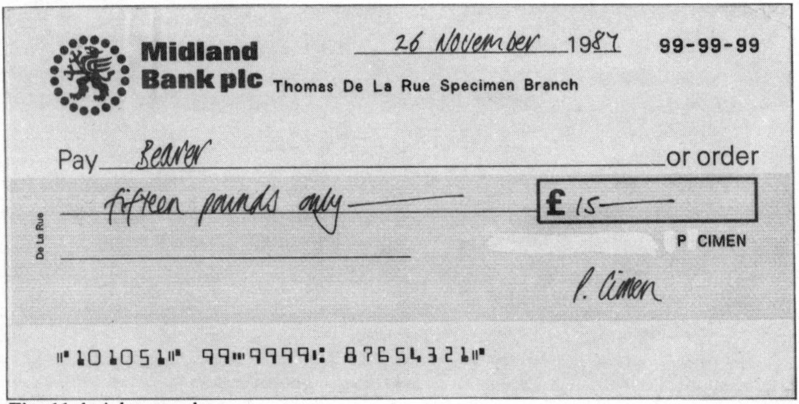

**Fig. 11.4** A bearer cheque

### 11.4.3   Crossed cheques

If two parallel lines are drawn across the face of a cheque it becomes a *crossed cheque*. (Figures 11.5 to 11.8 are all crossed cheques.) The bank will not pay cash over the counter on a crossed cheque, because the crossing indicates that the cheque must be paid into a bank account. If a thief pays a stolen crossed cheque into the wrong account, it will be possible to trace the account to which it has been credited. The fact that a crossed cheque is made payable to J. Smith does not mean, however, that it has to be credited to J. Smith's account – he may want it paid to his *order*. Thus if he owes money to B. Jones he can endorse the back of it *in favour of B. Jones*, and Jones can then pay it into his own account.

The cheque in fig. 11.5 carries a *general crossing*. Other general crossings appear on the cheques in figs 11.6 and 11.7. Some people maintain the old

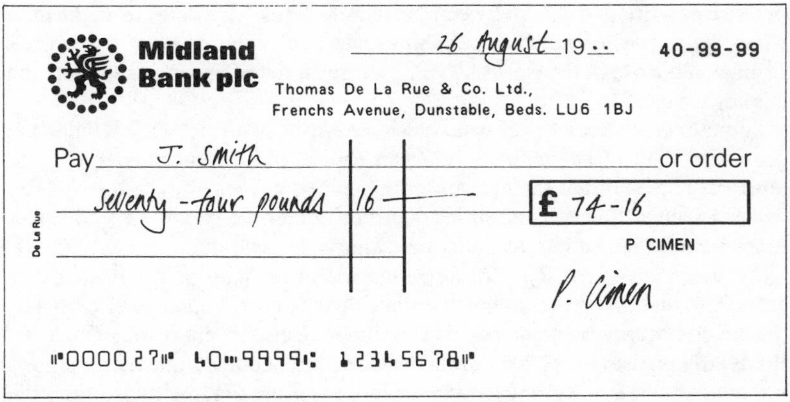

**Fig. 11.5** A crossed cheque

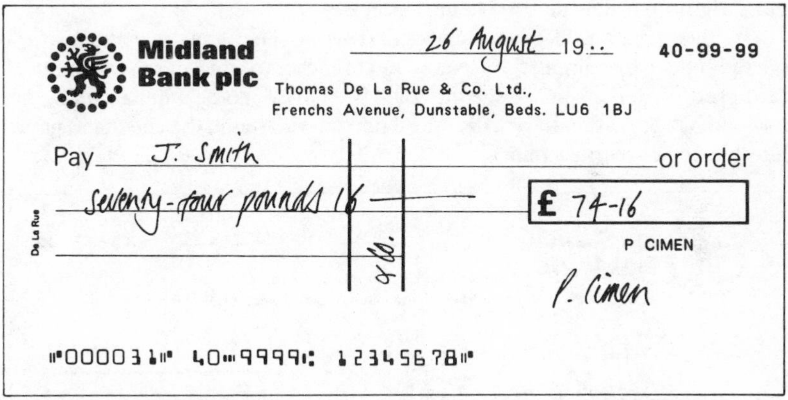

**Fig. 11.6** A general crossing

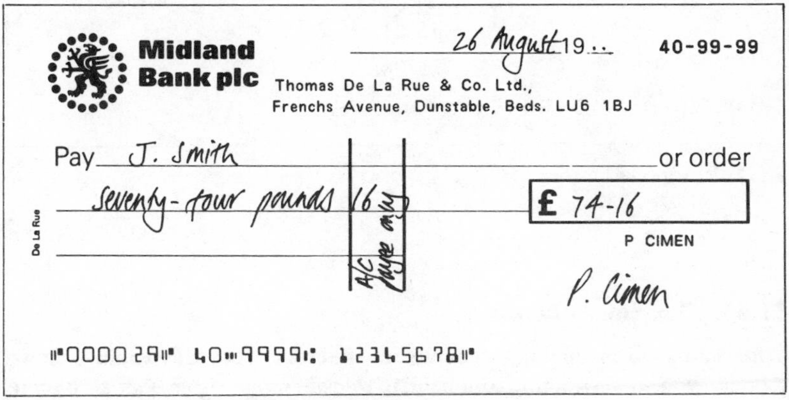

**Fig. 11.7** A general crossing

practice of writing '& Co.' between the parallel lines. This dates from the days when the drawer of a cheque who was uncertain of the name of the payee's bank would write in the words '& Co.', leaving it to the payee to complete the banker's name.

Sometimes a cheque is crossed *Account payee*, as in fig. 11.7. Under the provision of the Cheques Act 1992, such a cheque is non-transferable and must only be paid into the account of the named payee. Prior to this Act the words 'Account payee' had no legal authority and the cheques could some-times be paid into other accounts following a suitable endorsement.

*Not negotiable* crossings are also quite popular. The intention of such a crossing is that the payee cannot negotiate the cheque to someone else (that is, the cheque cannot be made payable to someone else by endorsing it). In fact this is *not* the case: the payee can still transfer the cheque if some reason arises, but the crossing is a warning to the recipient to ensure that the transferer is the real owner of the cheque. If the cheque has been stolen, the recipient has no more right than the thief to claim the money.

The cheque in fig. 11.8 bears a *special crossing*. Here the drawer is restrict-ing the cheque by naming the account and branch into which it must be paid. If the payee insisted, even this cheque could be paid into some other account, but it would be very difficult for a dishonest person who found the cheque to pay it into his or her own account.

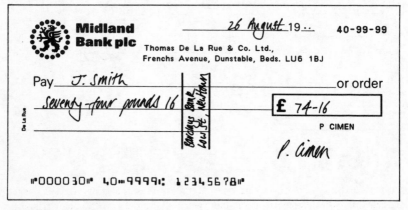

**Fig. 11.8** A special crossing

## 11.5   Clearing a cheque

When you write cheques in favour of your creditors – people to whom you owe money – you are instructing your bank to transfer money from your account to theirs. The process of dealing with a cheque once it has been paid in to your

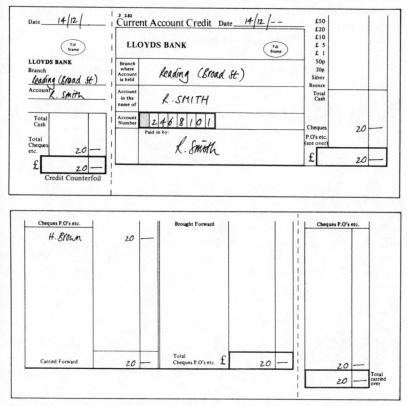

**Fig. 11.9** A paying-in slip (front and back)

creditor's bank is called *clearing* the cheque. The actual process will vary according to whether the drawer and payee share the same bank or have different banks. Two examples will show you in outline what happens.

**Example 1** (fig. 11.10(a))   H. Brown, who banks at Lloyds, Ipswich, pays £20 by cheque to R. Smith, who banks at Lloyds, Reading. Smith pays the cheque into his account, using a paying-in slip like that shown in fig. 11.9.

The counterfoil of the paying-in slip is stamped by the bank and kept as a receipt by Smith, who thus has a permanent record of his in payments. The two branches will be linked by computer to head office and via this system Brown's account will be debited with £20 and Smith's credited with a similar amount.

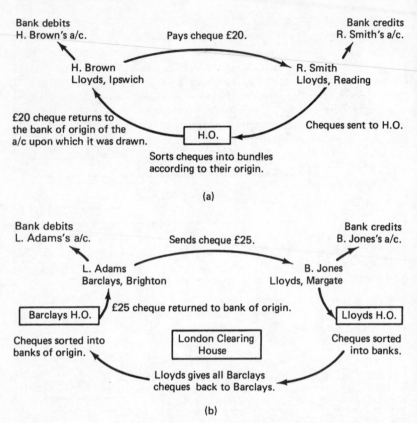

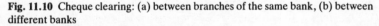

**Fig. 11.10** Cheque clearing: (a) between branches of the same bank, (b) between different banks

If Brown and Smith actually had accounts at the same branch the adjustment could, of course, be made there. However, there are more procedures if drawer and payee have accounts with different banks.

The processing of such cheques is supervised by the Association for Payment Clearing Services (APACS).

### 11.5.1  Association for Payment Clearing Services

APACS operates through three limited companies.

(a) The bulk of cheques are handled through the Cheque and Credit Clearing Company. The procedure formerly called the General Clearing is illustrated in fig. 11.10(b) and an example is given below.

**Example 2**  L. Adams, who banks at Barclays, Brighton, sends a cheque for £25 to B. Jones, who banks at Lloyds, Margate. The cheque is paid into Jones's account in the same way as before, the account is credited with £25 and the cheque sent off to Lloyds' head office. Lloyds divides all the cheques it receives according to their bank of origin. Thus there will be great racks of cheques drawn on Barclays, Lloyds itself, Midland, National Westminster and other smaller banks. We will confine our attentions for the moment to those cheques, like that of Adams, drawn on Barclays Bank and paid into Lloyds. When they have been assembled, they are delivered in vans to a central site. They are handed over to the Barclays' representatives together with a note of their total value, for this is the sum that Barclays owes to Lloyds. At the same time the Barclays' representatives present Lloyds with cheques received by Barclays, drawn on Lloyds. Any necessary payment between the two banks is made through the accounts they operate at the Bank of England (see Unit 12.7).

Adams's cheque is now taken back to Barclays' head office with all the others that have been received, and from there it is returned to Barclays' Brighton branch, where Adams's account is debited £25. The payment is now complete.

The Cheque and Credit Clearing Company handles around 2500 million items each year with a value of about £1200 billion in 1991. Over 90 per cent of the items were cheques, the remainder being paper credits.

(b) The general APACS company is the CHAPS (Clearing House Automated Payment System) and Town Clearing Company which operates two high value clearings every day, ensuring that cheques are settled on the day that they are drawn. The Town Clearing deals with cheques of £500000 or more, originating from and paid into bank branches in the City of London. The CHAPS clearing is a nationwide electronic transfer service for items of £1000 or more. The average value of each item through CHAPS and the Town Clearing is over two and a half million pounds.

(c) The Bankers Automated Clearing Service Ltd (BACS) provides for the processing of automated credits, direct debits and standing orders. In 1990 BACS handled 1600 million transactions valued at over £660 billion.

## 11.6 Dishonoured cheques

It sometimes happens that when the cheque arrives back at the drawer's branch via the clearing system there is insufficient money in the drawer's account to cover the payment. In this case the cheque may be sent back to the payee marked 'Refer to drawer', which means that the payee should ask the drawer for an explanation. Sometimes the returned cheque is marked 'Refer to drawer, please re-present'. This would imply that the bank cannot honour the cheque at the moment but has reason to believe that there will soon be sufficient funds in the account to meet it. (Perhaps the drawer's salary is due to be paid in shortly.)

Lack of funds is not the only reason for cheques being dishonoured by the banks: there are at least three other possibilities.

(a) The amount written in words and the amount written in figures may be different. In this case the drawer will be asked to remove the discrepancy.

(b) The signature may not correspond with the specimen given to the bank when the account was opened (see Unit 11.3.1). This will arouse the bank's suspicions, and they will ask the account-holder to verify that the signature is genuine. Some accounts need the signatures of two people before money can be transferred, and cheques will be dishonoured if there is only one signature on them.

(c) If more than six months have elapsed between the date of the cheque and the day it is presented to the bank, the cheque is *stale*. It is possible that the cheque has passed through many hands in this time, and the bank will want to make sure that the drawer knows what is happening to the cheque.

## 11.7    Bank giro credit system

Cheques are the most important method of payment provided by the banks but there are others, and the *bank giro credit system* is one of them. Figures 11.11 and 11.12 show the main documents used. This system allows payment to be made at any branch of any bank to any branch of any bank in the country, and it is available to those who do not have a bank account as well as to those who do. The system was formerly known as the 'credit transfer system'.

In fig. 11.11, Bloggs & Co. is using the system to pay £228.24 to the account of A. J. Smith, who has presumably supplied it with goods to this value. The cheque will be cleared in the ordinary way outlined in Unit 11.5, and Smith's account will be credited with the amount in a few days.

The bank giro system offers several advantages.

(a) You do not need a bank account to pay by this method, although your creditor must have one.

(b) Since you pay your cheque (or money) directly into the bank, you do not have to worry about it going astray in the post.

(c) If you are an account-holder you can pay money into your account from any part of the country.

For businesses there may be considerable economy in using the bank giro credit system to pay wages and salaries. Figure 11.12 shows what happens. Bloggs & Co. Ltd wants to pay the monthly salaries of its eight branch managers. The firm *could* instruct the wages department to send eight separate cheques to these employees. Instead, the bank giro summary form is completed as shown, with the name, bank branch and account number of each payee as well as the amounts with which they are to be credited. At the same time an individual giro slip is prepared for each payee, but this does not need signatures. The main form is totalled and signed, probably by a director of the firm, and a single cheque is drawn to cover the total salary bill. Thus by using a multiple bank giro credit form, the director has to sign one cheque instead of

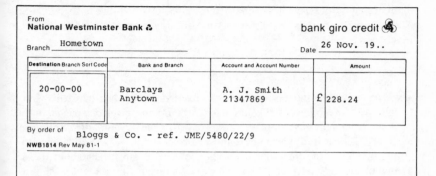

**Fig. 11.11** A bank giro credit slip

# National Westminster Bank PLC &

To_____ Hometown _____ Branch

To be completed in
duplicate if a receipt
is required

Date_____ 20 July 19.. _____

**Cashier's Stamp**

### Bank Giro Credits - Summary List

Please distribute the undermentioned sums in accordance with the ___8___ bank giro
credits attached as arranged with the recipients.

Our cheque for £ 6886.83 _____ is enclosed.

C. Parker

For Bloggs & Co. Ltd     Signature(s)

| Code Number | Bank and Branch | Account and Account Number | Amount |
|---|---|---|---|
| | Barclays, Anytown | M. D. Davis 23456789 | 921.29 |
| | Lloyds, Downtown | H. Hancock 34567890 | 836.50 |
| | Midland, Hometown | R. Carter 45678901 | 848.78 |
| | Nat West, Sometown | A. Williams 56789012 | 893.34 |
| | Lloyds, Anytown | P. Chambers 32109876 | 851.92 |
| | Barclays, Sometown | P. J. Jones 21987654 | 845.37 |
| | Midland, Downtown | W. Kelly 43210987 | 839.15 |
| | Nat West, Hometown | J. Cobb 54321098 | 850.48 |

**Fig. 11.12** A bank giro summary form

eight. Imagine the saving of time if there are 5000 employees to be paid. Today, large firms may give these instructions by means of computer disk or tape.

## 11.8    Standing or banker's orders

If you have to make regular payments of a fixed amount, you can instruct your bank to pay the money out of your current account on a given day each month or year. You might have standing orders covering the payment of your house mortgage, life assurance premiums and a club subscription. The advantage to you is that once the form has been completed you can forget about these annual or monthly payments. A slight disadvantage is that the bank will not inform you each time it makes the payment, so if you keep only a small balance in your account you may inadvertently overdraw the account and not realize this until the bank sends you a statement.

The advantage to the payee of a standing order is that reminders do not have to be sent to the payer, and this saves much paperwork. The only disadvantage is that if the payments have to be increased, a new form has to be completed by the account-holder, and people are notoriously slow at completing the forms. This problem has been overcome by the introduction of direct debit.

## 11.9    Direct debit

This system is a cross between the bank giro and the standing order systems. Here, however, the initiative lies with the creditor, who informs the debtor's bank of the amount owed, and this is then transferred to the creditor's account. Of course, the debtor's prior authority must be obtained for this system to be used.

Its main advantage over the standing order system is that it can be used when the size of the payments is likely to vary from month to month. Also, for a payment such as an annual subscription, an increase can be put into effect without a new form having to be filled in. To the payee there is the further advantage over the bank giro system that it is not necessary to rely on the debtor's punctuality to secure payment.

## 11.10    Bank drafts

This method of payment is used where large sums are involved and where the payee, being unacquainted with the debtor, is not happy to accept a cheque. If Retailer Co. Ltd owes Wholesaler Co. Ltd £500 it can obtain a bank draft like that in fig. 11.13 by paying £500 plus a small commission to the bank. The draft is sent to the wholesaler, who now has a cheque drawn on the bank itself. This is clearly much safer than a cheque from a little-known retailer. Once regular transactions are taking place between the two, it is likely that payments will be made by cheque.

**Fig. 11.13** A bank draft

**Fig. 11.14** A travellers cheque

The *travellers cheque* is a more familiar kind of bank draft. If you are travelling abroad you may not want to carry large amounts of foreign currency with you. Instead, you can buy travellers cheques, like the one shown in fig. 11.14, from a bank. As a safeguard you should sign the cheque immediately. When you want to exchange it for foreign currency, you countersign the cheque, and it will only be cashed if the two signatures are identical. The recipient now has a cheque drawn on the bank itself: this is much more acceptable than a cheque drawn on the account of an unknown person.

Although travellers cheques are normally used abroad, there is no reason why you cannot use them in your own country. In the UK, however, there is generally no need to carry large amounts of money on your person because you can nearly always find a branch of your bank where you can withdraw money

from a cash dispensing machine (see fig. 11.2) or use a cheque with the backing
of a cheque card (see Units 11.12.7 and 11.12.8); if not, a bank where you are
unknown will telephone your branch to get authority before making the
payment.

## 11.11    Loans and overdrafts

An important role of the banks is to lend money to people and businesses who
are temporarily short of funds. The early bankers soon found that they had
surplus funds on their hands which could be lent at a profit, and this activity has
been the basis of their business ever since. You must remember that most
people, once they have deposited money in the bank, will not want to withdraw large amounts of cash. They are normally happy to make payments by
cheque or bank giro. As long as the bank retains sufficient money in its tills to
meet its day-to-day requirements, it will be able to use the balance to its
advantage. Experience has taught modern bankers that they need to keep
very few of their assets in the form of cash. As we can calculate from Table
11.1, the position of the main UK banks in December 1991 was that cash
accounted for just over 1 per cent of their sterling assets.

**Table 11.1**  UK banks: main assets and liabilities December 1991

| Sterling assets | £m | Sterling liabilities | £m |
|---|---|---|---|
| Cash and balances at | | Sight deposits | 174000 |
|     Bank of England | 6000 | Time deposits | 338000 |
| Market loans: | | Total deposits | 512000 |
|     Loans to discount houses | 9000 | | |
|     Loans to other financial | | | |
|     institutions | 125000 | | |
| Treasury bills | 4000 | | |
| Other bills of exchange | 9000 | | |
| Investments | 31000 | | |
| Advances | 382000 | | |

The table includes all UK banks. The main retail banks keep a rather higher
proportion of cash.

In order to make profits the banks make loans, but they have to ensure that
they can always obtain more cash if they need it. To maintain an adequate level
of liquidity (see Unit 11.3.1) the banks have to achieve a balance between
*short-term* and *long-term loans*.

Short-term loans fall into two groups.

**Market loans** are made to other institutions in the money market, notably the
discount houses (see Unit 12.2). Sometimes the loans are made to other

commercial banks on what is known as the *inter-bank market*. Most of these loans are for a very short duration and many are repayable on demand (*at call*). The banks earn only a low rate of interest on many of these loans but this is preferable to keeping cash reserves idle in their tills and vaults.

**Bills** *Treasury bills* are paper securities issued by the Government for three months. They are extremely useful to the banks in that, having Government backing, they are absolutely safe. The banks know that they will get their money back (with interest) in three months at the most.

*Commercial bills of exchange* are also issued for three months. They are a means of financing trade and industry and, as in theory they carry a slightly greater risk than Treasury bills do, they earn the banks a higher rate of interest.

These short-term loans provide the banks with a second line of defence in case there should be heavy and unexpected cash withdrawals.

While liquidity is important to the banks' survival, they also have to make profits. This is achieved through the last two assets in Table 11.1. The main investments are British Government stocks, which are more fully discussed in Unit 13.5.1, and investments in other financial institutions.

However, the banks obtain most of their revenue from *advances* made to customers in the form of loans and overdrafts.

### 11.11.1   Forms of advance
The bank may allow you to borrow by means of either an overdraft or a loan.

**An overdraft** is an informal way of borrowing from the bank for a short period. Thus, if a business's bills are greater than its cash and bank balance at a given moment, it may ask the bank manager to allow its account to be *overdrawn* for a few weeks to cover the difference. If the bank manager agrees to an overdraft of £1000, the firm is entitled to draw cheques totalling up to £1000 more than the balance in the account. Interest will have to be paid, but only on the exact amount by which the account is overdrawn. If the rate of interest goes up during the period of the overdraft, the business will have to pay at the higher rate. When money is paid into the account the overdraft is reduced, and the bank manager will expect it to be paid off entirely by the stipulated date.

**A bank loan** is a more formal means of borrowing. If a business wants to spend £5000 on a van but has only £1000 available, it may apply to the bank manager for a loan to cover the difference. An application form will have to be filled in, stating the amount needed, the purpose of the loan and the length of time for which it is required. Whether or not the loan is granted depends on the factors discussed in Unit 11.11.2. Assuming that the bank agrees to the loan, the business's current account is credited with £4000, and the rate of interest is fixed for the duration of the loan. The bank normally requires the loan to be paid off in equal monthly instalments. When the money is credited to the business's account, the bank also opens a *loan account* in its name, and this is debited with £4000 plus the interest. The monthly payments are then credited to the loan account until the total has been repaid.

### 11.11.2    Creditworthiness

Banks do not lend to everyone who asks for a loan. Their ability to make loans may be restricted by Government policy, but it is more likely that their own caution will cause them to refuse to lend to some applicants.

There are several factors to be taken into account with every application for a loan.

**The suitability of the applicant**    The following are the factors that need to be taken into account with every application for a loan. First, the manager will need to be assured of the applicant's honesty and general creditworthiness. Since the applicant is normally an account-holder with the bank, the manager will have some idea of this already. The amount of the loan and the likelihood of the customer being able to meet the repayment will also be considered: the manager will not be keen to lend either to individuals or businesses if the repayment of the loan is likely to place too great a burden on them. Where the loan is to a business, the most important factors are its past record and the likelihood of its continuing profitability. It is the manager's job to assess the risk involved.

The banker will often want some *collateral security* for the loan. This means something that is left in the bank's possession until the loan is repaid and which may be easily sold if the borrower defaults on the repayment of the loan. Stocks and shares quoted on the Stock Exchange are usually acceptable because they are easy both to value and to sell. Life assurance policies or property deeds are equally acceptable. If none of these is available, the borrower may have to find a *personal guarantor* for the loan – that is, someone who will undertake to repay the loan in the event of the borrower defaulting.

Not all loans are secured in this way, however. Many businesses in their early days possess no acceptable securities, and the bank manager may take a calculated risk in lending to them. Furthermore, most of the banks run a personal loan scheme under which they lend to private individuals for a variety of reasons without security. Figure 11.15 shows us that the personal sector accounts for the largest proportion of bank loans. In fact, about two-thirds of loans to persons are for house purchase. As far as business loans are concerned the diagram reflects the data displayed in fig. 1.3 in that over 70 per cent of the loans go to firms providing services. Overall, manufacturing accounts for less than 10 per cent of the business.

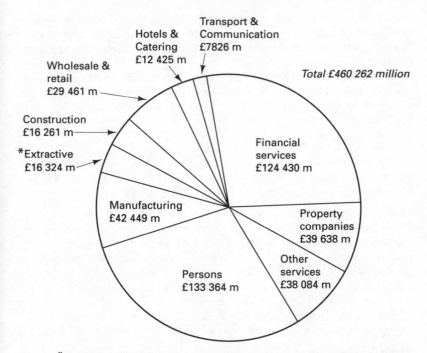

Transport &
Communication
£7826 m

Hotels &
Catering
£12 425 m

Wholesale &
retail
£29 461 m

Total £460 262 million

Construction
£16 261 m

*Extractive
£16 324 m

Financial
services
£124 430 m

Manufacturing
£42 449 m

Property
companies
£39 638 m

Other
services
£38 084 m

Persons
£133 364 m

*Includes agriculture, forestry, fishing and energy and water industries.
**Fig. 11.15** Bank lending in the United Kingdom, November 1991 (£ million)

### 11.11.3 *How do the banks make a profit on loans?*

Like all financial institutions, the banks aim to make a profit by charging a higher rate on the money they lend than they pay on the money they borrow. Approximately one-third of their deposits are held on current accounts, on which banks have traditionally paid no interest. In recent years competition has forced the banks to pay interest on some current accounts, mainly those where the account-holder maintains a high minimum deposit. If they relend the 'free' current account money, it is not difficult for them to make a profit. When money is left in deposit or savings accounts, however, the bank must pay interest on it. Whenever they make loans, however short-term they are, they will want to receive a higher rate than they pay out on these deposits. In general they follow this principle: *the greater the risk, the higher the rate of interest*. Thus the rate of interest charged for overnight loans to a discount house is likely to be lower than that charged for a three-year loan to a manufacturer.

All the banks work from their own *base rate*, which they establish in the light of prevailing economic conditions. The rates they offer on deposits, and the rates they charge for loans, are then related to this base rate. In those years when rates of interest are high (perhaps because the Government wants them to be) the banks should make good profits because of the big gap between any interest paid on a current account and the rates charged on loans and over-drafts to borrowers.

It should be remembered also that the banks sometimes make charges for many of their services. For example, there is often an administration fee for setting up a loan or overdraft, and a fee if the bank has to deal with dishon-oured cheques.

## 11.12   Other functions of the banks

We have now looked at the traditional functions of the banks: safekeeping money, transferring money and lending money. They have developed a range of other subsidiary but still important functions, which we shall now examine.

### 11.12.1   Savings

There are various savings schemes to supplement the traditional deposit account. Higher rates of interest are available to people with sums of over £2000 to invest, and for sums over £10000 quotations can be obtained for the investment of the money for periods ranging from twenty-four hours to twelve months. A monthly income can be arranged, and there are schemes for regular savers and for the younger generation.

For large organizations or wealthy individuals the banks may issue a Certifi-cate of Deposit in exchange for large sums of money (see Unit 12.2.4).

### 11.12.2   Home loans

Banks entered the mortgage market in the early 1980s, and at the end of 1991 they had almost £90000 million outstanding on house-purchase. Their home loans are similar to those of the building societies, with the borrowing normally repayable over a maximum of twenty-five years. Interest on these loans is imposed at a separate rate from interest on other loans. While the banks will want to adjust the rate when base rates change, they will also have to take account of the rates being charged by the building societies.

### 11.12.3   Safeguarding valuables

As well as looking after cash for its customers, a bank provides facilities for the storing of valuable documents such as property deeds, wills and items of jewellery.

### 11.12.4   Night safe facility

The retail banks are normally closed to the public by 4.00 p.m., with only a few branches open on Saturdays and none on Sundays, except in special locations such as international airports. Many small businesses collect money from their customers after the banks have closed and do not have the facilities to keep it safe until the banks re-open. The night safe facility overcomes this: the customer is provided with a wallet, into which is locked the cash to be deposited in the bank. The customer takes this to the bank, unlocks a small trapdoor in the outside wall, and 'posts' the wallet inside, where it slides straight down a chute to the strong room. When the bank staff arrive in the morning, either the wallets are unlocked and the money is credited to the appropriate accounts or they are locked away until the customers call to collect them.

Large stores, whose takings may run into tens of thousands of pounds, may consider it too great a risk to transfer the money themselves and they often employ a security firm to do it for them.

### 11.12.5    Bank statements

Statements are provided at regular intervals, to help customers keep a check on their finances. Of course, they should do this anyway, but the bank statement provides a double check. It is particularly useful where standing orders or direct debits are regularly drawn on the account, or where bank giro credits are paid in.

It also enables the account holder to check on any charges that the bank has levied on the account. Although the general level of such charges is published in advance, customers are not normally aware of charges on their accounts until the statement arrives.

### 11.12.6    Credit cards

A credit card enables the holder to obtain instant credit. The best known in the United Kingdom are Barclaycard, Access and Trustcard. Other cards are available but they all operate in basically the same way.

The way in which a credit card is used to obtain goods and services on credit is explained in Unit 6.3.2. The card may also be used to obtain a cash advance from any of the banks operating the scheme, up to the cardholder's credit limit. In this case interest is charged from the day the cash is withdrawn. All the card companies have links with credit card companies abroad, and UK credit cards are accepted worldwide.

The advantage of credit cards to the holders is the availability of instant credit – not for them the formalities involved in buying goods on hire purchase. One disadvantage is the temptation to buy too much and then spend many months in making repayments. Another is that retailers may increase their prices to cover the commission that they pay to the credit card companies.

The advantage to the trader is the increase in turnover that results from participation in the credit card system. The disadvantage is the proportion of turnover that has to be paid to the card company.

To the banks who operate the schemes, they provide a profitable outlet for funds which are temporarily surplus to requirements. The fraudulent use of cards has sometimes caused them problems, however.

### 11.12.7    Debit cards

A more recent development is the introduction of debit cards which are the main example of the Electronic Funds Transfer at the Point of Sale (EFTPOS). Debit cards such as Connect and Switch replace cheques and allow retail payments to be made electronically from personal accounts to the accounts of retailers. The main components of such a system are:

(a) electronic equipment installed at the retail outlet;
(b) magnetically striped plastic cards with associated Personal Identification Numbers (PINs) issued to the banks' customers;
(c) an automatic system for transmitting messages between the retailer's terminal and the banks.

These systems are provided by British Telecom and by Mercury (Unit 16.3).

Payments are effected by the customer's card being inserted into a terminal at the retail outlet. The card is electronically read and, provided there is sufficient money in the account, the right amount will then be transferred to the retailer's account.

Clearly there is a high degree of security in such a system in some respects, but if customers are to be convinced of the benefits they need to be persuaded that it is impossible for other people to transfer money from their account.

### *11.12.8   Cheque cards*
Cheque cards (fig. 11.16) should not be confused with credit cards (although the Barclaycard acts as a cheque card for Barclays Bank and cheque cards sometimes double as debit cards). Many shoppers prefer to use cheques rather than cash when buying expensive items. But retailers are sometimes reluctant to accept cheques in case they are dishonoured, which could involve the retailer in considerable work to secure payment. The banks issue cheque cards to their creditworthy customers, guaranteeing to the payee that a cheque drawn by a cardholder will be honoured by the bank even if there are insufficient funds in the account on which it is drawn. Certain conditions have to be fulfilled – in any single transaction one cheque of up to £50 or more for some customers is guaranteed provided that

(a) the cheque has been signed before the expiry date of the card in the presence of the payee, and the signature corresponds with that on the card;

**Fig. 11.16** A cheque card

(b) the cheque has been drawn on a bank cheque form bearing the name and code number shown on the card (the cardholder's branch code);
(c) the card number is written on the back of the cheque by the payee;
(d) the card has not been altered or defaced.

The advantages of the cheque card lie in the guarantee it affords to retailers and the assistance it gives to the banks' customers in getting cheques accepted. A further advantage to customers is that with the support of a cheque card they can withdraw cash from any branch of any bank issuing cheque cards, though there may be a charge if they use a branch of a bank other than their own. (Separate uniform Eurocheque cards have to be used on the Continent.)

Cheque cards are an example of a service provided by the banks for the benefit of their customers which really carries no advantages for the banks themselves.

### 11.12.9  Automatic teller machines (ATMs)
These enable bank customers to obtain cash quickly, even when the bank is shut, as machines are sited both inside and outside banks. The customer is provided with a coded plastic *cash card* (or the cheque card may also serve this purpose) and a secret Personal Identification Number (PIN). The card is inserted into the dispenser and the customer then taps out the number and the amount to be withdrawn. Varying amounts can be selected, and the money is forthcoming only if there are sufficient funds available in the account. Some machines can also be used to order a new chequebook, or to request a statement of the account.

### 11.12.10  Bankers' references
These are especially important to businesses. If you are about to sign a large business contract with a firm with which you have not dealt before, you can ask your bank to find out about its financial standing. The bank will do this either by consulting its own records, if the business concerned also uses that bank, or by approaching the firm's own bank. It will then be able to give you an assessment of the firm's creditworthiness. Similarly your bank may be willing to issue a reference on your behalf, as testimony of your own financial stability.

### 11.12.11  Income tax, insurance, executorship
The banks provide services in each of these fields. They employ specialists to help individuals and businesses with advice on taxation and insurance and can usually quote you competitive rates for all kinds of insurance. They are also able to help you to draw up your will and, more important, act as the *executor* – in other words, see that the provisions of the will are carried out. Many people appoint their bank as executor because they know that the bank's employees are experts who will do the job properly, and that the bank is always there.

### 11.12.12  Advice and information

The banks have built up a wide range of intelligence services.

**Advice on borrowing**   A bank cannot always lend to a customer, but will probably be able to give expert advice about alternative sources of finance.

**Advice on investment**   If you have only a small amount of savings you are unlikely to have your own stockbroker (see Unit 13.7.1). If you want advice on how to invest your savings you can consult your bank manager, who is sure to have some useful ideas. Furthermore, if the sum involved is too small to interest an individual stockbroker, you can use the bank's stockbroker to obtain your shares.

**Economic advice** of all kinds is provided by banks to trade and industry. Market advice on individual overseas countries and their economic conditions is one example. Banks will also draw up reports on particular industries in overseas countries at the request of a customer.

### 11.12.13  Overseas services

These range from the supply of foreign currency and travellers cheques for people going abroad to the provision of large-scale long-term loans to overseas governments to enable them to construct major projects such as power stations or chemical factories. Importing and exporting companies can borrow in either sterling or foreign currencies, and the banks operate sophisticated systems for the international transfer of money.

## 11.13   Questions

1. Who were the original bankers in England? Why were they suited to perform this function?
2. What are the advantages of having your money in a current account rather than a deposit account at the bank? Name any disadvantage of a current account.
3. Distinguish between the following in connection with a cheque: (a) drawer, (b) drawee, (c) payee.
4. On the same day you receive two cheques payable to you. One has no crossing; the other is crossed 'not negotiable, a/c payee only'. Explain the difference between these two cheques from your point of view.
5. A. Lamb is an exporter awaiting payments of £3000 which will arrive in three instalments of £1000 at the end of each of the next three months. In the meantime he wants to arrange a bank overdraft to cover the amount involved.

   (a) Why would an overdraft be preferable to a loan in these circumstances?

   (b) On what basis will the bank calculate the interest on the overdraft?

   (c) How will the overdraft be repaid?

6. You receive a letter from your motoring organization, stating that they can no longer accept payment of your annual subscription by banker's order. They ask you to complete a direct debit mandate instead.

   (a) What problems do banker's orders create for the motoring organization?

   (b) Why do such organizations prefer direct debit?

   (c) What disadvantages may there be for you in paying by direct debit?

7. Many personal bank transactions are facilitated by plastic cards. Your cousin is shortly to arrive in this country for the first time. Explain to her the difference between a cheque card and a cash card, showing the circumstances in which each is useful.

8. You have applied for and received an Access card with a credit limit of £250. You intend to use the card just to buy £50 of petrol per month, settling your Access account in full each month.

   (a) If you keep to this policy, how much interest will you pay per month?

   (b) How do petrol retailers and others benefit from accepting Access and other credit cards?

   (c) How does the credit card company make a profit?

   (d) In what ways does a card such as Access differ from the cards issued by individual stores?

9. (a) In what ways can you borrow from your clearing bank?

   (b) What factors will the bank manager take into account before granting a loan?

10. Describe the services which the retail banks offer to the small businessman.

11. Explain the importance of the cheque as a means of payment. What steps can be taken to ensure that a cheque reaches the correct account?

# The banking system: other financial institutions

## 12.1 Introduction

Although the retail banks are the most important financial organizations to the trader, they are only the most obvious of a variety of institutions that make up the financial markets. Some of these are primarily concerned with lending and borrowing on a long-term basis and are part of the capital market, which is considered in Unit 13. Others borrow or lend on a short-term basis and belong, like the retail banks, to the money market. They are considered in this Unit.

## 12.2 Discount houses

Discount houses specialize in raising money over short periods for the Government, as well as for trade and commerce. We saw in Unit 11.11 that the retail banks like to make some loans that can be recalled at short notice, so that they can restore their cash balances quickly in an emergency. Many of these loans go to the discount houses. They are repayable at twenty-four hours' notice or at a maximum of seven days, though in practice they are normally renewable. However, the discount houses obviously have to bear in mind the possibility of early repayment when using the loans to make a profit.

The discount houses use their resources to finance both public and private sector organizations by investing in a range of securities, as follows.

### 12.2.1 Treasury bills

Even the Government needs to borrow sometimes. Each week the Treasury calculates how much it will need to borrow to meet the excess of Government expenditure over tax revenue. This amount is obtained by issuing *Treasury bills*, which are in effect IOUs redeemable 91 days after issue. They have nominal values up to £100000 and buyers must take a minimum of £50000 worth. The bills are always sold to the highest bidders at less than their nominal value. For example, a £50 000 bill might be sold for £48 500. Then the purchaser will make a profit of £1500 by selling it back to the Treasury in 91 days.

Most of the bills are sold to the discount houses (who in any case guarantee to buy them all if necessary each week, so the Government knows that it can always borrow the money it needs). Sometimes a discount house will keep the bills for the full three months, but more often it will sell them to one of the retail banks.

One very important feature of a Treasury bill is that the Bank of England will always advance money against it if the discount house finds itself in need of immediate cash.

### 12.2.2   Bills of exchange

The traditional outlet for the funds of the discount houses was in providing temporary funds for traders by discounting commercial *bills of exchange*. These are examined in detail in Unit 20.6.2, but certain points must be noted here.

Where the purchaser of goods requires temporary credit which the seller cannot afford to give, the latter may draw a bill of exchange, setting out the debt and demanding payment, normally in three months' time. By signing the bill the purchaser acknowledges the debt and at the same time promises payment in three months. If the purchaser has a good reputation in the business world, the bill will be accepted by an accepting house for a small charge (see Unit 12.3). This guarantees that the accepting house will settle the account if the debtor defaults. The supplier of the goods who drew the bill of exchange now has a document which can be passed on to anyone else in exchange for cash.

Suppose the bill of exchange is for £10 000, payable in three months' time and that it has been 'accepted': the drawer of the bill takes it to a discount house and sells it at a discount, the amount of which depends upon the current rate of interest. Perhaps the discount house offers £9750 for the bill. The drawer has the advantage of immediate cash (for which he pays interest of £250), the customer has three months' credit and the discount house can make a profit of £250 by holding the bill for three months and then presenting it to the drawee for payment. In the unlikely event that the drawee is unable to pay, the accepting house can then be called upon.

In practice the seller of the goods will adjust the price so that the customer pays the charges incurred in using the bill of exchange.

In the nineteenth century this was a highly important function, since the sources of finance and credit for industry were much more limited than they are now. In recent years the volume of business in bills of exchange has declined, and the discount houses have found other areas for the profitable use of their funds.

### 12.2.3   Local authority bills

A large proportion of the revenue of local authorities comes from taxes collected in April and October, which are respectively the beginning and halfway mark of their financial year. It is not unusual for them to run short of funds just before these months and they sometimes issue bills for three months in anticipation of revenue. The discount houses are usually prepared to purchase such bills on the same basis as Treasury bills.

### 12.2.4   Certificates of deposit

If you wish to keep your savings at one of the high-street banks, you will have to accept whatever rate of interest it offers. However, if you happen to have £50000 or more to deposit for a fixed period, you will be able to arrange a special rate of interest with the bank, which will issue you with a *certificate of deposit* promising to repay you on a specified day, normally six or nine months hence. If you require your money earlier you can sell the certificate, probably to a discount house which will pay you now and collect the money from your bank on the appropriate day.

### 12.2.5   British Government stocks

These represent long-term borrowing by the Government, and a small proportion of the discount houses' funds is invested in them. Although they are not as liquid as Treasury bills and bills of exchange, Government securities can always be sold on the Stock Exchange, though the prices they fetch tend to vary.

Although the discount houses may seem remote from the high-street banks, they clearly occupy an important place in the financial system for some kinds of borrowers.

The discount houses themselves occupy a privileged position as borrowers. They alone among the financial institutions can borrow direct from the Bank of England. In practice they do not often borrow but they obtain funds by selling Treasury bills or suitable bills of exchange to the Bank. It is through the discount houses that the Bank of England ensures that the retail banks never run short of money.

## 12.3   The merchant banks

The term *merchant bank* is applied to many institutions nowadays, but refers specifically to the sixteen members of the *Accepting Houses Committee*, which include such names as Morgan Grenfell, Rothschild, Hambros and Baring. Such banks grew to prominence through their skill in accepting the bills of exchange used in the finance of international trade. As we have already seen, the discount houses advance money against bills of exchange, but are more willing to do so if the bill has been accepted by one of the major accepting houses and thus rendered a *bank bill* which, if necessary, can be used by the discount house to obtain advances from the Bank of England. (As the acceptance of a bill is a guarantee that the acceptor will meet the debt in case of default, the accepting house clearly needs a detailed knowledge of the traders concerned.) By guaranteeing the value of paper securities, the accepting houses contribute to the smooth running of the money market. Merchant banks are involved in many other activities as well. In addition to the original trading or merchanting functions from which they derived their name – and which some maintain today – they provide important financial services for industrial concerns, including the following.

(a) They accept deposits from customers, usually stipulating a minimum of perhaps £50000. Many of these deposits are made in return for the certificates of deposit mentioned in Unit 12.2.4.

(b) They make medium-term fixed-interest loans to their customers – to finance the installation of new machinery, for example.

(c) Sometimes firms do not want to purchase machinery; they prefer to rent it. Merchant banks may buy the machinery and lease it to the manufacturer (see Unit 13.11).

(d) When a company wishes to issue shares to the public, it will normally engage the services of a merchant bank since the necessary arrangements are highly technical and mistakes can be expensive.

(e) *Underwriting* is an important function related to the issue of shares. Suppose a company is planning to finance expansion through a share issue worth £5 million. If the public subscribe only £3½ million the expansion will be in danger. The merchant banks will often underwrite the issue, which means that they guarantee to buy any shares that remain unsold.

(f) Some organizations, such as pension funds, have large funds available for investment in property or on the Stock Exchange. Merchant banks often advise on the placing of these so-called wholesale deposits.

(g) An extension of this investment management is the establishment and management of many of the unit trusts discussed in Unit 13.4.4.

(h) Many merchant banks continue ordinary trading activities, such as dealing in gold bullion and silver and in the main commodity markets – sugar, coffee, tea, oil and non-ferrous metals.

(i) Most of the merchant banks have a foreign-exchange department which buys and sells foreign currencies for the bank's customers. It will also act on the bank's own account, since there is profit to be made from the timely buying or selling of currencies, as we shall see in Unit 21.4.

## 12.4   Other banks

A variety of other banks exist, offering specialized services to their customers. One of these – the Bank of England – is dealt with separately in Unit 12.6, but there are some others of which you should also be aware.

**Overseas banks** Something over 250 foreign banks have branches in London, competing in various ways with the main London banks. There are two particular reasons for the presence of these banks.

(a) They are able to provide a better service for their own nationals who import from or export to the United Kingdom.
(b) For many years there have been no restrictions on the movement of foreign currency into or out of the UK. Many overseas banks and their customers may see the opportunity to make profits by moving currencies around to take advantage of changes in exchange rates or interest rates. A branch in London may be helpful in this.

**Girobank** provides a full range of banking services through the 20 000 post offices throughout the country. Details are given in Unit 15.6.

## 12.5   Finance houses

We have already examined the role of finance houses in our discussion of hire purchase (Unit 6.4.2). They obtain their funds mainly from banks and other financial organizations though ordinary commercial firms may also place money with them. The interest received may be slightly higher than that paid by the retail banks. Originally this may have been because of a greater degree of risk associated with the finance houses. This is no longer the case. Indeed many of the larger finance houses are owned by a retail bank: for example National Westminster owns Lombard North Central and Barclays owns Mercantile Credit. The reason for higher interest rates is more easily explained by the higher rates that finance houses often charge for loans, the majority of which are used for the purchase of motor vehicles and other consumer durable goods.

Their other activities include home improvement loans and the leasing of equipment to industry (see Unit 13.11).

## 12.6   The Bank of England

The Bank of England is at the centre of the UK financial system, exercising a general control of the monetary and banking system on behalf of the Government. It was founded in 1694 as a private institution, but even then it had close links with the Government. These links gradually strengthened until the Bank was nationalized in 1946. Nationalization formally recognized what had long been the case: that the Bank of England was the Government's bank. But as long as it was a private sector institution there was the possibility of conflict between the Government and the Bank. This did not often occur, but the situation could arise if, for example, the Government wanted interest rates to increase while the Bank wanted them to fall or remain stable. Although there

**Fig. 12.1** The Bank of England in Threadneedle Street, London. It is from this famous building that the whole of the British banking system is supervised

may from time to time be differences of opinion between the Bank and the Government about the kind of policies appropriate at a particular moment, it is the Government that has the final word: the Chancellor of the Exchequer, advised by the Treasury, can dictate policy to the Governor of the Bank of England.

In most countries the Government's bank is referred to as the *central bank*, and indeed the functions of the Bank of England are equivalent to those of many central banks. Its most important functions are discussed below.

You will probably find it helpful to refer to Table 12.1, which is typical of the balance sheets published each week for the Bank of England.

### 12.6.1 The Government's accounts

One of the most important aspects of the work of a central bank is the administration of the Government's bank accounts, which appear under the heading *public deposits* in Table 12.1. There are two principal accounts here: the *Exchequer Account*, into which all taxation receipts are paid and from which all current expenditure is met, and the *National Loans Fund*, the Government's capital account for borrowing and lending. Although there are subsidiary accounts, run by individual Government departments, these two accounts between them are responsible for the majority of Government transactions. Since Government expenditure runs at over £180000 million per annum it is perhaps a little surprising that the public deposits are so small. This is a matter of deliberate policy on the part of the authorities (who in this

**Table 12.1** The Bank of England's weekly balance sheet, 31 December 1991 (£ million)

| Assets | | Liabilities | |
|---|---|---|---|
| *Issue Department* | | | |
| Government securities | 11 921 | Notes in circulation | 17 156 |
| Other securities | 5 239 | Notes in Banking Department | 4 |
| | 17 160 | | 17 160 |
| *Banking Department* | | | |
| Government securities | 1 516 | | |
| Advances and other accounts | 1 842 | Capital | 14 |
| | | Public deposits | 100 |
| Premises, equipment and other securities | 1 778 | Bankers' deposits | 1 608 |
| | | Special deposits | 0 |
| Notes and coin | 4 | Reserves | 3 418 |
| | 5 140 | | 5 140 |

instance are the Treasury and the Bank): rather than allow a great balance to accumulate in the form of public deposits, they prefer to pay off part of the National Debt (see Unit 12.6.3). On the other hand, the Bank takes steps to ensure that there is always enough in the accounts to meet the requirements of the Government, and on rare occasions the Bank itself lends to the Government (overnight) in the form of *ways and means advances*.

### 12.6.2   The note issue

The Government reserves the right to issue notes and coins, and these reach the public via the Bank of England. The size of the note issue is governed by the Currency and Bank Notes Act 1954, which set a limit of £1500 million, but this can be increased to meet public demand, subject to Treasury approval. Requirements vary seasonally (demand for notes reaches a peak at Christmas and during the summer holiday periods) and according to the general level of prices and economic activity. There has been a great increase in the issue since 1954, mainly because of rising prices.

At the Bank of England the notes are transferred from the Issue Department to the Banking Department. From there, they are passed on to the retail banks and it is from the retail banks that the notes eventually reach the general public.

### 12.6.3   The National Debt

Sometimes the Government needs to spend more money than it can raise through taxation. It resorts to borrowing to do this, and the total borrowing is known as the National Debt. In March 1991 the Debt amounted to over £198 000 million. The Bank of England looks after the Debt for the Government and in that capacity it has four main responsibilities.

(a)  To issue new securities when the Government wants to borrow. These may be very short-term Treasury bills (see Unit 12.2.1) or longer-term gilt-edged stocks (these are examined in Unit 13.5.1).
(b)  To keep a register of stockholders, so that the interest can be paid to the correct people.
(c)  To pay interest on the securities every half-year. The rate of interest is fixed for each security and does not vary during its life.
(d)  To redeem securities as they mature.

### 12.6.4   Lender of last resort

We saw in Unit 12.2 that the discount houses often borrow money at call and re-lend it for longer periods. It sometimes happens that those who have lent money to the discount houses demand immediate repayment. In these circumstances the discount houses are in difficulty, for they have committed their borrowed funds for three months or sometimes longer. They try to obtain the money they need from any likely source but *in the last resort*, if all else fails, they turn to the Bank of England, which will always provide the money they require against the security of Treasury bills or suitable bills of exchange.

### 12.6.5   External functions

The Bank also discharges a variety of other functions on behalf of the Government which really relate to the international rather than the domestic economy. Three of these are mentioned here.

**Exchange Equalization Account**   The UK's gold and foreign exchange reserves are held at the Bank in the Exchange Equalization Account. It is from this account that the foreign currency ultimately comes when it is needed by an importer to buy goods or by a traveller to spend abroad. Similarly, foreign currency earned by exporters eventually arrives here.

**European Community (EC)**   One of the UK's obligations as a member of the Community is to maintain the value of sterling against currencies of other member countries. This is done through the Exchange Rate Mechanism (ERM) and it is the duty of the Bank of England to act on behalf of the Government within the ERM, using the resources of the Exchange Equalization Account.

**International Monetary Fund**   The Bank's expertise is often called for in complex international monetary negotiations, particularly in connection with the International Monetary Fund, the body which supervises foreign exchange rates.

### 12.6.6   The bankers' bank

The Bank of England provides an essential link between the Government and the other banks. Policy initiatives of all kinds reach the banks via the Bank of England. In addition all the banks also run accounts there, which they treat in the same way as private individuals treat their bank accounts, except that the Bank of England does not allow overdrafts. The accounts are used to replenish the banks' stocks of cash if their own holdings – the money in their tills – are running low. They are also used to settle debts which arise between the banks themselves as a result of the daily clearing of cheques (see Unit 12.7).

### 12.6.7   Private customers

These are mainly a legacy from the past, when the Bank of England used to carry on an orthodox banking business as well as fulfilling its special responsibilities to the Government. Today the Bank runs accounts for its employees, as well as for some families who have held accounts there for generations.

## 12.7   The Bankers' Clearing House

In Unit 11.5 we looked at the route taken by an individual cheque, which allows the payee's account to be credited and the drawer's to be debited. We saw that the cheque passes through the Bankers' Clearing House, but we did not examine the Clearing House in detail.

Every working day millions of cheques are drawn and paid into bank accounts. It would be impossible for each of those cheques to be cleared individually: the job of the Clearing House is mass clearing.

### 12.7.1   General clearing

Most cheques are dealt with at the general clearing. A typical day might see around 8 million cheques processed, involving a sum of perhaps £20000 million.

Each branch of a bank sends the cheques it receives to the clearing department at its head office. There the cheques are sorted and their value added up. If there are four banks in the system, each bank will have three groups of cheques drawn on the other three banks. In order to credit its customers' accounts with the amounts shown on individual cheques, it must obtain the money from the banks on which the cheques have been drawn.

Suppose that Barclays customers have paid in cheques worth £10 million drawn on Midland Bank; Barclays must obtain the £10 million from Midland. Meanwhile, Midland customers have paid in £7 million of cheques drawn on Barclays. If Midland pays £3 million to Barclays the books will be balanced.

**Table 12.2** A hypothetical clearing (£million)

| Receiving bank | Paying bank | | | |
|---|---|---|---|---|
| | Barclays | Lloyds | Midland | National Westminster |
| Barclays | – | 8 | 10 | 3 |
| Lloyds | 6 | – | 4 | 6 |
| Midland | 7 | 2 | – | 8 |
| National Westminster | 4 | 1 | 9 | – |

Each bank could deal individually with each of the others on this basis, but the Clearing House eliminates the need for this. Table 12.2 summarizes the position at the end of a hypothetical clearing.

We can see the position of each bank in relation to each of the others from this table. Barclays is owed £8 million by Lloyds but owes £6 million to Lloyds, and an adjustment of £2 million is required. But we can also see the net position of each bank: Barclays is owed a total of £21 million (8 + 10 + 3) and owes a total of £17 million (6 + 7 + 4). We may summarize the net position of each bank as follows:

| | |
|---|---|
| Barclays | is owed £4 million |
| Lloyds | is owed £5 million |
| Midland | owes £6 million |
| National Westminster | owes £3 million |

Each of the banks runs an account at the Bank of England through which these debts can be settled. In this example Midland pays £5 million to Lloyds and £1 million to Barclays, while National Westminster pays £3 million to Barclays.

Not only cheques are dealt with in this way: bank giro credits and other means of payment via the banks also go through the Clearing House. Each day the debts arising from that day's town clearing and the previous day's general clearing are settled. In this way millions of payments are made by a minimum of transactions.

The organizations that we have been looking at in this Unit are all part of the *money market*, dealing essentially with the short-term movement of funds. In Unit 13 we shall examine the bodies which deal with the long-term movement of funds and which together form the *capital market*.

## 12.8   Questions

1. What are the main differences between the Bank of England and other banks in the United Kingdom?

2. The Government decides to issue Treasury bills with a face value of £100 million.
   (a) If current rates of interest are 10 per cent, make an estimate of how much the Government will receive.
   (b) For how long will the Government have the use of this money?
   (c) Which institutions are the most likely to purchase the Treasury bills?
   (d) How do those institutions obtain the money they need to buy the Treasury bills?
3. (a) Describe the function of a bill of exchange.
   (b) Why is it usually necessary for a bill of exchange to be 'accepted' by an accepting house?
4. What is meant by *discounting* a bill of exchange? How does a bank make a profit by discounting bills?
5. (a) How do the customers of the merchant banks differ from those of the retail banks?
   (b) Describe the services which the merchant banks provide for their customers which are not normally provided by the retail banks.
6. (a) Why are there over 250 overseas banks in London?
   (b) What are their main activities?
7. (a) What is meant by the term *clearing a cheque*?
   (b) D. Green, who banks at Barclays in Leicester, receives a cheque from A. Hendry who banks at Lloyds in Chelmsford. Describe the procedure by which the money is transferred from A. Hendry's account to D. Green's account.
8. Describe the main services provided to the Government by a central bank.

# The capital market

## 13.1 The basic market

All markets consist of some organizations or people supplying a good or a service and others demanding or buying that good or service. In the capital market the commodity being bought and sold is long-term finance. The underlying process and the main institutions involved are indicated in fig. 13.1.

Suppose that a large company needs several million pounds to buy some machinery or to open a new factory. Not having the resources itself, the company can approach an *issuing house* which will arrange to issue shares on

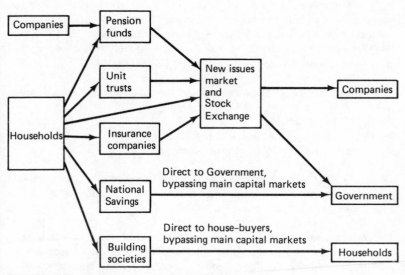

Fig. 13.1 The capital market

behalf of the company (this represents the *demand for capital*). The shares are purchased either by individual citizens or by large financial concerns (this represents the *supply of capital* – savings that are temporarily not required by their owners).

At a later date the buyer of the shares may want to sell them. Since the company will have used the money to buy machinery, it will be unwilling (and unable) to re-purchase the shares. This is where the Stock Exchange becomes important: it ensures that the holders of all approved shares are able to sell them.

We may summarize by saying that the capital market consists of those institutions that bring together savers and borrowers.

## 13.2    The borrowers

As you can see from fig. 13.1, the borrowers fall into three groups: households, companies and the Government. Households and companies both appear in the diagram as savers too. This may at first seem odd. At the simplest level, however, you know that some households will save money in building societies this year while others will borrow from the societies: this is why they appear on both sides of the market.

Let us first consider the borrowers in a little more detail. Why do they need to borrow on a long-term basis?

**Households**    Almost the only reason for individuals to borrow on long term is for house purchase. Very few people could afford to pay cash for a house, nor would most of us have the patience to save up. So people borrow the money, normally from a building society or a bank, and repay it over the subsequent period – usually a maximum of twenty-five years, though most loans are repaid early. The annual demand may total some £40000 million.

**Companies**    Limited companies may need capital for perhaps three reasons:

(a) to build new factories,
(b) to buy plant and machinery to put in their factories,
(c) to finance the take-over of other companies.

To some extent a company could finance these projects out of its previous profits, but companies as a group find it necessary to issue shares worth around £8000 million each year.

**The Government**    While it would be possible for the Government to increase taxation to meet all its expenditure, this might be politically unpopular and economically unwise. So, like the companies, the Government often borrows. In 1991–2 the Government borrowed about £14000 million. About £5000 million of this came from selling Government stocks (these are similar to shares and are discussed in Unit 13.5.1) and the remainder by attracting money into National Savings.

The Government needs this money for all kinds of reasons: partly to meet some of its day-to-day expenditure, but especially to pay for construction works of various kinds – hospitals, schools and motorways, for example – financed either directly by the central Government or indirectly by grants made by central to local government.

Occasionally, the Government has not needed to borrow and has actually been able to repay some earlier loans. However, households and companies continue to borrow. Where do the funds come from?

## 13.3 The savers

The most important savers are households, but it will be convenient if we leave them till last. Let us first consider the Government and companies.

**The Government**   Normally the Government does not save. This is why it is omitted from the left-hand side of fig. 13.1. The last time the Government spent less than its revenue from taxation was in 1988–9 when the savings (or surplus) was about £14 billion. More recently in 1991–2 the Government had to borrow about the same amount.

**Companies**   It might not be obvious how a company saves. At the end of the year, after paying tax, a company will have profits left to distribute to its shareholders. It would be very unusual to dispose of all the profit in this way. Some will certainly be kept within the company. This proportion is the company's savings and will probably be used eventually to buy new equipment, or perhaps to buy shares in other companies. It is unlikely, however, that much of these company savings will reach the capital market. Companies are not, therefore, much help in providing the money we are looking for, except that if a company uses its own savings to finance its activities the demand in the capital market is correspondingly reduced.

**Households**   In the UK, every encouragement is given to individuals to save. A large number of organizations, ranging from the National Savings Bank to pension funds, are eager to attract money from individuals.

Clearly there must be advantages for the savers in leaving their money with these concerns. But you can rely on it that there must also be advantages for the savings institutions – otherwise they would not compete as vigorously as they do.

What happens is that a large number of individuals contribute relatively small amounts to organizations which make the combined savings available to the central capital market. Some of the organizations you will readily recognize as savings organizations – National Savings and building societies, for example. You might not have regarded others, such as insurance companies, in the same way. Let us look at some of them more closely.

## 13.4    Savings institutions

We have seen that borrowers in the capital market need billions of pounds each year. If it were left to individuals to provide this sum directly, the market would fail. It is only because the financial organizations draw individual savings together that the market works.

### 13.4.1    Building societies

In 1991 there were 116 building societies. The general position of the societies is shown in fig. 13.2. They are the main destination for personal savings in the UK, and despite competition from the retail banks and elsewhere they are the source of finance for house purchase, which was, of course, their original purpose.

Changes in the law, including the Building Societies Act 1986, have enabled the societies to widen their activities. For example, they are allowed to lend up to 17½ per cent of their assets for purposes other than house purchase – furniture, cars, boats, holidays for example. Many have branched out into estate agency and insurance. However, the main area of expansion has been in competition with the retail banks in the provision of current account services and automatic teller machines.

While the building societies are part of the capital market (because they are concerned with long-term lending) they tend to bypass the main capital market since the majority of their funds is lent to people for house purchase – usually between £40 million and £50 million per year. Although the societies are allowed to invest through the Stock Exchange the main effect on the central capital market is to divert funds away from it.

The societies illustrate an important feature of capital market institutions: they borrow funds on a short-term basis, often promising repayment on demand, and lend on a long-term basis. To ensure that they can make repayments when depositors require them they must keep a reasonable proportion of their assets in a fairly liquid form.

### 13.4.2    Insurance companies

The business of insurance is discussed in Unit 19. Here we are interested only in the contribution of the insurance companies to the capital market, which means that we confine ourselves to life insurance.

A large number of people have a life assurance policy, under which the

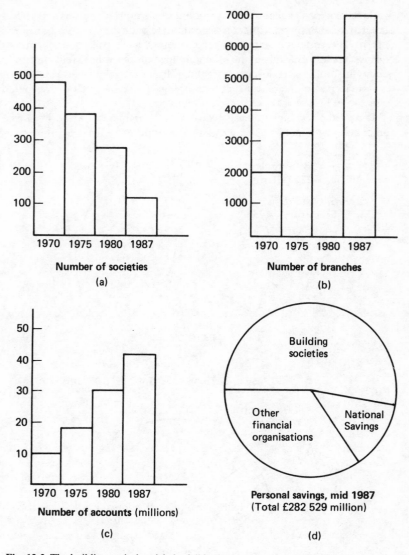

**Fig. 13.2** The building societies: (a) the fall in the number of societies, (b) the rise in the number of branches, (c) the increasing numbers of shareholders, (d) the societies' share in the personal savings market

insurance company collects weekly, monthly or annual premiums and undertakes to pay a lump sum, either on a specific date or on the death of the insured person. The company is able to repay more than it collects in premiums because it invests the bulk of the premiums in securities which yield interest or dividends (profits). At the end of 1990, UK insurance companies held investments in respect of their life assurance business of £208 000 million, distributed as shown in fig. 13.3(a).

Most of the funds that reach industry and commerce via the insurance companies would not be available to them without the existence of the com-

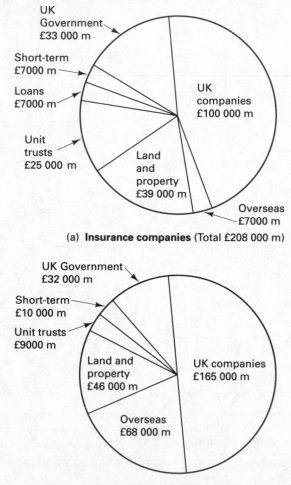

(a)  **Insurance companies** (Total £208 000 m)

(b)  **Pension funds** (Total £330 000 m)

**Fig. 13.3** The investments of the insurance companies and the pension funds (1990)

panies, since individually the contributions would be too small to be worth investing. In any case, the people paying their insurance premiums are probably only concerned about the financial security of their families, and not so much about how the money is invested. This is also true of the next group of savings institutions.

### 13.4.3 Pension funds

Pension or superannuation funds operate on a similar basis to the insurance companies: they collect weekly or monthly contributions from employees and employers over the working life of the employee, invest the income in the capital market, and guarantee to pay a weekly or monthly pension to the employee from the date of his or her retirement.

Since a high proportion of employees (and of self-employed people as well) are in a pension scheme of some kind, these funds are very important to the capital market. Again, the people making contributions are probably unaware of the destination of their money. Figure 13.3(b) shows the distribution of pension fund investments.

### 13.4.4 Unit trusts

Most people (even unknowingly) invest part of their savings on the Stock Exchange via the insurance companies and pension funds. The number who invest via a unit trust is much smaller. Small savers are able to buy units in a unit trust fund, sometimes simply by sending money in response to newspaper advertisements. In return for a commission, the managers of the trust then use the money raised to buy securities in the particular sectors of industry to which the trust is committed. (The deeds of individual unit trusts indicate the areas to which funds will be applied.) All earnings on the shares are payable to the trust managers, who then redistribute them to unit-holders who may, however, choose to convert them into further units. The chief outlets for unit trust funds are shown in fig. 13.4.

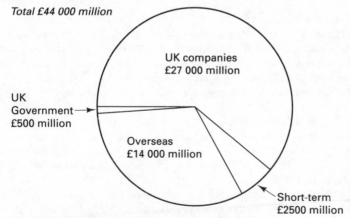

Total £44 000 million

UK companies £27 000 million

UK Government £500 million

Overseas £14 000 million

Short-term £2500 million

**Fig. 13.4** The investments of the unit trusts (December 1990)

One advantage of a trust for investors is its relative security, for it is able to spread its investment across a large number of companies and industries, thereby eliminating the danger of complete loss if one company collapses. But for precisely this reason the unit-holders cannot expect spectacular returns on their investment, even though they have the advantage of expert professional advice in the handling of their money. There is, however, an important difference between the trusts and, for example, the building societies. If you put £100 in a building society for one year, you will be able to withdraw £100 plus interest of perhaps £8 at the end of the year. If you invest £100 in a unit trust, you may find at the end of the year that you can sell the units for £150 if the value of the underlying shares has increased. On the other hand you may be able to obtain only £70 if these shares have fallen in value. That is the risk that you take.

### 13.4.5   Investment trusts

These are really ordinary limited companies that use their capital to buy shares in other businesses, in order to make a profit for their shareholders. Shares in investment trusts are bought in the same way as shares in other businesses and are therefore not as easy to obtain as units in a unit trust.

Like the unit trusts, investment trusts apply the funds mainly to commercial (as opposed to Government) investments, and approximately 90 per cent of their capital is invested in company shares. The main advantage of the investment trust over the unit trust is that it is not restricted in its activities by a trust deed, and thus retains greater flexibility for switching funds from relatively unprofitable to more profitable uses.

The savings institutions discussed above are all private sector organizations – they have no direct connection with the Government. We must also take note of the significance of National Savings, however.

### 13.4.6   National Savings

You can see from fig. 13.5 that a significant proportion of personal savings in the UK is lodged with the National Savings Bank, through the Post Office. Like the money going to the building societies, this money bypasses the main capital market and is made available through the Post Office to the Government. National Savings schemes are discussed in more detail in Unit 15.7.

### 13.4.7   Direct investment

As an alternative to putting your savings through one of the channels examined above, you could use your money to buy some shares direct, either when they are first issued (see Unit 13.6) or second-hand through the Stock Exchange (see Unit 13.7).

The programme of privatization of the public corporations since 1979 (see Unit 9.8) has resulted in a large increase in the number of individuals holding shares. Since the prices of most shares gradually increase over time, this can be

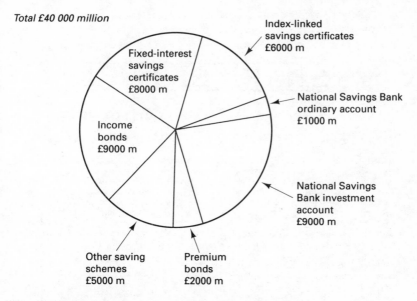

Total £40 000 million

Fig. 13.5 The main forms of National Savings (December 1990)

a profitable investment. There is, though, always the possibility of a fall in price (and the certainty of commission charges on both buying and selling), so it would be unwise to commit all one's savings to the purchase of shares.

## 13.5 Types of security

In Unit 8.6 we looked briefly at the ordinary shares and preference shares issued by companies. It is now time to look at these and other securities in detail.

### 13.5.1 Government securities

When the Government (or, sometimes, a public corporation) needs to borrow, the Treasury issues *gilt-edged securities*. These are generally known as *stock* rather than shares. Stock is traded in £100 lots, while shares are traded by number. Thus if you buy stock you might buy £800 worth, but if you buy shares you might buy, say, 750 shares.

Gilt-edged securities nowadays are issued for a fixed period of time and at a fixed rate of interest. They can be regarded as an absolutely safe investment, because the holders know that the Government will pay out £100 when the security matures, as well as paying interest each year. The trouble is that inflation will generally erode the value of £100 over the life of the security: £100 bought far less in 1992, say, than it would have bought in 1980.

# SHARE SERVICE

## DRAPERY & STORES

| 1991/92 High | Low | Stock | Price | + OT − |
|---|---|---|---|---|
| 90 | $28^1_2$ | Asda Group | 35 | $-^1_2$ |
| 107 | 75 | Acatos & Hutch | 78 | |
| 133 | 59 | Albert Fisher | 67 | |
| 338 | 243 | Argyll Group | 324 | |
| 118 | 25 | Ashley Group | 25 | −13 |
| 545 | 415 | Ass Brit F'ds | 421 | +2 |
| 158 | 112 | Assoc. Fish. | 141 | |
| 164 | 130 | Banks. Sidney | 149 | |
| 41 | 14 | Berisford | $18^1_2$ | $+^1_2$ |
| 490 | 411 | Booker | 443 | −1 |
| 43 | 29 | Borthwicks | 39 | |
| 437 | 266 | Brake Bros | 436 | |
| 55 | 26 | Budgens | 42 | |
| 476 | 317 | Cadbury Sch | 434 | +1 |
| 165 | 103 | Carr's Milling | 103 | |
| $61^1_2$ | 36 | City Centre Res | 61 | |
| 528 | 450 | Clifford Foods | 514 | |
| 237 | 155 | Clifford Fds A | 205 | |
| 468 | 361 | Compass Group | 432 | −3 |
| 39 | 17 | Copson F | 36 | |

## BRITISH FUNDS
### Over Fifteen Years

| 1991/92 High | Low | Stock | Price | + OT − | Yield (%) |
|---|---|---|---|---|---|
| $130^{15}_{32}$ | $118^{23}_{32}$ | Treas. $13^1_2$pc 04-08 | $125^1_8$* | $-^7_{16}$ | 10.8 |
| $99^3_8$ | $88^{31}_{32}$ | Treas. 9 pc 2008 | $95^5_{16}$* | $-^5_{16}$ | 9.4 |
| $90^{23}_{32}$ | $80^5_{16}$ | Treas. 8 pc 2009 | $86^7_8$* | $-^5_{16}$ | 9.2 |
| $99^{15}_{32}$ | $88^7_{16}$ | Conv. 9 pc 2011 | $95^5_{16}$ | $-^3_8$ | 9.4 |
| $67^1_4$ | $58^{21}_{32}$ | Tr. $5^1_2$pc 08-12 | $64^1_{16}$ | $-^1_4$ | 8.6 |
| $87^1_8$ | $77^7_{32}$ | Tr. $7^3_4$pc 12-15 | $83^5_{16}$ | $-^5_{16}$ | 9.3 |
| $127^3_{16}$ | $113^{15}_{16}$ | Exch. 12 pc 13-17 | $121^7_8$ | $-^7_{16}$ | 9.8 |

#### Undated

| High | Low | Stock | Price | + OT − | Yield (%) |
|---|---|---|---|---|---|
| $26^{25}_{32}$ | $23^5_8$ | Consols $2^1_2$ pc | $25^{15}_{32}$* | | 9.8 |
| $38^1_{16}$ | $33^5_{16}$ | War Loan $3^1_2$ pc | $36^1_4$ | $-^1_{16}$ | 9.6 |
| $61^3_8$ | $57^{13}_{16}$ | Conversion $3^1_2$ pc | $59^5_8$* | $-^1_{16}$ | 5.9 |
| $31^1_2$ | $28^1_4$ | Treasury 3 pc | $30^3_{16}$* | | 9.9 |
| $42^5_{16}$ | $37^{11}_{16}$ | Consols 4 pc | $40^9_{16}$ | $-^1_{16}$ | 9.9 |
| $26^1_2$ | $23^{15}_{32}$ | Treasury $2^1_2$ pc | $25^3_{16}$* | | 9.9 |

**Fig. 13.6** Stock Exchange prices

Some examples of gilt-edged stocks are shown in the right-hand column of fig. 13.6. The entry for the fifth one says:

| 67¼ | 58²¹⁄₃₂ | Tr. 5½pc 08−12 | 64¹⁄₁₆ | −¼ | 8.6 |
|---|---|---|---|---|---|

This is not as difficult to understand as you might think at first.

The first two columns show the highest and lowest price in pounds at which this stock has been bought and sold over the previous twelve months. (Notice that, although we have decimal currency, these prices are quoted in quarters, eighths, and sometimes in sixteenths and thirty-secondths.)

'Tr. 5½pc' indicates that we are talking about Treasury stocks whose holders receive 5½ per cent interest per year (£5.50).

Then we learn that the stockholders will be repaid sometime in the years 2008 to 2012, at the Government's convenience.

Next 'yesterday's' price for the stock is given: this was £64$\frac{1}{16}$, and it was £$\frac{1}{4}$ (or 25 pence) lower than the previous day's price. The final figure shows the *percentage yield* – that is, the interest payable (£5.50) as a percentage of the current market price (£64$\frac{1}{16}$).

Local authorities and overseas governments issue similar securities which can be held by investors, and they are quoted in the same way.

### 13.5.2 Company securities: ordinary shares

These are the most important shares and are issued by all limited companies. They are sometimes known as *equities*, because each share entitles its owner to an equal share of the profits of the company. They have several important features.

(a) The money that is handed over to the company in exchange for ordinary shares is never returned to the shareholders, for (as we have seen) the company uses the money to purchase plant and machinery.

(b) Normally the holders of ordinary shares have the last claim ᴏʳ company profits, which they receive in the form of payments called *dividends*. In profitable years the dividend may be paid at a very high rate per share, while in other years the ordinary shareholders may get no dividend at all. This danger may be minimized by buying shares in well-established companies, such as Shell or Unilever. These are known as 'blue chip' shares.

(c) The ordinary shareholders thus run the risk that their money will not earn them anything. In return for this risk they are entitled to vote at the firm's Annual General Meeting, where general policy is discussed and the board of directors is elected. It would be an exaggeration to say that the ordinary shareholders control the company, however, for, as we saw in Unit 8.9.2, this control really rests with the board of directors.

(d) Some companies issue two or three categories of ordinary shares, one category being entitled to receive a dividend before the rest. A special category is known as *deferred ordinary shares* or *founders' shares*. As their names imply, these shares are issued to the founders of a business, often when it becomes a public company, and they are the last to receive a dividend. But founders' shares often carry disproportionate voting rights, to enable the founders of the business to retain control over it.

In the left-hand column of fig. 13.6 you can see some Stock Exchange prices for company shares. One of them reads:

| 476 | 317 | Cadbury Sch | 434 | +1 |
|-----|-----|-------------|-----|----|

Following the procedure used in respect of gilt-edged stocks, we can deduce that the price has varied over twelve months between 476 pence and 317 pence; the shares are those of Cadbury Schweppes Plc. 'Yesterday's' price was 434 pence, one penny more than on the previous day.

### 13.5.3   Company securities: preference shares

These are designed to attract funds from investors who do not want to take the greater risks associated with ordinary shares and who want to be more certain of an annual income from their investment. They carry a fixed rate of dividend per year, which is payable before ordinary shareholders receive any payment but after interest has been paid to debenture-holders (see below). Similarly, if the company is wound up, the preference shareholders will receive their share of the proceeds before the ordinary shareholders do.

There are three kinds of specialized preference share.

(a) *Cumulative preference shares* differ in that if the company cannot afford to pay a dividend one year, it must be carried forward to the next year and be paid before the ordinary shareholders are paid.

(b) *Participating preference shares* carry a fixed rate of dividend, but they entitle their holders to a further share of the profits once they reach a certain level.

(c) *Redeemable preference shares* can be bought back by the firm in a few years' time. They are issued when the company wants money only temporarily, and this is an inexpensive way of obtaining it.

The voting rights of preference shareholders vary according to the articles of the company, but generally a shareholder who receives a fixed return on an investment does not have a voting right. If preference share dividends are in arrears, however, the shareholders normally can vote. In some companies preference shareholders have limited voting rights – perhaps one vote for every five shares, as against the ordinary shareholder's one vote for every share.

### 13.5.4   Company securities: debentures

These are *not* shares, as they do not give their holders any part of the ownership of the firm. They are stock, similar in many ways to gilt-edged stock, and are in effect long-term loans to the company, which normally undertakes to repay the holder on a specific date. Each year, debenture-holders receive a fixed rate of interest whether or not the company is making a profit. If the company goes into liquidation, the debenture-holders must be paid before any of the shareholders.

It is clear, then, that debentures involve very little risk for the holders, but to make them even safer for investors the debentures are often issued as *mortgaged* or *secured debentures*. This means that a particular part of the firm's property is earmarked for sale in order to repay the debenture-holders in the event of difficulty.

One respect in which debentures differ from other loans to a company is in the fact that the lenders (the debenture-holders) can sell their claim against the company to someone else. So someone who holds debentures worth £1000 in an approved company can sell them through the Stock Exchange for the highest price obtainable. The company is then in debt to the new holder, to whom the annual interest will in future be paid.

## 13.6 The central capital market: new issues

If a public limited company in the UK needs to raise long-term capital it will normally go to the New Issues Market, a group of institutions arranging for the sale of new shares. (The Stock Exchange, as we shall see, deals only in second-hand shares.) The procedures vary if the firm wants to make an issue on the Unlisted Securities Market (see Unit 13.9). Here we consider what is necessary for an issue of shares that are to be traded on the main Stock Exchange.

The company must already have a good trading record for this to be worthwhile: the Stock Exchange Council needs to see evidence of the firm's good record and current standing before it will grant a *quotation*, that is, permission for the shares to be traded on the Stock Exchange. The company must have a market value of at least £500000 before a quotation is allowed, and it is a further requirement that a single category of shares must have a value of £200000 before dealings can begin. In addition, the process of issuing capital is expensive in itself. The number of firms in a position to apply for a quotation is thus very limited.

Once a firm has decided to make a new issue, whether it is for the first time or the issue of additional stock, it will consult a merchant bank (see Unit 12.3) for advice. The merchant banks that specialize in new issues are known as *issuing houses*, and many of them are the accepting houses we saw in Unit 12.2.2 performing a different job. Their main functions in this connection include:

(a) advising on the timing of the share issue – it would be inconvenient if several firms were trying to raise tens of millions of pounds on the same day;
(b) advising on the price at which the shares should be offered for sale;
(c) arranging for the *underwriting* of the issue, that is, arranging a guarantee that any shares not bought by the public will be bought by the financial institutions – a kind of insurance function;
(d) carrying out all the necessary paperwork, including checking the applications and allocating the shares.

New shares are issued in several different ways, as follows.

### 13.6.1 By prospectus

The prospectus amounts to an invitation to the general public to subscribe capital. It contains full details of the company's history and future plans, and an application form for shares. Normally applications are opened on the stipulated issue day, and it is hoped that all the shares will be disposed of that day. Whether or not they are sold depends on the view taken by the investing public of the potential of the company in relation to the price of the shares. To allow time for this assessment, the prospectus must appear at least three days before issue day.

### 13.6.2   By offer for sale
This is similar to issue by prospectus, except that initially all the shares are taken up by the issuing house. Subsequently, the issuing house offers them for sale to the public, giving the same details that are set out in the prospectus.

In both the above methods of issue the public has not only the detailed information presented by the issuing house but also the views of the financial press, for most new issues are discussed in its columns.

### 13.6.3   By placing
The issuing house will recommend this method of issue when it knows that it can place the shares with a few large institutional investors. Details of the company do not have to be so widely advertised as with other methods, so the expenses are lower.

### 13.6.4   By tender
When shares are issued by the methods discussed above, they may be resold by their initial holders at a premium (that is, at a price higher than their nominal value) if the demand for them is high. For example, when British Telecom shares were first issued, investors had to pay 50 pence per share, but within a week they were being resold for 90 pence. The initial buyers thus made a quick profit. To reduce the possibility of this, the shares may be issued *by tender*: details of the company and its prospects are again set out in the press, and tenders (or bids) are invited above a certain price. When all bids have been received, the shares are issued at a price that just disposes of all the shares. Those who bid below this 'striking price' receive no shares, while those bidding above the price receive a cash rebate. In this way the company hopes to increase the capital it raises.

### 13.6.5   By issue to existing shareholders
When the amount of capital to be raised is not very large, it is sometimes possible to raise it from existing shareholders, by making a *rights* issue. This means that shareholders have the right to buy one new share for, perhaps, every ten that they already hold. The rights issue may be part of a larger issue to the public, with existing shareholders having the right to buy shares on more favourable terms than the public.

Sometimes an open offer may be made to existing shareholders, enabling them to subscribe for new shares but imposing no limit on the number that they may buy. Both methods have the advantage of being relatively inexpensive to the company.

A *bonus* or *scrip issue* should not be confused with a rights issue: in a bonus issue the shareholder receives the new shares free. A bonus issue is usually made when the real value of the company is much in excess of the nominal value of the shares.

Once shares have been issued, they can be traded on the Stock Exchange, as long as the prior agreement of the Stock Exchange Council has been obtained.

## 13.7 The central capital market: the Stock Exchange

### 13.7.1 The members of the Stock Exchange

New shares are bought by investors through the New Issues Market. However, virtually all second-hand shares in public companies are bought and sold through the Stock Exchange, and are traded through *stockbrokers*.

All members of the Stock Exchange, both individuals and institutions, are stockbrokers. As such they buy stocks and shares on behalf of their clients, earning a commission on each transaction. Most brokers are also dealers or *market-makers* – that is, they undertake to 'make markets' and are prepared to buy and sell shares at any time. As dealers, they make a profit by buying at one price and selling at a higher one. They must, however, tell the client whether they are acting as a broker or a dealer in any transaction: they are not permitted to act as both at once – there would be a strong temptation to push up the price of shares if they were selling them on your account and at the same time acting as a broker for the buyer!

Most deals between brokers are conducted by telephone. This could mean that dealers are not always aware of prices prevailing in the market at any particular instant. This is avoided by the new *Stock Exchange Automated Quotation* system (SEAQ), a computer system which enables any Stock Exchange transaction to be recorded within minutes and to be displayed as quickly on terminals throughout the UK and in some overseas centres.

### 13.7.2 Buying shares

If you want to buy some second-hand shares, there are several things you could do. (You have a similar choice of actions if you want to sell shares.)

(a) You could contact a *stockbroker*, though most of them deal directly only with individuals who have large amounts of money to invest.
(b) You could visit one of the relatively new *share-shops* which can be found in some town centres. These are really branches of some of the big stock-broking firms.
(c) You could contact a *licensed dealer*, which is often cheaper than using a stockbroker as there may be no commission to pay. There can be unforeseen risks about this, however, since these dealers are not yet bound by the same rules as stockbrokers.

(d) You would most probably contact your *bank* or (in some cases) your *building society*, who would arrange to buy or sell through its own stock-broker.

Because of the link-up with SEAQ, you can be informed almost immediately of the price that you have to pay. To this must be added stamp duty of ½ per cent (a kind of tax imposed by the Government) and the broker's commission of perhaps 1½ per cent. These details will subsequently be confirmed in a *contract note*.

Payment will be made some time later. The Stock Exchange year is divided into trading periods known as *accounts* of two (sometimes three) weeks, and deals struck during a trading period must be paid for by the account settlement day, which is ten days after the end of the account.

### 13.7.3    The importance of the Stock Exchange
The Stock Exchange is a rather remote institution to many people, but it serves several very important functions in the commercial and economic life of the country, including the following.

**Capital raising**    Although no one can actually raise capital on the Stock Exchange, it would be impossible to raise long-term capital without it. Investors are not prepared to commit their money to a company permanently, but the company needs it permanently. It is only through the Stock Exchange that this conflict is overcome and investors are able to turn their shares into cash.

**Investor protection**    The Stock Exchange offers protection to investors by insisting on the highest standards of behaviour from its members and by closely examining companies before allowing a quotation. Without this protection it would be much more difficult for companies – and indeed the Government – to raise the money they need. The question of supervision of the capital market is a complex one, however, and not everyone is happy that it should be left to the City institutions to regulate themselves, as they do at the moment through the Securities and Investments Board.

**Pension funds and insurance companies** are able to offer a better service to their clients because of the existence of the Stock Exchange, which gives them a profitable outlet for their funds.

**Services to Government**    By providing a ready market in gilt-edged securities, the Stock Exchange allows the Government to implement the various aspects of policy which depend upon the sale and purchase of Government securities.

**The administration of taxation** depends in some cases upon Stock Exchange prices. Capital gains tax is levied to a large extent on the profits made by buying and selling shares. The information provided on the contract notes enables the Inland Revenue to ensure that the right amount of tax is being paid. Similarly the valuation of stocks and shares for inheritance tax purposes relies upon their Stock Exchange valuation.

**Indicator of opinion**   The Stock Exchange is an important economic indicator. Stock Exchange prices reflect the underlying economic conditions in the country and within particular industries. Low prices reflect pessimism and a grim outlook; high prices indicate optimism. Potential investors can assess the various possibilities open to them by studying the achievements of different securities as shown in the share indices. However, the Exchange does tend towards extremes of optimism or pessimism, which exaggerate the actual trends.

## 13.8   Share prices

Dealers alter their prices according to whether their holding of a particular share is increasing or decreasing. This follows simply from the operation of the economic principles of supply and demand. But the changes in supply and demand only reflect deeper influences on the prices of shares. We can divide these influences into three groups.

### 13.8.1   Factors affecting a particular share's price

**Performance**   Much depends on the recent performance of the company that issued the share. If profits have been good and are expected to be buoyant, the price of the shares is likely to be high, as many people will try to acquire them. Poor profits will encourage shareholders to sell their holdings.

**Mergers**   The possibility of a merger with another company may cause the share price to change and, although the price will normally rise, the amount of change will depend on the view that shareholders in general take of the proposed merger.

**The development of new products or techniques** by a company may lead to optimism and higher share prices. Likewise, new developments by competitors may lead to a fall in the price of the share.

**Government policies** aimed at a particular industry may affect share prices of companies in that industry. For example, if restrictions are placed on the hire purchase of motor vehicles, the shares of car manufacturers may well fall in price.

### 13.8.2   *Factors affecting share prices in general*

**General economic atmosphere**   This affects all share prices. Sometimes the Government does all it can to persuade people to spend money. This will normally mean a period of rising profits, and many investors will instruct their stockbrokers to buy shares, causing a general rise in share prices. At other times the Government takes steps to reduce the level of spending. In this case, lower profits are expected and share prices fall.

The reasons for changes in Government policy are complex and you can study them more fully in *Success in Economics*. We need only note here that the Stock Exchange is extremely sensitive to changes in economic policy.

**Political factors** may also be important. The prospect of a change of Government often makes the Stock Exchange very jittery. The assassination of a foreign political leader has a similar effect.

### 13.8.3   *Speculation on the Stock Exchange*

By *speculation* we mean the practice of trying to make a quick profit by anticipating changes in the prices of shares. There are three ways in which this can be done.

(a) If a share is priced at £1 today and you have reason to think that by next week it will be worth £1.25, you could buy 1000 shares today for £1000 and, if your speculation is correct, sell them next week for £1250, making a quick £250 profit. People who speculate in this way, expecting a rise in price, are referred to as *bulls*. They may buy shares even if they have no money, hoping to pay at the end of the account out of the proceeds of the sale.

(b) On the other hand, if you own 1000 shares priced at 50 pence today and you think that they will be worth only 40 pence next week, you could sell them today for £500 and, if your speculation is correct, buy them back for £400 next week, leaving yourself with £100 profit. Speculators of this kind are called *bears*. They may even sell shares they do not own, hoping to be able to buy them back at the lower price before the end of the account. Both bulls and bears are likely to operate on much narrower margins than those indicated, and often over a much shorter period of time.

(c) It has often happened in the past that newly issued shares have risen in price quite rapidly, since the price of the share may be low considering the expected dividend that will be paid on it. Accordingly some speculators make a practice of buying new shares, hoping to sell them very quickly at a profit. Such speculators are called *stags*.

Bulls, bears and stags are names applied to speculators who behave in these ways at particular times, whether they are Stock Exchange members or not. They are not labels applied forever to individuals. An investor may behave in a 'bullish' way one day, but be 'bearish' the next. And, of course, speculators do not always make a profit. If prices move in the opposite direction to the one they expect, they may be in financial difficulties.

Bear dealers expect the price of XYZ shares to fall during the next few days. Although they do not own any of these shares, they undertake to sell some of them at today's price of 50 pence each. They hope that before they have to honour their commitment the price of the shares will fall so that they can buy them at perhaps 40 pence and sell them for 50 pence. If XYZ shares do not fall in price they are faced with the choice of buying them at a high and perhaps unprofitable price in order to honour their commitment, or of paying fees to their clients for postponing settlement. These fees are known as *backwardation*, and apply when prices have not fallen as anticipated.

Bulls, on the other hand, expect the price of XYZ shares to rise. They therefore agree to buy some at today's price so that they can sell them at a higher price in a few days' time. The proceeds of this sale would be used to settle the debt they incurred when they agreed to buy the shares. If the price does not rise, they may persuade the original seller of the shares to postpone settlement in exchange for a payment known as *contango*.

There are thus many influences on share prices. It is sometimes helpful to be able to assess the general feeling of the Exchange and the general movement of share prices. A *share index* is constructed to make this possible. A cross-section of shares is chosen by the compilers of the index, and their average price on a certain day is called 100. Subsequent changes in the average price of the shares are related to 100. So if the average price of the shares rises by 75 per cent, the value of the index is 175. The most widely consulted indices in this country are those compiled by the *Financial Times*, and you will find it an interesting exercise to follow them for a few weeks.

## 13.9   The Unlisted Securities Market

The expense of a full public issue and Stock Exchange quotation has always prevented medium-sized firms from acquiring capital from independent investors. In 1980, however, the Stock Exchange established a second-tier market known as the *Unlisted Securities Market* (USM). The requirements for companies entering this market are less stringent than for those seeking a full quotation, but they provide adequate safeguards for investors.

The company need only sell 10 per cent of its shares (as compared with 25 per cent for the full Stock Exchange), so that more or less full control can be retained. Costs are rather lower than for a full listing, but safeguards for investors are maintained.

Recently, over 600 companies had raised capital via the USM, 90 of them moving later to the full Stock Exchange list.

An even more recent development is the establishment of the *Third Market*, which enables small and young companies to raise extra funds even if they do not meet the requirements of the USM. There is probably more risk attached to such investments, but the potential rewards are greater and at least the investor has the advantage of knowing that the company has met certain Stock Exchange requirements.

## 13.10   3i

Sometimes a company may want long- or medium-term capital without the formalities of a share issue, even one made on the USM or the Third Market. This may not be something in which the banks want to involve themselves, because there may be a degree of risk. One of the organizations likely to be helpful is 3i (formerly Investors in Industry), an independent private sector group owned jointly by the London and Scottish clearing banks (85 per cent) and the Bank of England (15 per cent).

Finance may be provided in a number of ways. 3i may actually take shares in a company, thus providing capital on a permanent basis (although, like all investors, 3i can subsequently sell its shareholding). An alternative is the provision of long- or medium-term loans for the purchase of machines, the development of new products or other projects.

Apart from finance, 3i offers an important consultancy service which can provide advice to companies on a wide range of management services and procedures.

## 13.11   Leasing

One possibility that is quite popular is for a company to *lease* machinery rather than buy it. In this case an organization such as a merchant bank or finance house buys the machinery and rents it to the user. The advantage to the user company is that it can choose the machinery best suited to its needs, but can normally allow responsibility for repairs and maintenance to remain with the owner. The disadvantage, of course, is that the user never owns the machine.

## 13.12   Questions

1. Write a brief explanation of what is meant by the *capital market*.
2. Describe the main channels through which personal savers can make their savings available to Government and industry, showing the benefits to the individuals concerned.
3. 'Most savers want to withdraw their money at short notice, while most borrowers want long-term use of their loans.' Choose two savings organizations and show how they manage to satisfy both savers and borrowers.
4. 'In the 1980s there was a large increase in the number of people holding shares in British industry, mainly because of the policy of privatization.'
   (a) What is meant by the phrase *policy of privatization*?
   (b) What benefits might individuals obtain from holding shares in privatized companies?

(c) In what circumstances might the holders of those shares lose money?

5. (a) Name three kinds of security that a company may issue.
   (b) Why is it often necessary for a company to issue different kinds of security?
   (c) Show what advantages and disadvantages an individual may have from holding each of the securities mentioned in your answer to (a).

6. What is the *New Issues Market*? What services are provided by institutions in that market for companies wishing to issue shares?

7. Describe the main characteristics of the Unlisted Securities Market. Why is it important to medium-sized firms?

8. Many Stock Exchange transactions may be for speculative purposes.
   (a) What is meant by *speculation*?

---

# British Telecommunications plc

### Offer for Sale

by

### Kleinwort, Benson Limited

on behalf of

### The Secretary of State for Trade and Industry

of up to

### 3 012 000 000 Ordinary Shares of 25p each

### at 130p per share

50p is payable now
40p is payable on 24th June 1985
40p is payable on 9th April 1986

### and underwritten by

| | |
|---|---|
| Kleinwort, Benson Limited | S.G. Warburg & Co. Ltd. |
| Barclays Merchant Bank Limited | Baring Brothers & Co. Ltd |
| Charterhouse Japhet plc | County Bank Limited |
| Robert Fleming & Co. Limited | Hambros Bank Limited |
| Hill Samuel & Co. Limited | Lazard Brothers & Co. Limited |
| Lloyds Bank International Limited | Samuel Montagu & Co. Limited |
| Morgan Grenfell & Co. Limited | N.M. Rothschild & Sons Limited |

J. Henry Schroder Wagg & Co. Limited

---

**Fig. 13.7** An advertisement for British Telecom shares

(b) Explain two situations in which a speculator may hope to make a profit.

9. Describe briefly all the sources of finance – long-term and short-term – available to an industrial organization.

10. 'If the Government cannot raise sufficient money through taxation it will borrow the extra money required by issuing gilt-edged securities.'
    (a) What is the accumulated Government borrowing called?
    (b) Explain what is meant by *gilt-edged securities*.

11. The advertisement shown in fig. 13.7 was published in November 1984.
    (a) British Telecommunications plc was formerly a public corporation.
        (i) What is the main difference between a public limited company and a public corporation?
        (ii) Give one word for the process of turning a public corporation into a public limited company.
    (b) (i) Explain what is meant by the phrase 'underwritten by'.
        (ii) What do the firms named gain from underwriting?
    (c) What is the general term given to banks of this kind?
    (d) Which organization named in the document is the issuing house?
    (e) If you had applied for 200 shares in November 1984, how much would you have had to send with your application?
    (f) Assuming your application was successful, how much would you eventually have had to pay for your shares?
    (g) Suppose that in 1986 a dividend of 13 pence per share was paid. What would have been the percentage yield on your investment?
    (h) In March 1987 the price of the shares was 256 pence. What influences might have brought about this price increase?

# The arithmetic of business

## 14.1   Introduction

At the end of a *trading period*, which is normally a year, the owners of a business will review its performance. They will want to know how much profit has been made. Would they have been better off by investing their money in a building society or a unit trust? They will also want to know how much the business is worth. In a large limited company the calculations required are very complicated, but in a small business they are reasonably straightforward. For a detailed study of this subject you should consult *Success in Principles of Accounting*, but this Unit will enable you to understand the basic principles.

## 14.2   The capital of a business

In Unit 8.6 we saw that the capital of a limited company can mean the shares issued by that company. That is one way of measuring capital, but there are also several others. Let us consider the setting up of a small retail business. The owners will have to set aside from their savings a sum of money with which to start the business. Perhaps they decide that they need £60000, and put this into a special bank account. This is the initial capital of the business, and it is also one of the business's *liabilities*: a liability is any money owed by the business to someone outside it. So even the initial capital of a business is a liability, because it is owed to the owners. In a large company the same principle applies: the capital is owed to the shareholders.

As the business gets under way, some of the capital has to be spent. The proprietors need business premises from which to work, and perhaps a van for collecting and delivering goods. If they are manufacturers, they will need stocks of raw materials to work with, as well as stocks of finished products to sell. Wages have to be paid to employees, and there may be bills for stationery, gas, electricity, and so on. Already the initial capital is being divided up and put to different uses. We may identify four kinds of capital.

### 14.2.1   Fixed capital

Suppose the new firm starts by buying a small shop for £30000, some shop fittings for £12000, and a second-hand van for £3000. Things belonging to the firm are its *assets*, and the shop, shop fittings and van are called *fixed assets*, because they will probably remain in the business for many years, being used over and over again to help make a profit. Our proprietors have now spent £45000 of the firm's capital on fixed assets. The *capital* of the firm, however, remains at £60000, having simply assumed a different form: instead of holding all the capital in the form of cash, the firm now holds only £15000 in that form, and the rest as fixed capital in the form of various assets.

### 14.2.2   Working capital

Next the proprietors buy stocks of goods for resale. Perhaps they cost £10000 and, since this is a new business, it may well have to pay cash until the suppliers know the owners to be reliable. Again the nature of the capital has changed, leaving the business with only £5000 in cash. However, the purchase of stock is different from the purchase of the shop and other fixed assets: the object is to sell the stock as quickly as possible at a profit, thereby raising the cash to buy more stock for sale. Capital used like this for the day-to-day running of the business is known as *working capital*.

To establish how much working capital this firm has, imagine the balance sheet after a few months' trading. The balance sheet shows the position of the firm at a particular moment in time, rather like a photograph. Table 14.1 shows our firm's balance sheet after six months' trading.

**Table 14.1**  A balance sheet

| Assets | £ | Liabilities | £ |
|---|---|---|---|
| Shop | 30000 | Capital | 60000 |
| Shop fittings | 12000 | Bank loan | 4000 |
| Van | 3000 | Creditors | 6000 |
| Stock | 13000 | | |
| Debtors | 9000 | | |
| Cash at bank | 1500 | | |
| Cash in till | 1500 | | |
| | 70000 | | 70000 |

The formula for establishing working capital is

working capital = current assets − current liabilities

'Current' here means short-term, usually a year; so current assets and liabilities are those whose nature may be expected to change shortly. The current assets shown in the balance sheet are stock, debtors (people to whom the firm has supplied goods, but who have not yet paid for them), cash at the bank, and cash in the till, making a total of £25000. The current liabilities are a bank loan of £4000, and £6000 owed to creditors for goods supplied but not yet paid for. The working capital is therefore

$$£25000 - £10000 = £15000$$

Working capital is important for two reasons. First, every time cash is spent on stock and the stock is sold for cash, the business should be making a profit and this, after all, is the purpose of running a business. Secondly, any short-term liabilities have to be paid for out of working capital, so the ratio of current assets to current liabilities needs to be adequate. In our example it is 25000/10000 = 2½, which means that the firm could easily meet any bills that arrive. If its current liabilities were £25000 and its current assets £10000, the firm would be in a much more precarious position.

### 14.2.3   Liquid capital
*Liquid capital* is capital in the form of cash, or capital that can easily be turned into cash. This is one respect in which our firm is *not* in a strong position: it has very little liquid capital in relation to its liabilities. If we exclude debtors, since we don't know how soon they will pay, the firm has only £3000 liquid capital, half at the bank and half in the till, and would be in difficulty if all the creditors wanted payment tomorrow. Perhaps the firm is carrying too much stock for safety. (If it held less stock it would have more cash or fewer creditors.)

### 14.2.4   Capital employed
This measure of capital is also sometimes used: it means the sum of the assets the firm is using, whether borrowed or not. In this example the *capital employed* is £60000, consisting of the total assets minus the debts owing.

## 14.3   Adding to capital
According to our balance sheet, the capital has remained at £60000, even after some months' trading. While it is possible for this to happen, it is unusual: it implies either that no profits have been made in the period or that they have all been withdrawn by the proprietors for their personal use. In fact there are several ways in which the capital employed in the business can be increased:

(a) by leaving some of the profits in the business,
(b) by borrowing from banks or elsewhere,
(c) by obtaining credit from suppliers, which really means using their capital to run the business,
(d) by converting the business into a larger unit, either by bringing in a partner or by forming a limited company, or
(e) by issuing shares to the public, although this can only be done by a public limited company.

It is also possible for the capital employed in a business to *fall*. The proprietors may withdraw too much money for their own use, for example, or creditors may insist on payment.

Whether capital is increasing or decreasing, the important thing is to be able to understand from the balance sheet whether the firm is in a strong or a weak position to continue trading. Potential suppliers, customers and shareholders can learn a lot about a company by studying its balance sheet.

## 14.4  Profit

The purpose of business activity is to make a profit by supplying goods and services to consumers. This is done by buying goods at one price and selling them at a higher price, often after changing their condition. A rough indication of profits can be obtained by subtracting the cost of the goods from the money obtained by selling them, but we need to be more precise. There are several points to consider.

### 14.4.1  Turnover
The turnover of a business is another term for its sales. *Gross turnover* is the total value of goods sold, but the *net turnover* is more significant. This is the gross turnover minus the value of any goods returned by customers. The turnover of a business is important because if the firm doesn't sell anything (that is, if it has a zero turnover) it cannot make a profit. If turnover is high the profits are likely to be high, but it does not follow that profits rise in direct proportion to turnover.

### 14.4.2  Cost of goods sold
This can be obtained from the invoices received during the year. It does not include all the firm's purchases, however, because some of them, like the van and the shop fittings, are not intended for resale, and so are not included.

### 14.4.3  Gross profit
Gross profit is the difference between turnover and the cost of the goods sold. If during the year a firm sells goods for £90000 which cost £70000 to buy, the gross profit is £20000.

### 14.4.4  Net profit
In selling goods for £90000 the proprietors of the business will have incurred some expenses. Wages, fuel, power and rates will all have been paid during the year. If these amount to £9000, the firm will have made a net profit of £11000 at the end of the year.

### 14.4.5  Percentage profit
Whether or not the profit figures of £20000 and £11000 are satisfactory to the proprietors depends partly on the kind of business they are running and partly

on their own needs. In order that different kinds of businesses can be compared, or that the proprietors can easily compare one year with another, it is often useful to quote gross and net profits as a percentage of turnover. This is obtained by the formula

$$\text{percentage profit} = \frac{\text{profit}}{\text{turnover}} \times 100\%$$

Of the £90 000 turnover, £20 000 was gross profit, so the *gross* profit percentage was

$$\frac{£20\,000}{£90\,000} \times 100\% = 22.2\%$$

The *net* profit percentage was

$$\frac{£11\,000}{£90\,000} \times 100\% = 12.2\%$$

The use of percentages in accounting makes the comparison of different firms much easier. For example, consider the figures in Table 14.2 for two different firms, A and B.

**Table 14.2** Comparison of profits (£)

|  | Firm A | Firm B |
| --- | --- | --- |
| Turnover | 50 000 | 30 000 |
| Cost of goods sold | 40 000 | 22 500 |
| Expenses | 4 000 | 2 000 |
| Gross profit | 10 000 | 7 500 |
| Net profit | 6 000 | 5 500 |

If we look only at the profit figures, A seems to have had a better year than B, though the difference between their net profits is less than that between their gross profits, because B has kept its expenses down. The percentage profit figures on the other hand give a different picture. A's gross percentage profit is 20 per cent and B's is 25 per cent, while their net percentage profits are 12 per cent and 18.3 per cent respectively. B has had a much more satisfactory year than A in relation to turnover.

### 14.4.6 Level of profits

The owners will examine the annual profit figures in detail. (Indeed they will probably want half-yearly or even quarterly profit figures calculated so that they can keep a close watch on the firm's performance.) If profits are significantly lower than expected, the causes must be investigated.

(a) If *gross* profits are up to normal but *net* profits are lower than usual, some of the expenses must be higher than expected. Perhaps too many staff are being employed, or electricity is being wasted. Some staff may be using the firm's vehicles outside working hours at the firm's expense. Perhaps wage rises or other increases in costs have not been passed on to the customer.

(b) A reduction in the *gross* profit percentage may be more serious, and the cause may be more difficult to trace. It could be that money or stock is being stolen: either has the effect of reducing turnover while not reducing costs. In some businesses stock may be wasted. For example, bakers, grocers and other food retailers may find themselves throwing stock away if they have over-estimated the demand for their goods. In other businesses a change of fashion, breakages or gradual deterioration of goods may cause goods to be disposed of or sold off at very low prices. The firm probably needs to tighten up on its activities and make sure that it does not carry more stock than it needs. There may, of course, be a simpler explanation: perhaps the firm is paying more for its stock, or selling at lower prices than it should. This raises the question of the rate at which the stock is sold, which is dealt with in Unit 14.5.

### 14.4.7  Profits and capital

Profit figures in relation to turnover convey important information about a business. But the proprietors will also be interested in their profits in relation to the capital they put into the business at the beginning. After all, we suggested in Unit 14.1 that they might be better off by putting money in a building society or unit trust.

Suppose the firm whose balance sheet we looked at in Table 14.1 made a net profit of £12000 in the first year. The return on capital invested is obtained by the following formula:

$$\text{return} = \frac{\text{net profit}}{\text{capital}} \times 100\%$$

$$= \frac{£12000}{£60000} \times 100\% = 20\%$$

This is more than could have been earned by investing in building societies or unit trusts, but you must remember that the owners are not necessarily better off. If the £60000 had been put into building society accounts, it could have been withdrawn intact – with interest – at the end of the year. As it is, much of the money is now invested in shop fittings and a van, and there is no guarantee that these could be sold for the same amount that was paid for them. That is one of the risks of business. In addition, the owners may have contributed a year's work to the firm. They will need to compare their profits with what they could have earned by working for somebody else.

## 14.5   The rate of turnover

We saw in Unit 14.4 that every time goods are sold the firm expects to add to its gross profit, and that firms should try to ensure that stocks are not left on their hands for too long. These two points come together when we consider the *rate of turnover* (also known as the *rate of stockturn*), which means the number of times that a firm sells its stock each year. To calculate the rate of turnover we need to know the average stock that the firm carried through the year and the amount of stock sold. However, since the stock held is valued at cost price and the stock sold is valued at selling price, we must first reduce them to the same terms. We can do this if we know the gross profit percentage on goods. For example, if we know that sales are £15 000 and that there is a gross profit on sales of 33⅓ per cent, then the cost of goods sold is £10 000. (One-third of the £15 000 is profit, so the remaining two-thirds, £10 000, is the cost of the goods.)

Once we know the cost of goods sold, we need to work out the average stock held, which is given by the formula:

(stock held on 1 January + stock held on 31 December) ÷ 2

Finally we are ready to calculate the rate of turnover, for which the formula is

$$\text{rate of turnover} = \frac{\text{cost of stock sold}}{\text{cost of average stock}}$$

Thus, if a trader has a turnover of £36 000, with a gross profit of 25 per cent, and his opening stock was bought for £2000 and his closing stock for £3000, the rate of turnover is calculated as follows:

$$\text{Cost of stock sold} = £36\,000 - £36\,000 \times \frac{25}{100}$$
$$= £36\,000 - £9\,000$$
$$= £27\,000$$

$$\text{Cost of average stock} = \frac{£2\,000 + £3\,000}{2} = £2\,500$$

$$\text{Rate of turnover} = \frac{27\,000}{2\,500} = 10.8$$

This means that the average stock has been sold 10.8 times during the year. (The rate of turnover is always expressed as a number.) However, we cannot tell whether a rate of 10.8 represents a good or bad performance unless we know what kind of business it is. A fishmonger, for example, makes a profit of only a few pence on each fish, and therefore needs to sell a lot of fish to make a living (that is, fishmongers must have a high rate of turnover). A car dealer, on the other hand, may make hundreds of pounds on each sale and can survive with a much lower rate of turnover. Furthermore, unless fishmongers dispose of their stock fairly promptly it is useless – this is a less urgent matter for car dealers.

One way of increasing net profits is to increase the rate of turnover. If the average stock is sold twelve times during the year rather than ten, we will expect profits to rise. (The supermarkets provide the best example of firms which make huge profits by a high rate of turnover. We saw in Unit 3.5 that they have many advantages over traditional shops, but one of the most important is their much higher rate of turnover.) However, this does not always happen, for it may be that various expenses have increased also. If the increase in expenses is greater than the increase in gross profit, the result will be a reduction in net profit. Or if the increase in the rate of turnover is achieved by reducing prices, the level of net profit may again be reduced.

## 14.6  Questions

1. Distinguish between the *assets* of a business and the *liabilities* of a business.
2. (a) Give examples to show the differences between fixed assets and current assets.
   (b) Why is it normally necessary for a firm to have a mixture of fixed assets and current assets?
3. A firm has opening stocks worth £10000 and closing stocks worth £12000. During the period under review, purchases of new stock were £60000 and total sales were £120000.
   (a) Calculate the gross profit of the firm.
   (b) What further information would you require in order to calculate the net profit for the period?
4. Outline three ways in which the capital of a business may be increased.
5. (a) Explain what is meant by the *rate of turnover*.
   (b) Why does the rate of turnover vary between different kinds of business? Give examples to illustrate your answer.
6. A local business has sold goods which had cost £150000 to buy. Its opening stock was £20000 and the closing stock £40000. Calculate the rate of turnover.
7. A market greengrocer always adds 25 per cent to the cost of his goods before selling them to the public.
   (a) One day he buys goods for £240. How much should he receive if he sells them all?
   (b) The following day he sells all that day's purchases and his takings are £240. How much did he pay for the goods?
8. A trader manages to increase the turnover from £1000 per week to £1500 per week. Despite this 50 per cent rise in sales, the trader's profits have risen by only 10 per cent. Explain how this might have occurred.

# UNIT 15

# Communications: the Post Office

## 15.1 Introduction

Trade and commerce can flourish only if the individuals and institutions concerned can communicate with each other. This communication can take various forms, which are discussed in this and the three following Units.

The earliest kind of communication required the parties to a business deal to be in the same place. Traders or merchants would travel in order to conduct their business. Obviously transport was important for this and it remains important, perhaps more for goods than for people. This physical movement of goods and people is the subject of Unit 18.

Traders need the services of transport to obtain goods and materials and to deliver them, but they also have to establish a market for their goods in advance. They may communicate with potential customers by means of advertising, and this is covered in Unit 17.

Sometimes it is necessary for a trader to contact a supplier or customer some distance away – even abroad, perhaps – in a hurry. In the United Kingdom, facilities for this are provided mainly by British Telecom and they are examined in Unit 16.

At all times traders require written records of their transactions in a form similar to the documents described in Unit 5. In the UK, the physical movement of these documents and millions of others is the responsibility of the Post Office, whose work is the main subject of this Unit.

The services provided by the Post Office fall conveniently into two groups: (a) the traditional mail services and developments deriving from them and (b) financial services of various kinds.

## 15.2 Inland letters

The basic Royal Mail service, originating in 1635, remains essential to business and social communication. The Post Office delivers to over 24 million addresses in the UK and handles over 60 million items each day. This total has increased significantly in recent years. The aim is to deliver 90 per cent of first-class letters on the following working day, and 96 per cent of second-class by the third working day after collection: the achievement according to Post Office figures is 86 per cent and 93 per cent respectively.

The reasons for the increase in the number of letters include the following.

(a) Encouragement has been given to social letter writing by the Post Office, including competitions and advertising campaigns.

(b) There has been a fairly spontaneous increase in what the Post Office calls 'financial mail' – bills, invoices, bank statements, insurance matters. This is attributable to a number of developments, including a growth in the number of households each receiving and paying gas, electricity and other bills, more people opening bank accounts which inevitably generate correspondence between banks and their customers, and the increasing number of credit cards in use. All of these generate more mail.

(c) The Post Office has made considerable efforts to increase direct mail advertising materials sent direct to consumers. There seems to be plenty of scope for further increases here, since each household in the UK receives three such items per month, much below other countries (in The Netherlands householders receive on average eleven items per month, and in Switzerland twelve).

(d) The Post Office has offered special incentives to business users.

In addition, the development of a range of special postal services has encouraged further increases in the volume of mail. Some of these services are listed below.

**Business Reply Service**   This enables members of the public to send short replies to businesses without having to pay for a stamp. It is used mainly by traders who are advertising their goods and are anxious to encourage replies from the public. Before the service can be used, a licence must be obtained from the Post Office and a deposit paid to cover the likely costs of delivering the letters. When they are delivered, the letters are subject to a small surcharge over the ordinary letter rate. Almost 50 000 licences are in operation for the Business Reply Service.

**Freepost** offers two different services. A firm may send out pre-printed labels or envelopes to potential or existing customers, including the word 'Freepost' in the address. This may be on a first- or second-class basis, and in either case the firm pays a surcharge for the service. Alternatively the firm may invite customers to reply to a Freepost address by including it in advertising material, having first made appropriate arrangements with the Post Office.

**Admail** enables a company to invite replies to any particular address, perhaps a local or prestigious one, and have them automatically forwarded to its head office (or anywhere else). A company might, for example, use a number of regional addresses in order to attract local customers who might not respond to a remote Head Office address.

There are some further refinements of the basic postal service of which you should be aware, and these are described below.

**Postcodes** allow the automatic sorting of letters. By means of a code of letters and numbers, each item can be sorted – automatically in many places – down to the final stage for the postman to put them into the right order. Letters carrying the postcode are likely to arrive more quickly than those without it.

**Certificates of posting** For a small charge, the Post Office will issue a certificate providing proof that you have posted a package to a particular address.

**Recorded delivery service** This service provides proof not only that you posted a letter but also, more important, that it was delivered. A charge is made for the service, and the Post Office clerk gives the sender a slip of paper certifying that the letter has been sent. When it is delivered, the letter has to be signed for, preferably by the addressee. In the event of non-delivery, a limited amount of compensation is payable. For an additional fee the Post Office will inform the sender when delivery has been made, though no extra care is taken of letters under this service.

The recorded delivery service is often used by traders who want to ensure that debtors receive their bills, and by solicitors sending important documents by post. Limited compensation will be paid for loss of documents. The system should not be used for sending cash or anything which is of monetary value, since no compensation will be offered for loss of articles like these. Where valuable items are concerned, the registered post system should be used (see Unit 15.5).

**Franking machines** It is no trouble for us, as individuals, to buy stamps and stick them on our letters as we send them. But some large companies dispatch several thousand letters from their head office every day, and it would be laborious and time-consuming to have to stick stamps on each one. To avoid this, the Post Office allows customers with a heavy outward mail to use a franking machine, which prints the postage payable on each envelope. The machine contains a meter which records the total postage payable on the letters passed through it, and the amount is payable to the Post Office periodically, normally in advance.

This system is time-saving, not only for a business but also for the Post Office, because it saves them cancelling stamps on the letters when they arrive at the sorting office. There is a further advantage to the business in that it can advertise itself by incorporating a short message or symbol in the postage-paid mark. The only drawback is that the users may try to defraud the Post Office by franking letters with a lower amount than is strictly payable, but this is discouraged by a system of spot checks.

**Cash on delivery** is an additional service which is useful to traders. The Post Office undertakes to collect payment for the goods being delivered before they are actually handed over. The sender of the goods pays for the service, though of course the cost is generally included in the price paid by the consumer. Cash on delivery provides a safeguard to both sellers and buyers. Sellers do not have money tied up in bad debts and do not have to keep sending reminders to debtors, while mail order customers do not have to send off money in advance, perhaps to obscure companies that may take months to deliver the goods.

## 15.3   Inland parcels

Despite increasing competition from other carriers, the Post Office parcel service showed continuous growth in the 1980s, with the number of parcels carried rising to almost 200 million per year. The main reasons for the steady expansion seem to be the nationwide scale of the distribution network, effective advertising prompted by competition from other carriers, and special arrangements made with mail order companies and other heavy users of the service. The maximum parcel weight accepted is 25 kilograms.

## 15.4   Datapost

While the Post Office aims to deliver 90 per cent of ordinary first-class letters on the following working day, there appears to be a rising demand for absolutely certain punctual delivery of some items. Datapost has been developed to meet this demand. Originally designed to guarantee that computer data collected from contracted customers one day would be delivered by the following working morning, Datapost now carries parcels and paperwork of all kinds. The bulk of the work deals with documents whose delivery is critical, but there is a growing proportion of parcels for delivery in the United Kingdom and abroad.

There is a 'Freefone' link (see Unit 16.2.1) to all Datapost service centres so that customers can almost instantly arrange collection times for their urgent packages. In effect Datapost provides a courier service for such material, with guaranteed delivery.

## 15.5   Payment through the Post Office

Apart from the transmission of mail, the Post Office has an important role to play in the payments system of the United Kingdom, both in accepting payments at the counter for onward transmission to many businesses and Government departments, and in making payments of Social Security benefits. Increasingly the Post Office receives or disburses money in its role as an

**Fig. 15.1** Priority is given to Datapost packages to ensure that they arrive on time

agent for Girobank transactions but there are other, separate, means of payment.

**Postal orders** are the basic method of payment provided by the Post Office. They are issued for any amount from 25 pence to £20 on payment of a fee which is related to the value of the postal order.

Postal orders are a convenient way of making payments if you do not have many to make. Their disadvantage is that you have to go to the post office to get them, as they are not issued in books like cheques. The payee's name has to be filled in, because postal orders are not negotiable – only the payee can collect the money from the post office.

Postal orders can be crossed in the same way as cheques (see Unit 11.4.3) to ensure that they are paid into a bank account. As they are not negotiable, it is advisable to check that the payee does have a bank account before crossing an order.

Approximately 54 million postal orders were used in 1986, but with the increase in the number of people with bank accounts there has been a decline in their use in subsequent years.

**Registered post**    On the rare occasions when cash (or valuables) has to be sent through the post, the safest way to send it is by registered letter. This must be handed in at a post office (not put in the letter-box) and a receipt obtained. A fee is payable in addition to the first-class letter rate. The fee varies according to the value of the contents of the packet; it provides for compensation in the event of loss, up to certain limits (specified in the *Post Office Guide*). Naturally the Post Office takes special care of registered packets, and it is very unusual for one to go astray.

## 15.6    Girobank

Girobank offers a wide range of bank services for personal and business customers (over two million in all) through a network of 20 000 post offices. All accounts are held centrally at a computer centre in Bootle. Money can be cheaply and efficiently transferred from one account to another, or deposited from outside the system, or indeed paid outside the system.

Girobank became a subsidiary of the Alliance and Leicester Building Society in 1990 and offers a range of services similar to those of the other retail banks.

### *15.6.1    Personal current accounts*

Anyone aged fifteen or over can apply to open a Girobank current account. All account-holders are provided with a cheque book and, apart from using cheques to pay bills in the usual way, they can cash a cheque for £50 at post offices offering Girobank services or for £100 at their 'home' bank.

Standing orders and direct debits operate through the current account on the same basis as in the other banks. For payments between Giro accounts a transfer system operates. Many household bills are paid in this way. If you have a Giro account you simply fill in the transfer form attached to the bill and send it to Girobank headquarters; on receiving it, the appropriate sum is transferred.

Since 1985 Girobank has been a leading member of *Link*, a group of financial organizations, including some building societies, which provides a network of automatic teller machines (ATMs) enabling customers to withdraw cash via personal cards (a further example of the way in which Girobank competes with the other banks). Girobank is also fully involved with other developments concerned with the electronic transfer of funds.

In addition to cash transfer services, loans of up to £5000 are available for customers, and customers are allowed to overdraw their accounts.

### 15.6.2   *Business services*

As it has developed, Girobank has offered a wider range of services to business customers. Apart from the ordinary current account services, there are special facilities for the payment of wages, salaries or pensions, the rapid transfer of large amounts from Giro accounts, and a range of international money payment systems.

### 15.6.3   *Paying in*

Paying money into a Girobank account is quite straightforward: a deposit form is completed and handed in with the money at any post office. If cheques are being paid in they will not be credited to a Girobank account until they have been cleared.

   If someone without a Girobank account wants to pay money into an account, he or she completes either a *Transcash* form or a form specially prepared by the payee and hands the form and the cash into the Post Office, which makes a nominal charge for the service.

### 15.6.4   *The advantages and disadvantages of Girobank*

The relative merits of Girobank and clearing banks are debatable. Several points should be borne in mind.

**Speed**   Payments between Girobank account-holders are usually quicker than those between customers of different bank branches. Once the Girobank transfer form reaches the computer, the transaction is complete. The bank cheque has a longer journey to make.

**Cost**   There is very little difference in cost as long as the bank account remains in credit. Girobank account-holders make a limited payment for stationery, which is specially printed with the name of the customer. On the other hand they are provided with pre-paid first-class envelopes for their remittances through the Girobank centre.

**Convenience of use**   Post offices are more convenient than high-street banks in that they are open not only for longer hours, but also on Saturday mornings.

**Statements**   Girobank sends frequent statements showing the position of the account. Business customers can receive them whenever the balance in the account changes, while other customers receive statements whenever money is paid into their accounts or after every ten debit entries. Clearing banks do not normally send statements as often as this, although special arrangements can be made for individual customers.

The Girobank system has its disadvantages, however, and there are several ways in which it compares unfavourably with other retail banks.

**Range of services**    All in all, the banks provide a more comprehensive range of financial services than Girobank does. In the long run this may count against Girobank, because people sometimes need advice on matters outside its scope.

**Post office congestion**    A minor disadvantage of Girobank is that post offices have all kinds of other business to contract. It may be frustrating to the account-holder to have to queue up behind several people wanting to renew their television licences or inquire about the postage rates to Australia.

## 15.7    Saving through the Post Office

We saw in Unit 13.4.6 that National Savings are part of the capital market, collecting small amounts from individual savers and making the total available to the Government. The National Savings Bank operates through post offices, so it is appropriate that we now look at the main savings facilities.

### 15.7.1    The National Savings Bank

**Ordinary accounts** are intended for small savings and easy withdrawal. Interest rates are announced each November and guaranteed for the following calendar year. For 1992 the basic rate was 2.5 per cent, doubling to 5 per cent for balances over £500. Interest is tax-free up to £70.

**Investment accounts** offer a higher rate of interest (often about double that on ordinary accounts), but withdrawals require one month's notice and the interest rate may be changed at any time.

### 15.7.2    National Savings Certificates

These are issued for different amounts and on different terms from year to year. They are fairly liquid in that they can be cashed at about a week's notice, but they have to be held until they mature – normally after five years – to provide the best yield.

Some issues of the certificates are *index-linked*. They were first introduced when the rate of inflation was high. They are linked to the retail prices index (see Unit 10.3.2), so that the holder eventually recovers his or her original investment plus a payment to compensate for the fall in the value of money since the purchase of the certificate. When the rate of inflation fell to a low figure, extra interest was added by the Government to make these certificates more acceptable to savers.

Savings certificates have the advantage that no income tax is payable on the interest received.

### 15.7.3   Premium bonds

The holders of premium bonds receive no interest, but each bond qualifies the holder for a stake in a draw for cash prizes which takes place each week. The prizes, up to a maximum of £250000, replace the normal system of interest payments as the incentive for people to invest, and are paid out of the money that would be used to pay the interest if the Government borrowed from the public in the ordinary way. Subscribers must purchase a minimum of £100 worth of bonds, and there is a maximum holding of £10000. (Children under the age of sixteen may purchase bonds in £10 units.)

### 15.7.4   Other forms of saving

There are several other forms of saving available through the Post Office, including the purchase of gilt-edged securities (see Unit 13.5.1). Leaflets listing the securities currently available can be obtained from any post office.

## 15.8   Questions

1. Explain the various ways in which trade depends upon effective communications.
2. Describe the basic communications services provided by the Post Office.
3. Explain how each of the following may be of benefit to people and organizations using the postal services:
   (a) certificate of posting,
   (b) recorded delivery,
   (c) registered post,
   (d) Freepost,
   (e) franking machines.
4. Discover what you can about the Post Office services providing for the urgent delivery of documents, and write a report on those services.
5. In what ways are postal orders (a) a convenient, (b) an inconvenient method of payment compared with cheques?
6. (a) Describe the principal services provided by Girobank.
   (b) In what respects are they more convenient than the services offered by other clearing banks?
7. Units 13 and 15 discuss various outlets for personal savings. Compile a report examining the advantages and disadvantages of the various savings facilities from the point of view of someone with £2000 to save.

# Communications: telecommunications

## 16.1 Introduction

Telecommunications is one of the fastest growing industries in the world. In the United Kingdom, the provision of telecommunication services was the monopoly of the Post Office until 1981. In that year British Telecom became a separate organization, and in 1984 it was privatized (see Unit 9.8). It is now a public limited company. It was also in 1981 that British Telecom's monopoly was ended when the Government allowed other organizations to offer competing services.

In this Unit we shall examine the services provided by British Telecom and consider the alternatives that are being offered by other companies.

## 16.2 British Telecom services

### 16.2.1 The telephone

Business life today would be inconceivable without the telephone. The service was first provided by the Post Office in 1912, and in 1991 there were over 24 million subscribers to the service who between them made 28 000 million calls. Charges are made by a combination of a fixed quarterly rental and payments which depend on the number and length of the calls, the distance over which they are made and the time at which they are made.

Most subscribers are now linked to the *Subscriber Trunk Dialling* (STD) system, which enables one subscriber to dial direct to any other on the system. This is much cheaper than making calls via the operator, although the chances of misdialling are greater. Through the international direct dialling system, callers in the UK can reach over 700 million telephones in 201 countries.

The telephone's immediate advantage is speed. A trader can place an order for goods or get a quotation for them much more rapidly by telephone than by letter. Moreover, there may be details of the job or consignment to be

**Fig. 16.1** The British Telecom Tower is not only central to the UK telephone network but also sends television programmes from London to other regions and receives and transmits TV programmes by satellite from and to other countries

discussed, and this can be achieved more efficiently in a five-minute telephone conversation than by the exchange of three or four letters.

It is important, however, that agreements made by telephone are confirmed in writing as soon as possible, for two reasons. First, without written confirmation there is no evidence of a contract between the two parties, and it is easy to imagine the difficulties to which this can lead. Secondly, words can easily be misheard over the telephone, and a written follow-up avoids any confusion.

To ensure that the best use is made of the telephone system, British Telecom provides a number of ancillary services for subscribers, though not all of them are designed specifically for businesses. These extra services include the following.

**Directories**    In addition to the basic directories containing an alphabetical list of the subscribers in a given area, classified trade directories are also available for each area. The best known of these, the *Yellow Pages*, is issued to all subscribers in that area.

The advantages of the *Yellow Pages* are that the subscriber can readily obtain the telephone number of, for example, a plumber, because all the local plumbers will be listed in the same place in the directory. Thus plumbers and other businesses enjoy an inexpensive kind of advertising, and British Telecom enjoys extra revenue from the more intensive use of the system.

**Directory Enquiries services** provide assistance to callers unable to trace the number of the person they wish to call. (Some subscribers deliberately choose to have their numbers excluded from the directory, because they do not want them to be available to everyone. In such cases the Directory Enquiries service is unable to help.)

**Redirected calls**    Sometimes you may find it inconvenient to accept calls on your normal number. In this case British Telecom can intercept the calls and redirect them to a number where they can be dealt with. This service operates when people have to change their number or when, as happens with family doctors, they are temporarily unavailable.

**Miscellaneous services** provided by British Telecom include such things as alarm calls, where you can arrange for the telephone operator to ring until you answer, recorded weather forecasts, the time, and the latest score in a Test Match in progress. There is also a *Freefone* service along the lines of the Freepost service described in Unit 15. A full list of the miscellaneous services is to be found in the introductory pages of the telephone directory.

### 16.2.2    Telex services

*Telex* is best regarded as a combination of a telephone and a typewriter. Subscribers to this service have a teleprinter installed in their office and are given a number in the same way as telephone users. Messages can then be sent to other subscribers: the telex operator types the message out and it is automatically printed at the recipient's office, even if there is no one there to receive it.

The main advantage of this system is that messages can be received at any time of the day or night, so, when offices open in the morning in London, written information is already to hand about price changes or other developments that have occurred in other parts of the world overnight. Subscribers to the service in the UK can contact over 1.5 million others in 200 different countries.

A further refinement, *Telex Plus*, enables a subscriber to transmit the same message to up to 1000 different destinations, feeding the message into the machine only once. If necessary the message can be personalized for each recipient, and Telex Plus will automatically confirm delivery.

A more recent introduction is the *Teletex System* (not to be confused with teletext, the television information system). Teletex permits the high-speed transmission of top-quality documents between terminals similar to word-processors or electronic typewriters. The finished item is of the same quality as if it had originated in the recipient's office.

Teletex is a development of the *Fax* system. A Fax machine scans documents and sends signals down the telephone system to the destination, where the receiving Fax machine converts them back to the original form within seconds. Fax can transmit diagrams and photographs, as well as handwritten, typed and printed text.

### 16.2.3 Datel services
*Datel* provides a means of transmitting information from one computer to another, using the public telephone network. Where a business organization has a substantial or continuous need for such a service, private lines or networks can be provided to meet its requirements. It is through such networks that the EFTPOS service (discussed in Unit 11.12.7) and other money transmission services operate.

### 16.2.4 Teleconferencing
The rapid expansion of the world's telecommunications network now allows businessmen in, say, New York, London, Tokyo and Paris to hold a meeting without the need and expense of travelling to an agreed location. Both 'videoconferencing' and 'audioconferencing' services are available. The former, which is the more expensive, is appropriate where there is a need to discuss drawings or plans. The latter is useful for a company needing perhaps to hold a meeting between salesmen spread around the world – people in up to twenty different locations can be accommodated in the same audioconference.

### 16.2.5 Prestel
Through the telephone network, the *Prestel* viewdata system allows a subscriber to have information extracted from a computer and displayed on an adapted television set. (This should not be confused with the Ceefax system on BBC and the Oracle system on ITV which are examples of the *teletext* system in which data is transmitted like ordinary television programmes.) The subscriber can 'dial' into any of 300 000 'pages' of information on a wide range of subjects. Many of these deal with current events and are constantly updated, thereby providing businesses with immediate checks on such things as commodity prices, interest rates and foreign exchange rates.

The importance of rapid and efficient communications in business cannot be exaggerated. As commerce and trade become more competitive and complex, the need for up-to-date information grows. Decisions about buying, production and marketing may commit a company to spending thousands of pounds – the better and more complete the information available to the firm, the less chance there is of wrong decisions being made.

To some extent the services outlined above represent the tip of an iceberg – there is a huge and growing range of services available. As far as international links are concerned, their growth depends on the use of satellites orbiting the earth. British Telecom is the Government's representative on the three international groups responsible for the satellite system:

(a) International Telecommunications Satellite Organization (INTELSAT),
(b) International Marine Satellite Organization (INMARSAT) and
(c) European Telecommunications Satellite Group (EUTELSAT).

### 16.2.6 Telemessages and telegrams

*Telemessages* have replaced telegrams as a means of communicating quickly with people within the United Kingdom without a telephone or telex. You dictate the message you wish to send over the telephone to the operator. The message is then transmitted by telex to the main post office nearest to the addressee, and British Telecom guarantees that it will be delivered with the first-class post the following morning. This is not as efficient as the former telegram service, which normally provided same-day delivery.

The overseas telegram service still remains. You can send a telegram by telephoning the International Telegram Service and dictating your message to the operator.

## 16.3 Private telecommunications services

When British Telecom was privatized, the Government introduced some competition by licensing Mercury Communications Limited to provide alternative services. Mercury is a subsidiary of Cable & Wireless PLC, a company with wide international experience of providing telecommunications services.

Among other things Mercury now provides its own telex services, using either its own lines or those of British Telecom, by means of a special access code. British Telecom has similar access to Mercury lines if it needs it.

Various private message networks are also available. These include

**Credit card validation**   Retailers can quickly establish whether a proposed purchase is within the limit of the cardholder, and that the card has not been reported as stolen.

**Electronic funds transfer**   These are discussed in Unit 11.12.7.

**Reservation systems** These are of various kinds. Travel agents operate one, for example: when you go into a travel agency to book a holiday, the staff can quickly check on its availability through this system.

**Specialist information** to people in particular industries where conditions may change quickly – banking and the foreign exchange market are examples.

Perhaps of greater significance is the alternative public telephone service that Mercury now provides, interconnecting with the British Telecom services. Mercury 2000 is primarily a business service and Mercury 2300 is a residential service; both provide good savings. Mercury also provides an itemized bill to the customer, making clear the destination, time and duration of each call.

**Fig. 16.2** Mercury communications satellites. Dishes such as these not only speed up international communications but also permit more simultaneous calls to be made

Like British Telecom, Mercury does not confine itself to inland communications. The company has worldwide satellite links, and it may be cheaper for users to make calls to areas such as North America and parts of the Far East via Mercury rather than British Telecom.

## 16.4  Questions

1. What is the main advantage of the telephone over the ordinary postal service?
2. What disadvantages does the telephone have compared with the postal service?
3. Explain how the telex system operates, showing the advantages it has over the post and telephone systems.
4. Describe the Teletex or Fax system of conveying information from one location to another.
5. Distinguish between Datel and Prestel, showing the circumstances in which each could be of benefit to business people.
6. (a) Describe the main forms of electronic communications systems available to businesses today.
   (b) Why have they grown in popularity in recent years?
   (c) Despite this growth, the basic postal services have continued to expand. How would you explain this?
7. (a) What is Mercury Communications Ltd?
   (b) Describe the main services that this company provides, showing how they may be of use to (i) a travel agent, (ii) a business with its head office in London and several branches in the north of England.

# Communications: advertising

## 17.1   Introduction

Many large firms have *marketing departments*, whose function is to identify the market for the firm's products and to ensure that those products reach that market. We shall take a general look at the work of the marketing department in Unit 17.10, but for most of this Unit we shall concentrate on one aspect of marketing: *advertising*, in its various forms.

Advertising is used for so many different purposes that it can only be loosely defined as the spreading of information or awareness. It is the means by which one party communicates with another. This covers, for instance, the Government's efforts to reduce cigarette smoking or encourage road safety. More commonly, however, the main objective of advertising is to increase, or at least maintain, the sales of a product or service.

Before we look at the different types of advertising, let us first consider the aims of commercial advertisers in more detail.

## 17.2   The aims of advertising

### 17.2.1   Higher sales

The main purpose of any business is to make a profit, and in general the more goods a firm sells, the higher its profits will be. Indeed, profits should rise at a higher rate than sales, because some of the costs of production do not increase with output. In commercial terms, as sales increase, the *cost per unit of production* is reduced. The cost per unit can be calculated by dividing the total costs by the number of units. Let us look at an example.

Suppose that the monthly cost of producing plastic trays can be broken down as follows:

cost of machinery                £8000
rent of factory                  £2000
cost of labour and materials     £100 per thousand units

and that sales have been running at 10000 units per month.

The total costs are thus £8000 + £2000 + £1000 (the cost of labour and materials for 10000 units). Therefore the cost per unit will be

$$\frac{£11\,000}{10\,000} = £1.10$$

The producer now tries to increase sales by advertising, at a cost of £2000 per month. The effect of the campaign is to increase sales by 25 per cent, so that 12500 are sold. The costs are now as follows:

machinery and rent    £10000
advertising           £2000
labour and materials  £1250
                      ─────
                      £13250

The cost per unit will therefore have fallen to

$$\frac{£13\,250}{12\,500} = £1.06$$

The overall cost of production per unit is lower, even though the advertising has cost £2000, so the producer can make a bigger profit per unit. If sales had increased by more than 25 per cent, the reduction in costs per unit would have been even more significant.

If you study advertisements on television and in the press you will find that, while their basic purpose is to increase sales, some of them have more specific aims.

### 17.2.2  New products
These have to be brought to the attention of the public if they are to catch on. Advertising seems capable of creating a demand for products that people didn't realize they needed. A few years ago, for example, it would have been inconceivable that the market for men's toiletries could grow to the size it is today. Much of the growth was achieved by clever advertising. Similarly the widespread use of video-recorders, automatic washing machines and micro-wave ovens owes much to the power of advertising.

### 17.2.3  Information
Many advertisements are designed to inform consumers of changes in the nature of the product. You have probably noticed how many products are described as 'new' or 'new formula' in advertisements.

### 17.2.4 Branded goods
Manufacturers' and retailers' branded goods are often advertised to keep the brand name in the public eye. Some producers identify their goods by a special sign or trade mark and advertise on the basis of this.

### 17.2.5 Retail outlets
Some advertising is restricted to the trade press, in an attempt to get more retailers to sell the product. Increasing the number of outlets in this way should result in higher sales.

### 17.2.6 The company's image
Businesses generally want to project a favourable image of themselves to the public – they like to be known for the reliability or high quality of their products, for giving value for money, for putting the customer first and so on. Many advertisements are designed purely to project the desired image and do not attempt to 'sell' goods directly.

### 17.2.7 Other objectives
The list above is by no means exhaustive. There may be many other objectives, such as the opening up of overseas markets. But whatever objective receives the heaviest emphasis in a commercial advertisement, the overriding aim – in the short run or the long run – is to increase sales, for without customers the business will fail.

## 17.3 Types of advertising
We can divide advertising into different categories, according to its approach or attitude, or according to its medium. We consider the media used for advertising in Unit 17.4: here we identify the various types of advertising.

### 17.3.1 Persuasive or competitive advertising
This type is aimed at consumers, and is the kind you see most often on television: it tries to persuade you to buy the advertiser's product rather than a competitor's. A good example is provided by the manufacturers of household detergents, who produce very similar products but who all try to persuade the consumer that their own particular brand has some special qualities. This form of advertising is the main type of non-price competition between producers. It is this kind of advertising that is sometimes criticized as being wasteful. However, it is essential for the individual firm to keep the public familiar with the names of its products if it is to maintain its share of the market.

### 17.3.2 Informative advertising
All advertising is informative to some extent, in that it is informing people that a product exists or an event is taking place. But the term *informative advertising* is normally reserved for the following goods and services.

**Advertising in technical and trade journals**   Such advertisements usually contain technical details of products and invite inquiries from interested parties.

**Advertising of particular events**, such as trade fairs, exhibitions, concerts and sporting activities. It is true that the advertisers hope to attract people to attend the event, but on the whole they do this by stating facts rather than by making persuasive claims.

**Advertising of employment opportunities**   Again you could argue that the advertiser is hoping to persuade people to offer their services, but these advertisements are more informative than persuasive.

### 17.3.3   Generic advertising

When all the producers in one industry combine to advertise the product in general rather than their own particular brands, we call the result *generic advertising*. Advertisements which exhort you to 'join the tea-set' or 'drink more beer' are familiar examples. Such advertisements belong to a special kind of persuasive advertising and are normally financed by the trade association to which firms in the industry belong. (A *trade association* is a body representing the interests of all the firms in an industry. In addition to this kind of joint advertising, a trade association might make itself responsible for research, information and negotiation with the Government or the trade unions.)

### 17.3.4   Sponsorship

An increasingly popular way of advertising is to sponsor a cultural or sporting event. Here a sponsor meets some of the expenses of the event, to which the sponsor's name is normally attached, and obtains a large amount of 'free' advertising, especially if the event is televised.

## 17.4   Advertising media

An *advertising medium* is a means or vehicle for advertising. Television and the press are familiar examples, but there are many other ways in which goods can be advertised. Some of these are suitable for small and highly localized markets, while others are more suitable for goods sold on a national or even international scale.

### 17.4.1   Television

Television is probably the best medium for advertising consumer goods. It has the advantage of providing a combination of sound and vision and, if necessary, of giving a national coverage, though it is unusual for an advertiser to buy time from all the independent television companies at once. A further advantage is that television advertisements can be shown at times appropriate to the market for the goods: for example, children's sweets and toys can be promoted between children's programmes, and household goods later in the evening when adults are more likely to be watching television.

Some people argue that television advertising has the advantage of a relaxed and therefore receptive audience but, on the other hand, some viewers find advertisements an unnecessary intrusion into their entertainment and find other things to do during commercial breaks.

Television advertising is expensive, but few doubt its effectiveness. When a sporting event is televised, many advertisers pay to place posters in places where they will catch the eye of the television camera. When football matches from Europe are shown on television, you will often see advertising hoardings around the ground, aimed specifically at British viewers.

### 17.4.2   Radio
A less expensive alternative is to advertise on commercial radio. While there is no independent national radio service (though one is planned), in July 1991 there were 79 independent local radio contractors in the UK, all of them funded through advertising. Local radio advertising has two advantages over television: it is less expensive, and it can probably be aimed at a more specific audience. Like television it has a fairly captive audience but, since it is cheaper, the message can be repeated more frequently.

### 17.4.3   The national press
To a large extent the national press depends upon advertising revenue for its existence. As newspapers are published every day, they are very suitable for advertising 'topical' products: 'Congratulations to John Smith who won yester-day's Grand Prix using Whiz petrol'. Another advantage is that advertise-ments can be placed in appropriate places in the newspaper: sports equipment on the sports pages, dresses on the fashion pages and so on. Magazines that specialize in particular subjects are also useful to advertisers.

One disadvantage is that the producer's advertisement may be submerged in a large number of others, although it can be shown more prominently if a higher rate is paid.

To the newspaper proprietor, however, advertising is essential. The price you pay for your newspaper covers only part of the producer's total costs: the balance and the profit margin are generated by the revenue from advertising.

### 17.4.4   The local press
This is not affected by commercial television in the same way as the national press is, though local commercial radio has taken over part of some papers' advertising. Local papers are very important to local advertisers: since they often have a monopoly in their area, the advertiser can be sure of reaching almost every household. Moreover, weekly papers are usually around the house for several days, so their advertisements are more likely to be seen by

potential customers. Once again, advertising revenue is of enormous importance to the newspaper proprietor: sometimes over 40 per cent of a paper is given over to advertisements.

A most important recent development in this sector has been the growth of free local newspapers, delivered to every household in the area. These normally carry fewer news items than ordinary local papers do, and are paid for entirely by their advertising revenue.

### 17.4.5  Posters

For some producers, posters provide an appropriate form of advertising. Posters have to be carefully designed and located if they are to deliver their message to the customer, but once in position they do not need much attention. Their effect comes from repetition, as many of the people who pass them do so every day. They tend to rely on visual effect rather than written information.

Similar considerations apply to the advertisements displayed in trains and buses, except that here the advertiser has a temporarily captive audience. Many passengers have nothing to do but study the advertisements.

### 17.4.6  The cinema

Producers and traders may ask an advertising agent to produce a short commercial for them to circulate to cinemas. In general these have the same advantages and disadvantages as television commercials, but they lack the cumulative impact of frequent repetition, since few people visit the cinema more than once a week.

### 17.4.7  Other media

The methods above are the main means of advertising, but many traders use other methods to keep their name before the public.

(a) They may carry an advertisement on their vans.
(b) They may advertise on the paper bags or plastic carriers that they provide to customers.
(c) They may have circulars delivered to local households.
(d) They may use some of the methods of sales promotion we discuss in Unit 17.9.

## 17.5  Advertising agents

If you have a second-hand car or washing machine to sell, you can draft an advertisement setting out the details and the price required and insert it in the local newspaper or shop window. Newspaper columns also provide a convenient means of advertising, both for retailers wanting to sell goods and for employers wanting to attract staff. But a national campaign to advertise a new brand of chocolate or a new model of car needs rather more care if it is to be effective. Few manufacturers have the particular skills that are needed to devise, make and place such advertisements. The advertiser normally consults *advertising agents* and selects one of them to plan and run the campaign for him. An advertising agent handles campaigns for many advertisers and can afford to employ specialists in many fields, a luxury which individual manufacturers could not afford for themselves.

The advertising agent has five main functions, as follows.

### 17.5.1  Creating the advertisement

This is done on the basis of information provided by the advertiser about the nature of the product, its strengths and weaknesses, and the market at which it is aimed. The amount that the advertiser is prepared to spend is also relevant, of course. The agency's work on behalf of each client is the responsibility of an *account executive*, an individual who organizes the campaign but does not actually create the advertisement itself. This job is done by *copywriters*: they are the people who devise the advertisements you see on television and in the newspapers.

### 17.5.2  Producing the advertisement

The agency's production department then goes to work on putting the ideas of the copywriter into practice: artists produce drafts of posters and the film department produces films in the agent's own studio or on location. The finished advertisement can then be shown to the client for approval and, if changes are wanted, amendments can be made.

### 17.5.3  Placing the advertisement

It will have been agreed in advance which advertising media are to be used for the campaign (see Unit 17.4). The agency normally books advertising time on television or space in the press in advance of its requirements, and then places its advertisements as necessary. The agency receives a commission from the television or newspaper company for the advertisements that it places with them, and of course the advertiser pays the television or newspaper company.

While these are their three main functions, advertising agents also offer other services to those clients who don't want to employ specialists on a full-time basis.

### 17.5.4  Market research

The purpose of market research is to provide manufacturers with as much information as possible about the market for their products. Often the research is carried out before the creation of the advertising campaign, so that the agent knows exactly who the advertisements should be aimed at. Manufacturers may conduct such investigations for themselves, they may employ a firm specializing in market research, or they may use their advertising agent.

The research is normally undertaken by means of carefully drafted question-naires. They are designed to obtain details of the number of potential customers, their location, their tastes as shown by their reactions to rival products, and the ways in which tastes may be changing. Many refinements can be included, such as the effectiveness of different kinds of packaging or different methods of selling, but the basic idea remains the same – to find out more about the market, so that more goods can be sold and more profits made.

### 17.5.5   Advice

Since the success or failure of a new product can depend upon the way in which it is presented to the public, it is important that the advertising agent is consulted in the early stages of the product's life. Agencies develop a sense of what will and what will not sell a product, and can often offer useful advice about, for example, the name of a new product or its packaging. They can certainly advise about the best media for advertising the product.

## 17.6   The case for advertising

Advertising is the subject of much debate between those who see it as a waste of valuable resources and those who see it as essential to the survival of our economic system. As usual, the truth lies somewhere between the two extremes. Among the main arguments in favour of advertising are the following.

(a) Advertising leads to higher profits, which the producer either can retain or can share with the customers by charging lower prices. In a very competitive industry most manufacturers do the latter.

(b) Without advertising it would be almost impossible to launch new products. Consumers would only know about them when they saw them in the shops or when other people spoke about them. Producers would never be prepared to invest vast sums in new products.

(c) Consumers can be better informed of the goods available and of their relative merits through advertising. This is often true even of competitive advertising.

(d) Many would argue that, by introducing new products to consumers, advertising improves the standard of living.

(e) Some people argue that advertised goods are of a higher quality than other goods, because the producer's reputation is at stake. If advertised goods turn out to be shoddy, subsequent advertisements will be ignored.

(f) An indirect benefit of advertising is that it keeps the price of newspapers at a reasonable level. Also, without advertising there would, of course, be no commercial television at all.

(g) On a broader scale, advertising may help to keep people employed. If a firm can sell more goods as a result of advertising, the labour force will almost certainly increase to meet the extra demand.

## 17.7 The case against advertising

Few people would want to abolish all advertising. The classified advertisements in local and national newspapers are an important source of information about houses, second-hand cars and many other things for sale. The same is true of display advertisements for jobs. But there are several criticisms which are frequently heard.

(a) Advertising can be very expensive. In 1990, over £7900 million was spent on advertising in the United Kingdom alone. A full-page advertisement in the national press costs several thousand pounds, and thirty seconds of television time can cost tens of thousands. The manufacturer's resources may be severely stretched to meet the costs.

(b) The cost of advertising may lead to higher prices for consumers if sales do not increase sufficiently to cover the cost of the advertising.

(c) Advertising uses scarce resources which could be better employed elsewhere. This is really an economic argument, but it is worth looking at. Many of the people employed in drafting and making advertisements are very talented. Some of the advertisements they produce are designed not to introduce new products or increase sales but merely to maintain the advertiser's share of the market. Advertisements for bread and detergent, for example, are unlikely to increase total sales. The people employed in the advertising industry might therefore make a greater contribution to the country's economic life if they worked in other occupations.

(d) Advertising is the main form of non-price competition. Consumers might be better off if there were less advertising and more competition over prices. (This argument must, of course, be balanced against the possibility that extra sales cover the cost of the advertisement and lead to lower prices.)

(e) Advertising can persuade consumers to buy things they do not really want and cannot afford. You may find that difficult to believe, but it is true. Extremely subtle techniques can be employed to persuade consumers that they should not be without the latest household appliance, for instance. For centuries people managed without deep-freezers: now many people regard them as a necessity. You can probably think of many other examples where advertising seems to create needs that were not there before.

(f) When people cannot immediately afford the goods being advertised, they may be tempted to live beyond their means, by buying the goods on credit or by hire purchase.

(g) Some people criticize advertising on ethical rather than economic grounds. They point out that it often exploits people – for example, in suggesting that only by using a certain product can they give their family the treatment they deserve. Other advertisements exploit sex by implying strongly that girls who wear the advertisers' products will be surrounded by the most desirable men (and vice versa). Yet others suggest that the consumption of alcohol and tobacco is a symbol of maturity, without

emphasizing the dangers associated with these products.
(h) There have been cases in the past of advertisements misleading the public. Today the Trade Descriptions Act offers some protection, and more detailed guidance is given by The Advertising Standards Authority (see Unit 17.8), but the danger remains.

There is thus much to be said on both sides. You must judge for yourself the desirability of heavy advertising, but we can safely conclude that advertising is generally worthwhile for producers.

## 17.8    Protecting the consumer

As we saw in Unit 7.1, the object of producers is to increase their profits, and there is a danger that they will be tempted to deceive consumers in their efforts to increase sales. We saw that the Trade Descriptions Act exercises legal controls over the contents of advertisements.

In addition, the advertising industry itself has established *The Advertising Standards Authority*, whose responsibility it is to maintain standards within the industry. The Authority represents a large number of bodies and supervises a

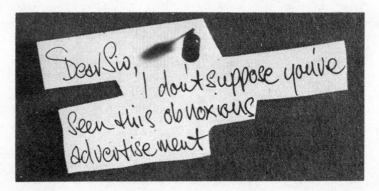

We welcome complaints from the public about advertisements in the press, on posters and in the cinema. It helps us keep advertising standards high. But we also monitor a considerable amount of advertising, and take the necessary action ourselves.

If you'd like to know more about our work, and receive a copy of the rules, please write.

### The Advertising Standards Authority.
### We're here to put it right. ✔

ASA Ltd., Dept. X, Brook House, Torrington Place, London WC1E 7HN.

This space is donated in the interests of high standards of advertising.

**Fig. 17.1**  A press advertisement by The Advertising Standards Authority

*Code of Advertising Practice* first drawn up in 1962. The code is a very detailed document setting out general principles to which advertisers and advertising agents should adhere. It is a voluntary code, but much more detailed in its requirements than the Trade Descriptions Act. There is provision for the investigation of complaints made by the public about advertisements, and for the Authority to make recommendations where appropriate.

## 17.9 Sales promotions

Advertising is just one of the ways in which producers try to increase sales. Other methods of winning the attention of the public belong to the general category of sales promotions. The aims are of course the same as those of advertising, but promotion schemes tend to demand more of the consumer than just watching or reading an advertisement. Various techniques are employed, of which the following are a selection.

### 17.9.1 Free samples

The best way of introducing consumers to a product is to let them try it out free. It is a very expensive method of promoting sales, especially where a sample is sent to every household. Accordingly it is a method reserved for things that are cheap and have a national sale. Often the distribution of free samples is backed up with a fairly extensive advertising programme.

### 17.9.2 Price reductions

These are so widely used that they are no longer regarded as special promotional activities. Customers have been conditioned to expect that household detergents will be offered at '10 pence off' the 'normal' price, and the cartons are printed with the price reduction.

Sometimes the price reductions are indirect or conditional. Some manufacturers distribute coupons to householders, for use in part payment for their goods; others allow a price reduction in exchange for the label from the previous packet bought. In either case the retailer is involved in extra work, either in redeeming the labels for cash from the manufacturers or their representatives, or in arranging for their use in part payment for purchases from the manufacturers.

Occasionally an item may be so heavily reduced in price as to almost eliminate the retailer's profit. The hope is that this 'loss leader', as it is called, will entice people into the store and that they will then buy other things as well. And, of course, many shops hold seasonal sales to dispose cheaply of outdated stocks and to make room for new lines.

### 17.9.3 Competitions

Sometimes producers organize competitions. A condition of entry is often the purchase of several packets of the producer's goods. This achieves an immediate boost in sales, which the producer hopes will be sustained as new customers become regular buyers.

### 17.9.4   Free gifts

Petrol stations try to increase their sales by giving away goods such as glasses, footballs or cups when a certain amount of petrol is bought. Cigarette manufacturers have a variation of this: they sometimes include coupons in their packets, which can be redeemed for a free packet of cigarettes at a later date or used in part payment for another packet of the same brand. Since the aim is to win the loyalty of consumers and retain their custom, the latter type of scheme requiring the collection of, say, ten coupons is generally preferred.

## 17.10   The marketing department

As we said in Unit 17.1, many large firms have marketing departments, whose function is to identify the market for the firm's products and to ensure that those products reach that market. We shall conclude this Unit with a summary of the work of such a department.

Before goods are produced, the firm must be sure that they can be sold. To be sold, they have to appeal to the public – they have to have a good 'image'. The creation of this image is the responsibility of the *brand manager*, who is accountable for a range of aspects of the selling of the goods.

**Packaging**   One way to distinguish your product from its competitors is to provide it with attractive packaging. This may result in higher sales, but it may also lead to higher prices for consumers. You will find it interesting to examine some of the articles you buy and to consider the packaging. Many carry three or four different layers of packaging – this is especially true of articles sold 'gift-wrapped' at Christmas.

**Advertising and sales promotion**   Each product has a budget allocated to it, in which a stated amount of money is set aside for publicity. The brand manager must decide how this money is to be spent.

**Market research**   In order to make the correct decisions, the manager must have detailed information about the product and its market and will therefore initiate research to obtain the required information.

**Sales**   The manager may also be responsible for a team of salesmen, or representatives, who visit retailers to introduce the product and provide display material and free samples. They also deal with complaints and queries, and generally maintain the link between the company and its customers.

# 17.11 Questions

1. What is meant by the term *advertising media*?
2. List as many different advertising media as you can.
3. 'Since advertising on television is expensive, it must increase the prices of the products which are advertised.' Explain carefully why this may not be the case.
4. Advertising is controlled partly by the Trade Descriptions Act and partly by the *Code of Advertising Practice*. Give examples to show how consumers may benefit from these controls.
5. (a) Describe the main services likely to be offered to its clients by an advertising agency.
   (b) Why do firms employ such agencies rather than provide the services for themselves?
6. What is meant by the term *market research*? In what circumstances would a manufacturer of chocolate sweets be likely to undertake market research? Of what benefit might it be to the manufacturer?
7. State which advertising media you would recommend to a company about to launch the following products:
   (a) a new brand of tea;
   (b) a new electric milk float;
   (c) a new range of fashion jewellery;
   (d) a low-priced personal computer.
   In each case give reasons for your answer.
8. Apart from advertising, what methods might an oil company use to try to increase the sales of its petrol?
9. Make a collection of advertisements to illustrate the different methods that advertisers use to persuade consumers to buy their products.

# Communications: transport

## 18.1 Introduction

The system of mass production relies on an efficient transport system for its very existence. This is because production is *indirect*, by which we mean that enormous amounts of goods are produced in one place for consumers who live all over the country or indeed all over the world. Economic activity would be impossible without transport, and our commercial system would collapse. Transport must be available first to deliver raw materials, components and even labour to factory sites, and then to distribute the finished goods to places where the ultimate consumers can acquire them. Therefore we need to consider two things: first, what features are necessary for an efficient transport system and, second, the extent to which the different forms of transport meet these requirements.

Every day of the year goods are on the move – products as diverse as newspapers, boxes of matches, generating equipment, personal computers, medicine and bricks are all travelling to their markets. Consignments can vary in many ways. Sometimes the journey is only a few miles; sometimes the goods are going to the other end of the country or the other side of the world. Some goods are needed only occasionally, and then urgently and at very short notice, while others are needed at regular intervals and on a continuous basis. Some are extremely valuable in proportion to their size, like diamonds; others are of low value but great bulk, like coal. Some are fragile; others are robust. An efficient transport system must be adaptable enough to deal with every possible kind of consignment.

The accessibility of the *terminal* (the place where the journey starts or ends) is another key factor. It was once the practice to build factories and warehouses close to canals and railway lines so that the delivery of large consignments could easily be arranged. As commercial life has expanded, shops and factories have multiplied and become more widely dispersed, while railways and canals have lost traffic to the roads, which can usually provide a more direct service. Several factors such as the development of the motorway network and the use of containers have added to the advantages of road transport in this respect, and we shall need to look at them in detail.

An efficient means of transport must be *regular* and *punctual*. Most goods are produced and consumed in a continuous flow: producers need to be able to dispose of their output promptly so that they can keep their spending on warehousing to a minimum. At the other end of the distributive chain, retailers require the steady flow of goods that is provided by regular deliveries, so that they do not have too many goods in stock and so that they can supply their customers with fresh or up-to-date items. Irregular or unreliable transport is therefore a nuisance both to producers and to retailers.

It is just as important that goods arrive punctually. In the complex factories of today, the whole workforce may be left idle if a batch of components arrives late. This is not the same, of course, as saying that *speed* is necessary: it may not matter if the components are delivered by horse and cart as long as they arrive at the right time. (There may. of course, be other reasons for not using a horse and cart!)

There are, then, many factors to be taken into account when assessing the efficiency of a transport system or the relative merits of different forms of transport. The overriding considerations are that goods must be collected punctually and be efficiently delivered in the right quantities in good condition at the correct time.

We can now look at the main forms of transport and the advantages that each of them offers. We should also be able to see why some forms of transport expand while others lose business.

## 18.2   Road transport

The road network in the United Kingdom extends to about 237 000 miles (358 000 km) and it constitutes the most important aspect of transport in the country. The usage of freight transport is normally measured in terms of tonne–kilometres. If, for example, a load of 50 tonnes is carried 100 kilometres, the journey represents $50 \times 100 = 5000$ tonne–kilometres (t–Km). Table 18.1 shows the extent to which road transport dominates other forms of inland freight transport.

**Table 18.1** United Kingdom inland transport

|  | 1980 Thousand mill.tonne Km | % | 1985 Thousand mill.tonne Km | % | 1990 Thousand mill.tonne Km | % |
|---|---|---|---|---|---|---|
| Road | 92.4 | 52.9 | 102.9 | 55.0 | 136.2 | 63.2 |
| Rail | 17.6 | 10.1 | 15.4 | 8.2 | 15.8 | 7.3 |
| Water | 54.5 | 31.2 | 57.6 | 30.8 | 52.5 | 24.4 |
| Pipelines | 10.1 | 5.8 | 11.2 | 6.0 | 11.0 | 5.1 |
|  | 174.6 |  | 187.1 |  | 215.5 |  |

It is clear that there has been a move away from the railways: the roads have increased their share by ten percentage points to around 60 per cent, and in fact have achieved over 47 per cent more tonne–kilometres in 1990 than in 1980.

It is sometimes argued that ways should be developed of moving less freight by road and more by rail. There must be some doubt as to the extent to which this would be possible. If the railways could take twice as much traffic as they do now, road freight would fall by only 11 per cent; in any case, such a change would require an enormous increase in railway investment to cope with the rise in traffic.

Why is it that such a large proportion of total inland freight is carried by road?

### 18.2.1  The advantages of road transport

**Flexibility**   Road transport provides a door-to-door service. Goods can be loaded at the factory and delivered straight to the customer. There is no problem of changing from one form of transport to another, with all the extra handling that this involves. Even remote rural districts, inaccessible to the railways, can nearly always be reached by road. To some extent the long-term increase in the movement of goods by road has been inevitable as the rail network in the UK has been reduced from 18000 miles in 1960 to about 10000 miles in 1992.

The frequency of road journeys can easily be adjusted, whereas the nature of a railway system requires that train journeys be carefully timetabled. A trader who has an urgent consignment cannot expect railway timetables to be amended to accommodate the goods: they must wait for the next appropriate train. On the other hand, it is quite likely that a road transport operator will be able to move the goods at fairly short notice.

Some things simply cannot be delivered by rail, but special facilities can be provided by road hauliers to deal with exceptional loads. The height and width regulations that necessarily restrict the loads that can be carried by rail are less severe for road transport.

**Economy**   The road haulage industry is very competitive, consisting of large and small firms based both nationally and locally to meet differing requirements. This competition is an incentive to efficiency and economy, often resulting in lower charges for customers. *Return loads* exemplify this: a driver who has delivered a consignment has to make a return journey, and the employer has to meet the costs of this journey. If the van can carry a return load on the way back, the employer's overall costs will be reduced even if the load is taken at a cheaper rate than normal.

**Motorways**   The continuing development of the British motorway system has linked up the main centres of industry and population, permitting the speedy

**Fig. 18.1** An awkward load accommodated by road transport

movement of goods by road. Speed of movement was formerly considered an advantage of the railways.

**Vehicles**   There has been a gradual increase in the size of vehicles over the years and this allows freight to be delivered more economically – almost 80 per cent of the traffic is carried in vehicles of 28 tonnes or more.

Another factor has been an improvement in the mechanical efficiency of vehicles. Engines have been improved to keep fuel costs down as oil prices have risen.

**Containerization**   Perhaps the most important advance has been in the use of containers. Freight can now be packed in large containers at the point of manufacture, and each container is sealed and not opened again until it reaches its final destination. The loading into the container does not have to await the arrival of the lorry, and containers are standardized and so are usable with any operator's vehicles. Special cranes lift the containers on and off lorries and ships, taking a matter of hours rather than days to load and unload a vessel.

Heavy initial capital expenditure is required to buy the containers, vehicles and handling equipment but considerable savings result from containerization. Nor are the benefits only economic. The goods are safer in sealed containers, protected both from the weather and from pilfering. Moreover the container system has been developed to accommodate different kinds of freight. Refrigerated containers are widely used, and there are special containers for bulk liquids, grain and powder.

### 18.2.2 Disadvantages of road transport

Clearly the advantages mentioned above are highly significant, otherwise it would have been difficult for road hauliers to have captured such a large share of the market. There are some problems associated with road transport that ought not to be overlooked, however.

**Bulk**  Road haulage is not suitable for transporting goods of great bulk for long distances. It would be uneconomic, for example, to transport coal from South Wales to London by lorry, when a freight train can carry so much more on a single journey. Labour and fuel costs put the road hauliers at a considerable disadvantage here. Even so, many bulk commodities *are* taken by road because of the convenience it provides, and because lorries would have to be used in any case once the rail journey is complete.

**Congestion and delays**  Road transport may be subject to delays which do not trouble the railways. Road congestion becomes more severe each year. Although one of the benefits of the motorways is that they bypass congested town centres, the problem has not entirely disappeared. Most road journeys begin and end in heavily industrialized urban areas. The existing housing makes the improvement of urban roads difficult, and problems of acquiring land and obtaining planning permission delay the construction of new motorways and bypasses, so the traffic of the 1990s is often delayed by the roads of the 1920s.

**The social costs** of road transport are very great. A road haulier's rates for a consignment are based only on what we may call the *private costs* – the costs to the business of making the journey and delivering the goods. Such things as the driver's wages, fuel, tax and insurance will enter into the calculations, so that the firm can be sure of making a profit. But no haulage company takes into account such things as the cost to other people of traffic congestion, atmospheric pollution and noise, the expense of keeping up the roads and the road signalling system, or the problems caused by accidents. These all have to be met by society as a whole, and are the *social costs* of road transport.

There are, of course, social costs involved in journeys by rail too, but it is unlikely that they are as high as those of road transport. This is why the Government makes efforts from time to time to divert freight traffic from the roads to the railways. They have little success, because the convenience of road transport to its users outweighs its disadvantages to society.

### 18.2.3 The organization of road transport

The road haulage industry in the United Kingdom consists mainly of a large number of very small firms. To operate a vehicle of over 3½ tonnes weight an operator's licence must be obtained from the Department of Transport, to ensure that standards of safety and competence are maintained. There are over 130 000 licence-holders, many of them operating only one vehicle. (The national average fleet size is around five.) The largest UK road haulage concern is the National Freight Consortium. This was formerly the national-ized National Freight Corporation, until it was purchased from the Govern-ment by its managers and employees.

Traders with goods to deliver can choose between using their own vehicles and paying a private haulier to deliver them. About one-third of road freight is carried in traders' own vehicles. This, of course, means that they must bear the expense of purchasing, maintaining, taxing and insuring the vehicles, so they need to be sure they have sufficient work for them. On the other hand, traders with their own vehicles can programme their journeys to suit their own requirements. However, organizations that do not have regular large amounts to transport usually hire a haulier to carry their goods.

## 18.3 Rail transport

As we saw in Unit 9.5, the railways in the United Kingdom are a nationalized industry. Nationalization was necessary in 1947 owing to the weak condition of the industry, which had been deprived of capital investment for many years. Since nationalization, the system has been extensively modernized – diesel and electric trains have replaced steam, many uneconomic lines have been closed down, and new services have been introduced to meet the needs of commerce and industry. However, Table 18.1 shows that as far as freight is concerned the railways lost ground during the 1980s: while the total amount of freight carried increased the amount carried by rail actually fell. Table 18.2 gives further indications of the decline of the railways, though it also shows that there were more passenger journeys in 1990 than in 1980.

### 18.3.1 The advantages of rail transport

**Speed between two areas** Once the journey has begun, rail transport be-tween, say, London and Manchester is faster than road transport. The difficulties arise at each end of the journey: in getting goods to the London terminal through heavily congested streets, and in dispatching them from the Manchester station.

In the competition for passengers between the railways and the airlines, on the other hand, the delays caused by road traffic congestion favour the rail-ways. An airport is bound to be outside the city centre, while a railway passenger terminal is usually in the heart of the city. Therefore the speed advantage enjoyed by the airlines over medium distances is partly eroded by

**Table 18.2**  Railway statistics 1980–1990

|  | 1980 | 1985 | 1990 | % Change 1980–90 |
|---|---|---|---|---|
| Tractive units | 8358 | 7101 | 6425 | −23.1 |
| Passenger carriages | 17042 | 14062 | 12451 | −26.9 |
| Freight wagons | 138600 | 54400 | 36100 | −73.1 |
| Length of track (Km) | 17645 | 16752 | 16584 | −5.0 |
| Passenger journeys (million) | 760 | 697 | 779 | +2.5 |
| Freight (million tonnes/Km) | 17640 | 15400 | 15800 | −10.4 |

the problems of access to and from city centres. The introduction of faster passenger trains with speeds of up to 125 m.p.h. has increased the time advantage, and the benefits can be expected to extend to freight transport in due course.

**Economy in the use of labour**  This would seem to be one of the great advantages of the railways. While every lorry has a driver and sometimes a driver's mate, it only takes two men – a driver and a guard – to run a train with fifty or sixty trucks. The wage bills for the two systems will obviously be very different. But the advantage to the railways may not be as great as these figures suggest: the railways require a larger team behind the scenes to programme trains and maintain the network.

**Bulk commodities**  Railways are particularly suitable for the transport of bulk commodities such as coal, petroleum and iron and steel over long distances: about 90 per cent of rail freight is of this kind.

**Containerization** (see Unit 18.2.1) has been helpful to the railways as well as to the road haulage industry. One of the main problems of the railways is that of the repeated handling of the goods. A consignment usually has to be loaded on to a lorry at the factory and then unloaded before being transferred to the train. At the other end it has to be taken off the train, loaded on to a lorry and finally unloaded again. In such circumstances delays, breakages and theft are difficult to avoid. Containers overcome most of these problems. Goods are packed into the container, which is then loaded on to a lorry, mechanically transferred from the lorry to the train and later transferred back to a lorry for final delivery (fig. 18.2). Only then is the container opened. British Rail has developed its own container system – Freightliner – with its own lorries, to exploit the advantages as fully as possible.

**Special facilities** are provided for industrial customers. Bulk deliveries of oil, cement, coal and motor cars, for instance, are often carried in the producer's own rolling-stock, painted with its own livery.

### 18.3.2  Problems of rail transport
Despite these advantages, the railways clearly find it difficult to compete with road transport. This is mainly because of the even greater advantages enjoyed by lorry operators, but there are also specific disadvantages associated with the railway system.

**The problem of transshipment**  Only a few industrial customers have their own sidings. For the others, lorries are necessary for at least part of the journey, so many customers prefer to use road for the whole journey.

**Delays**  While road transport suffers from congestion, there are correspondingly unavoidable delays for some rail freight owing to the need to timetable trains. Such delays may be expensive to customers because goods held up in this way represent capital tied up in stock.

**Overhead costs**  Taxation on road vehicles and fuel is high, and this can be regarded as contributing to the cost of building and maintaining the road system. The lorry operators do not actually have to provide their own track, however. On the other hand, the railways have enormous overhead costs (that is, costs that have to be met whether anything is produced or not). These costs include paying for the track, signalling systems and rolling-stock – passenger-carrying rolling-stock is particularly expensive, since much of it is used only for commuters at each end of the day and stands idle most of the time.

**Fig. 18.2**  At a container base, modern methods permit a lorry-load of goods to be shifted in one lift

**Short journeys** by rail usually waste time and money, particularly where the consignments are small. Only where bulk loads are carried on a continuous basis does the railway have a real advantage.

**Timetables** impose a rigidity on the railways which is unknown to the road transport industry.

**Changing output**   One long-term factor of importance is the changing nature of what is produced in the UK. The emphasis is very much on consumer goods which are conveniently delivered by the lorry-load rather than the train-load. The decline of the coal industry, steel and heavy engineering has reduced the need for rail transport.

We can conclude, therefore, that there have been many factors accounting for the increase in road transport at the expense of rail. We must not forget the other forms of inland transport, though. We will discuss these in the next section.

## 18.4   Other inland transport

**Airways**   Because the United Kingdom is a relatively small country, the airways are hardly used at all for freight transport except for postal services and some newspaper deliveries. In countries like Australia and the USA, however, they play a more important part.

**Water transport**   About a quarter of freight in the UK is now carried by water. Only 1 per cent is carried on inland waterways, however, and these are used mainly for recreational purposes. The bulk of water transport in the UK is therefore coastal shipping between its seaports – for example, for carrying crude oil to a refinery and finished products away from it.

**Pipelines** are frequently used for transporting oil and gas over long distances. Their capital costs are heavy, but once they have been installed they can make considerable savings for producers.

## 18.5   International transport

Road and rail can, of course, be used for international transport and are important in this respect in Europe and North America. Indeed a growing proportion of the goods traded between the UK and her European trading partners is carried by lorries using the ferries to and from Dover and other ports. In this section, though, we need to take note of sea and air transport.

## 18.5.1    Sea transport

**Liners** run on fixed routes to a fixed timetable. They carry general or mixed cargo. The liner operators belong to *shipping conferences*, which determine the fares, the freight charges and the frequency of journeys.

**Tramp ships** do not have fixed routes or timetables and do not normally carry passengers. They go where business takes them, and they may be *chartered* (contracted to a user) at the Baltic Exchange in London (see Unit 4.6.4) either for a specific period (*time charter*) or for a specific voyage (*voyage charter*). Their rates are likely to be highly competitive, for their owners need to keep them working at all times.

**Coastal shipping**, as we have seen, is really an alternative to inland transport for bulk trade. For example, it may be more economical to send coal or timber round the coast rather than inland. Also, access to some refineries is difficult for large ocean-going tankers, so their cargo may be discharged into coasters to complete its journey. Refined oil is often distributed in this way.

**Bulk carriers** are designed for special purposes. Oil tankers are the best example, though ships are also built specially to accommodate other minerals or timber. Refrigerated vessels are available for transporting perishables over long distances.

The nature and volume of the UK's external trade is examined in Units 20 and 21. The importance of sea transport can be gauged from the fact that 95 per cent of that trade by volume is carried by sea (about 80 per cent by value). Between a quarter and one-third of this is carried in British-owned vessels.

The great advantage of sea transport is of course that tens or even hundreds of thousands of tonnes can be carried at one time. Bulk oil carriers can deliver three or four hundred thousand tonnes in a single journey.

Sea transport also offers considerable flexibility. Every week vessels leave the major ports for all parts of the world, and an exporter can usually find accommodation for a cargo fairly easily. Of course the goods will not be delivered as quickly as they would be by air, but speed is not necessarily the most important consideration: punctuality is normally more significant. A manufacturer in the UK does not usually need raw materials to be delivered from Australia in thirty-six hours, but it is important that they arrive at regular intervals, so that production is not held up by shortages.

Specially built vessels give sea transport an added advantage. Perishable goods can be carried around the world and arrive in perfect condition, thanks to refrigerated vessels, and raw materials can be specially dealt with. Ships and terminal facilities are now often designed together, so that sophisticated loading and discharging methods can be used – for example, grain cargoes are

**Fig. 18.3** Two of the many forms of sea transport: a general cargo/bulk carrier, capacity over 12 500 tonnes (*top*) and a large container vessel, capacity over 57 000 tonnes (*bottom*)

pumped ashore at main terminals. The growth of containerization has been accompanied by the building of special container vessels, with special facilities to deal with them at the ports.

### 18.5.2   Air transport

Whereas 300 million tonnes of freight are annually moved to or from the UK by sea, less than 1 million tonnes is carried by air, over half of it through Heathrow airport. In terms of value, the airlines' share is about 20 per cent, however, because they are more suitable than shipping for high-value, low-bulk consignments.

There has been a steady increase in air freight over the years, and this is likely to continue for several reasons.

(a) New, larger aircraft are capable of carrying larger loads.
(b) Speed of delivery is important for some consignments. Mail, newspapers, medical supplies and other emergency requirements come into this category. An even more important factor in the growth of air transport is the need for machinery and components to be available at short notice. Office machinery, computer components and vehicle spares can now be rushed quickly from one side of the world to the other.
(c) Although the rate per tonne is higher by air than by sea, the cost of transport must be related to the value of the goods being delivered. If the goods are of low bulk and high value they can absorb the cost of air freight without a large increase in their price. Many UK exports, such as electrical machinery, belong to this category. On the other hand the price of iron ore would increase dramatically if it had to be sent by air.
(d) The incidental expenses associated with exporting are often lower when goods are sent by air. For example, when sea transport is used, goods may have to be well packed to protect them against the effects of weather or corrosion by sea water: less elaborate precautions are normally needed for goods sent by air. Moreover, since the goods are in transit for a shorter period, insurance charges are usually lower.

It is the comparative newness of air transport that is responsible for its main disadvantage: history has resulted in many industrial concentrations being close to the major ports, so that goods delivered by sea can quickly reach their final destinations and exports can quickly begin their journey. This is why almost all major steel works and oil refineries are situated on the coast. Airports are constructed away from the main industrial sites, and, although in time they exert their own magnetic pull on industries, the fact remains that a long secondary journey may be necessary for many goods arriving by air. However, the growth of the motorway system makes this less of a problem, since all the major UK airports are within a few miles at most of the motorway network, allowing for easy movement between the airports and industrial areas.

Another important limitation of air freight is the size of the loads that can be carried. Even the largest aircraft cannot compete economically with sea transport when the cargoes are of great bulk.

In the UK, air transport is dominated by British Airways (a limited company owned by the Government until 1987, but then privatized) and regulated by the Civil Aviation Authority, which has to ensure the provision of satisfactory services to all classes of users at reasonable costs.

## 18.6   Conclusion

We have seen that there is considerable variety in the transport facilities available to traders. The methods adopted by any single trader will depend upon several factors, the most important of which are the value and bulk of the consignment and the degree of urgency with which it must be delivered. However, the important point is that our industrial and economic system could not exist without transport to bring about the physical transfer of goods from their place of production to their place of consumption.

## 18.7   Questions

1. What is meant by the term *mass production*?
2. Explain why a system of mass production would be impossible without an efficient transport system.
3. What facilities are necessary in an efficient freight transport terminal?
4. State the ways in which the following characteristics may be essential to an efficient transport system: (a) frequency, (b) regularity, (c) punctuality, (d) speed.
5. Explain why most freight in the United Kingdom is carried by road.
6. (a) What is *containerization*?
   (b) In what ways has containerization improved (i) the security, (ii) the efficiency of transport systems?
7. Describe the main advantages of rail transport over road transport.
8. What factors should a manufacturer take into account when deciding whether to buy his own lorries for deliveries or to hire a road haulier?
9. (a) Why is an increasing amount of freight carried by air?
   (b) What factors might limit the growth of air transport?
10. Describe the main differences between liners and tramp ships.
11. State what methods of transport would be most suitable for
    (a) a human kidney from Paris to London;
    (b) 200 tonnes of coal from Cardiff to Ipswich;
    (c) a 30-tonne electricity generator from Birmingham to Penzance;
    (d) a consignment of diamonds from South Africa to Manchester.
    Give reasons for your answer in each case.

# Business risks: insurance

## 19.1 Insurable risks

All businesses take risks. They are an inherent part of our economic system. The risks taken differ in nature and, in this context, may be divided into two groups: *insurable risks* and *non-insurable risks*. The insurance companies will be prepared to safeguard you against insurable risks but not against non-insurable risks.

The difference between those two types of risk is that insurable risks are calculable, while non-insurable risks are not. That is, insurable risks occur regularly enough for the insurance company to calculate with some accuracy the likelihood of their occurring during the period of insurance. They can make this calculation on the basis of past statistics. If, on the other hand, no statistics are available, the necessary calculations cannot be made and insurance cannot be undertaken. Some examples will show you the difference.

A retailer can insure against his premises being burnt to the ground, because there are statistics which tell the insurance company how likely retail premises are to catch fire. Statistics can also show what sort of shops are most likely to catch fire, and in what areas the risk is greatest. On the other hand, suppose that a retailer holds a stock of girls' dresses worth several thousand pounds, which she hopes to sell over the next few weeks. She cannot insure against the possibility that she will not sell them because the fashion has changed, or simply because she has misjudged the demand for them. There are no records which show how quickly these particular dresses will go out of fashion, or how competent the retailer is at judging demand. These, therefore, are non-insurable risks.

A further requirement before a risk can be regarded as insurable is that there must be a large number of similar risks. Otherwise the basic insurance system of the pooling of risks cannot operate.

## 19.2 The pooling of risks

You probably know how a football pool works. Thousands of people contribute money to the pool, together with their forecasts of the results of the forthcoming games. A few of those people later receive money from the pools company for forecasting the results correctly: the lucky ones are paid by the unlucky.

Insurance operates on the same principle, but in reverse: a large number of people contribute money, called a *premium*, to a central pool which is operated by the insurer. Suppose the payments are made to insure against fire: those whose property is damaged by fire are then compensated by the insurer from the pool. Thus the risks are pooled – all the property is at risk but no one

**Football pool**

Losers

The winner – the unlucky
pay the lucky.

**Insurance pool**

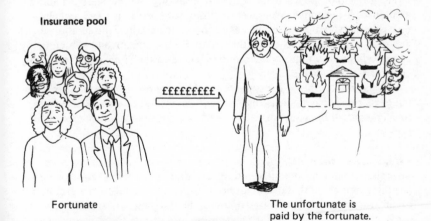

Fortunate

The unfortunate is
paid by the fortunate.

**Fig. 19.1** The football pool and the insurance pool

knows in advance which will suffer fire damage. Figure 19.1 illustrates the way in which the insurer organizes the pool.

Insurance is not simply a matter of a lot of people wanting to obtain cover, however. Certain important principles have to be observed before insurance can be arranged.

## 19.3    The principles of insurance

From the point of view of the insured person, the important thing is that, if an insured risk occurs, the insurer will compensate him or her. But compensation will be paid only if the *proposer* (the person taking out the insurance) has complied with the principles of insurance. The most important of these are discussed below.

### 19.3.1    Utmost good faith

If you wish to take out an insurance policy, you must fill in a *proposal form* and answer all the questions that this asks you. You must also give the company any additional information that is relevant to your application, so that it can make an accurate assessment of the risk and calculate the premium that you should pay. This proposal will form part of a legal contract between you and the insurance company.

Suppose I apply for insurance for my car. One of the questions I am asked is 'Have you been convicted of any motoring offences in the last three years?' If I have had no convictions during the last three years I can quite truthfully answer 'No' to this question. But if I am expecting to appear in court next week on a charge of dangerous driving, I must declare this to the insurance company, as it is likely to affect the size of the premium it will wish to charge.

The principle applies to all kinds of insurance. When applying for life assurance, for example, you must disclose your correct age and any chronic illnesses that you or your family have suffered from. The contract is invalid if any of the material facts are withheld from the company and subsequently come to light, and there is then no obligation on the company to meet any claim arising under the policy.

It is also important for the company to show utmost good faith, by explaining to its prospective clients the terms of the insurance and the exact cover being provided. In fact it normally does this by including all the details on the policy.

### 19.3.2    Insurable interest

Insurance companies permit you to insure against a risk only if you have an insurable interest in that event not occurring: that is to say, if the event does occur, *you* must suffer some kind of loss or incur some kind of liability. If your car is stolen or damaged you would suffer a loss and are therefore entitled to insure it against theft or damage. If *my* car is stolen or damaged you would not be affected and you cannot, therefore, insure it. Similarly if people are injured in my shop I may have to compensate them, but if they are injured in your shop I won't have to pay out; thus I can insure against the former but not the latter. I can insure my life or my wife's life but not the life of my neighbour, unless he or she happens to be my business partner.

There are two reasons for this principle. First, without it, insurance would become nothing more than a kind of gamble. You could look around for something that might happen (such as a favourite tennis-player being injured) and insure against it. If it occurs you win the gamble, if not you lose.

More importantly, if the event that you have insured against is not going to harm you, you might be tempted to bring it about. So you could insure someone else's car against fire, set light to it and collect the money! Apart from this being illegal, it would enable you to make a profit out of insurance, and this is not allowed under the third principle of insurance: the principle of *indemnity*.

### 19.3.3 Indemnity
The object of all insurance (except for life assurance and personal accident insurance) is to restore the insured to the position he or she was in before a stipulated event occurred. If your six-year-old car is damaged so badly in an accident that it cannot be repaired, the insurance company is not going to give you the money for a brand-new car; it will pay you sufficient to buy a six-year-old car of a similar model. If it bought you a new car you would be making a profit, and people might deliberately damage their cars. If, on the other hand, the company gives you only half the car's present value, you would be making a loss. It must try to compensate you precisely.

You might think that you can get round this principle of insurance by accepting the money payment made in exact compensation by the company and then selling the wrecked vehicle to the local scrap dealer. This is prevented by the rule of *subrogation*, which gives all the rights over the car to the company settling the claim. Any money raised through the sale of the car belongs to the insurance company, not the insured person.

If you were really dishonest you might not yet be satisfied: you might insure the car with two different insurance companies and claim from both of them when the vehicle is damaged. The rule of *contribution* determines that each company pays a proportion of the cost so that no profit is made by the insured.

Although the principle of indemnity is meant to put you, the insured, in the position you were in just before the accident, a limit to the compensation is set by the policy itself. If you insured the contents of your house for £12000 in 1988, £12000 is the maximum compensation you can expect from the insurance company if you make a claim. Suppose the contents are now worth £16000 because you have purchased some new furniture, electrical goods and jewellery. Now £14000 worth of your possessions are destroyed by fire. The insurer will not pay you £14000 because your premiums are linked to a maximum payment of £12000. It is unlikely that you will receive even £12000 since the insurer will apply an average clause: here goods worth £16000 are insured for £12000 or three-quarters of their value. The insurer will therefore be liable only for three-quarters of the value of the goods destroyed which is £8000. The rest of the risk is carried by the insured person.

Just as the principle of indemnity prevents you from gaining from *over*-insurance, the average clause prevents you from making a profit from *under*-insurance. It is obviously important to keep the value of your insurance policies closely linked to the value of your property, especially in times of inflation.

Sometimes, in return for higher premiums, the insurance companies themselves break the principle of indemnity by offering 'new for old' policies. Suppose you bought a new carpet for £500 in 1989, and it was damaged by fire in 1992. Under a 'new for old' policy you could obtain the money for a similar new carpet even if it now cost £750.

### 19.3.4 Proximate cause

Before an insurance company pays out on a claim, it will want to satisfy itself that the claim is for an event caused by something which is within the precise terms of the policy. The root cause of the event is known as the *proximate cause* and this must be covered by the policy for a claim to be valid.

You might insure the food in your freezer against the effects of a failure in the electricity supply, but the policy will usually exclude a failure caused by a strike of workers at the power station. If there is a power failure caused by such a strike, the insurer will not pay out, as the proximate cause of the power failure is not covered by the policy. If, on the other hand, the failure results from accidental damage to the power line, the company will pay out, because this cause has not been excluded from the policy.

Similarly, if you insure yourself against death by accident when flying but die from a heart attack during a flight, the insurer will not be required to meet any claim made under the policy.

Many insurance companies use standard policies which they modify by means of *endorsements* to meet the needs of particular clients. Before paying compensation, the insurance company will normally require a *claim form* to be filled in and will check that the claim is within the terms of the policy. What all this amounts to is that anyone taking out an insurance policy needs to examine the terms of that policy very closely.

## 19.4    The premium

The premium is the payment made into the central pool by each policy-holder. The payment is not the same for all policy-holders, so we must now look at what determines the size of the premium paid. Let us consider a policy for motor insurance, and look at some of the factors that are taken into account before the premium is fixed. The insurer will need the following information:

(a) *The age of the driver* Statistics show that drivers under twenty-five are more likely to make claims than older people are.

(b) *The type of car* There may be a greater chance of an accident if you are driving a 3 litre sports car than if you are driving a 1200 c.c. family saloon.

(c) *The value of the vehicle* It costs more to replace a Jaguar than a Mini.

(d) *The cost of repairs* The cost of repairing damage to a Rolls-Royce is likely to be greater than that of repairing a cheaper car.

(e) *The district where the driver lives* Accidents are more likely to occur in densely populated areas than in remote rural areas.

(f) *The driver's record* If you have a long history of colliding with telegraph poles or other motorists, the company will raise your premium, to allow for the increased risk it will incur. Likewise, if you have recently been convicted of motoring offences your premium will be higher.

(g) *The driver's occupation* Racing drivers are sometimes reluctant to adjust their driving to ordinary road conditions, and are often charged high premiums despite their obvious driving ability. Company representatives who cover huge distances each year, often under great pressure, may also pay high premiums, and students too are viewed with some suspicion by insurance companies. Other groups – teachers, for example – normally receive a discount on the basic premium, since the insurance companies' statistics show that they are involved in accidents less frequently than many other people are.

(h) *The driver's recent claims record* If you have made no claim on the insurer for a year your premium will normally be reduced by perhaps 20 or 25 per cent – a *no-claims discount*. (This does not normally apply to other kinds of insurance.)

The insurers employ experts called *actuaries* to calculate the premiums for them. It is essential that the actuaries do their calculations correctly so that the insurers don't run out of money through excessive claims. The principle behind the calculation of the premium is illustrated in simplified form in fig. 19.2.

When the first premium has been paid, the insurer may issue a *cover note* to certify that insurance has been taken out while the actual policy is being prepared.

## 19.5   The insurance market

Millions of businesses and individuals need insurance policies of various kinds. They are one side of the market – the demand side. The other side of the market offering them insurance policies may be divided into two groups: the insurance companies and Lloyd's of London.

### 19.5.1   The insurance companies

Many of these are nationally known organizations offering the whole range of insurance cover; others specialize in one branch only, such as motor insurance.

1. Assume that statistics show that 4 per cent of all houses are burgled each year, and that the average compensation paid to each household is £1000.
2. An insurance company has 5000 householders wanting to insure against burglary.
3. The total number of potential claims on the basis of past experience would be

$$5000 \times \frac{4}{100} = 200$$

4. On average each claim will be for £1000, so the total amount that the insurance company will expect to pay in compensation is

$$£1000 \times 200 = £200\,000$$

5. To accumulate this money, the company will require a premium from each householder of

$$\frac{£200\,000}{5000} = £40 \text{ per year}$$

6. Since the company will want to cover its costs as well, and make a profit, the premium will be higher than this.
7. In practice the premium will not be the same for each house since allowance has to be made for houses with thatched roofs, houses made of wood, and other matters.

**Fig. 19.2** Fixing the premium

Industrial life offices deal primarily in life policies, their branch offices collecting the premiums on a weekly or monthly basis. Most of the companies belong to the Association of British Insurers, which lays down standards of behaviour for the companies.

If you want to obtain insurance cover from one of the companies, you can either visit one of its branch offices or arrange for one of its agents to call on you. Alternatively you can consult an *insurance broker*, whose job it is to provide a link between the companies and members of the public wishing to buy insurance. Brokers are paid by the companies on a commission basis.

The companies may be divided into two groups: *proprietary companies*, which have shareholders who expect a share of the profits annually, and *mutual companies* which are owned by their policy-holders.

### 19.5.2   Lloyd's of London
The first thing to understand is that Lloyd's itself does not insure anything: it is a corporation which provides facilities for its members who wish to provide or

**Fig. 19.3** Lloyd's of London: from the street (*top*) and a view of the underwriting room (*bottom*)

negotiate insurance for businesses or individuals. Originating in the early eighteenth century, Lloyd's has grown to a position of pre-eminence particularly in marine insurance, largely because of the high standards of financial integrity it has traditionally demanded of its members. Those members are divided into two groups: underwriters and brokers.

**Underwriters** are the people who accept insurance at Lloyd's. Each underwriter must be nominated by one member, supported by five others, and then elected unanimously by all the members. An underwriter must be able to show considerable financial resources and deposit a large sum with the Corporation before beginning to trade. This is because any claims that have to be met on a Lloyd's policy are met from the personal resources of members.

It was once possible for a shipowner to find perhaps half a dozen underwriters who would insure a vessel between them. Today an ocean-going vessel and its cargo are worth several million pounds, and it might take several days to obtain insurance cover if each underwriter had to be contacted individually. To overcome this problem, underwriters have formed themselves into groups known as *syndicates*, which may have a couple of hundred underwriters as members, or a couple of dozen. The syndicate is represented at Lloyd's by an *underwriting agent* who is able to accept insurance on behalf of the whole syndicate. In this way the vessel and its cargo can quickly be covered.

Like most institutions, Lloyd's has adapted itself over the years and now offers cover on much more than marine risks. Fire and accident policies are also issued there, but ordinary life assurance policies are not available through Lloyd's. Short-term life policies are issued, however, to cover a particular journey or expedition.

**Brokers**    Members of the public are not allowed to deal directly with underwriters: they must deal through one of the authorized Lloyd's brokers. The broker's job is to obtain the best possible policy for the client – the member of the public requiring insurance – but the broker's commission is paid by the underwriters.

When a Lloyd's broker receives instructions to obtain insurance, the first step is to make out a *slip* – a sheet of paper setting out the details of the cover required. The next is to find underwriters who specialize in underwriting this kind of risk, and obtain quotations from them. The broker accepts the most favourable, and the underwriter writes down the amount of the risk he is prepared to accept and the rate at which the premium is charged. He initials the slip, and all concerned will regard this as binding. The broker then takes the slip round to other underwriters to get them to accept some of the risk, until eventually the whole risk is covered. It is the first underwriter who sets the premium, because all the others will accept the rate he has quoted.

Let us look at an example. Suppose that the owners of the oil tanker *Spillit* want insurance cover for £30 million: their broker will approach several underwriters specializing in this area of insurance. Perhaps a quotation is given for cover for £2 000 000 at a premium of 1 per cent. This means that the underwriter will cover damage or loss up to the value of £2 000 000 for a premium of £20 000. If this quotation is acceptable, the broker will then have to find other underwriters willing to accept part of the risk at the same rate, until the whole £30 million is covered.

If a claim later arises that has to be settled, it will be met by the underwriters in proportion to the amount they have agreed. So if the vessel is subsequently lost, the first underwriter (or his syndicate) will have to pay £2 000 000. If the vessel suffers £600 000 of damage, this underwriter – because he has covered one-fifteenth of the total risk – will have to pay £40 000 to the shipping company.

Once the whole of the risk is covered, the policy can be prepared. It is then sent to Lloyd's Policy Signing Office, where it is checked and then signed by members of the appropriate syndicates. It can now be sent to the client by the brokers.

While insurance remains the most important service provided at Lloyd's, the Corporation's long association with ships and shipping has given rise to some ancillary activities. The Corporation maintains a network of overseas agents who supply Lloyd's with information of shipping movements throughout their areas. These reports form the basis of two important daily publications: *Lloyd's List* and *Shipping Gazette Index*, each containing a mass of information on shipping movements. Both are consulted regularly by shipowners and merchants.

Between them the insurance companies and Lloyd's provide a wide range of cover to their clients. The main kinds of insurance cover available are discussed in the next section.

## 19.6  Insurance policies

There are two broad categories of insurance: life assurance and non-life insurance.

### 19.6.1  Life assurance

The term *assurance* is used when the event that is insured against will definitely happen. We use the term *life assurance* because everyone dies sometime – the only question concerns the timing. (In the other branches of insurance there is no certainty that the event insured against will ever take place.)

Normally the aim of insurance is to compensate the person for some loss or damage. The aims of life assurance are somewhat different, in that insured people themselves cannot be compensated. The aims also vary, which is why several types of life assurance policy are available.

**Whole life policies** are payable on the death of the insured. The sum assured may simply be enough to pay for the funeral, or it may be much larger to give some benefit to dependants.

**Term policies** provide benefit only if death occurs during a specified period. *Mortgage guarantee policies* are of this type. Someone who is buying a house on a mortgage (a *mortgagor*) is often required by the building society to take out a life assurance policy for the duration of the mortgage. In the event of the mortgagor's death, the proceeds of the policy are used to pay off the mortgage.

**Endowment policies** guarantee that a fixed sum will be payable on a specified date or at death, whichever is earlier. They are therefore a means of saving as well as a form of insurance. Some endowment policies are *with profits*, and holders of these policies receive a share of the profits made by the insurance company from investing their savings. Such policies require higher premiums than policies without profits.

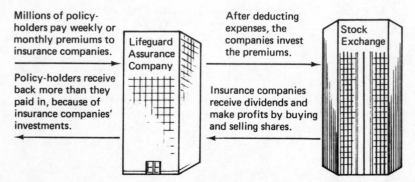

Millions of policy-holders pay weekly or monthly premiums to insurance companies.

Policy-holders receive back more than they paid in, because of insurance companies' investments.

After deducting expenses, the companies invest the premiums.

Insurance companies receive dividends and make profits by buying and selling shares.

Lifeguard Assurance Company

Stock Exchange

**Fig. 19.4** How with-profits endowment policies work

It is quite common for endowment policies to be arranged so that their maturity date coincides with an important event in the policy-holder's life. Some people take out policies which mature at about the time their children are likely to get married; others hope to receive a lump sum when they retire. A common practice is to take out a policy which matures at retirement, and then immediately use the proceeds to finance an *annuity*. Under an annuity, the insurance company undertakes in return for a lump sum payment to make weekly or monthly payments to the policy-holder (or *annuitant*) for a specified period. In this way the annuitant can arrange to have a regular income for the rest of his or her life.

**Family income policies** If the policy-holder dies, the dependants will be paid an agreed sum at regular intervals (£100 a month, for example) until an agreed date (usually from 15 to 30 years after the policy was taken out). Obviously this would be an important policy for the breadwinner of a young family.

**Special policies** have been developed by the insurance companies to meet particular requirements. *Group policies* provide cover for groups such as the employees of a firm; *house purchase policies* link the proceeds of an endowment policy to the purchase of a particular house; *unit-linked policies* permit investment in a unit trust as well as giving ordinary life cover.

Thus the life assurance companies offer a broad choice to their clients, and we can see that the purpose of taking out a life assurance policy may be to provide a lump sum or a regular income for dependants, or to save for one's retirement or some special occasion.

### *19.6.2 Non-life policies*
There is a wide range of these policies. Here we will mention only the main categories.

**Marine insurance** originated as early as the fifteenth century and is mainly available through Lloyd's. There are four branches of marine insurance.

(a) *Hull insurance* covers the vessel itself and its fixtures, either for a particular voyage or for a particular period of time.
(b) *Cargo insurance* covers the goods or merchandise carried by the vessel. These goods do not normally belong to the shipping company and if they were not insured the exporter would not send them till payment had been made, nor would the importer pay till the goods had arrived. Trade would almost come to a halt.
(c) *Freight insurance* 'Freight' is not the same as 'cargo' in this context: it is the charge levied by the shipping company for carrying the goods. It is usually paid in advance, even though the company is not strictly entitled to it until the cargo is safely delivered. If the goods are not delivered for some reason, the company may face a claim for repayment of the freight. It is customary for an insurance policy to be taken out against this possibility.
(d) *Shipowner's liability insurance* covers the shipping company against a multitude of events which may be its own fault or that of its employees: collisions with other vessels or dock installations, injury to passengers, crew or dock workers, pollution of the water or beaches, and so on. Substantial sums may be claimed in compensation for damage or injury in these circumstances, so the company carries a further insurance to cover it against this risk.

**Fire, motor, aviation insurance** These terms are more or less self-explanatory. Fire insurance originated soon after the Fire of London in 1666, and the first fire insurance companies had their own fire brigades. Fire insurance policies can often be extended, on payment of an additional premium, to cover other risks such as explosions, floods and even earthquakes.

Motor insurance is compulsory for all drivers and is summarized in fig. 19.5.

---

**1 Minimum legal cover**
Injuries to third parties on public roads only. (A third party is someone other than the insurer and the insured. The definition includes passengers.)

**2 Third party cover**
As 1, plus cover for damage to other people's property and for approved legal costs.

**3 Third party, fire and theft**
As 2, plus cover for theft of car and for fire damage. An extra premium is charged for theft in some areas.

**4 Comprehensive**
As 3, plus cover for damage to the insured's vehicle, personal injury to the driver, and loss of or damage to personal possessions while in the car.

---

**Fig. 19.5** The four categories of motor insurance

As air travel has increased so has the need for aviation insurance, covering the aircraft against accidental damage and the operators against claims arising from injury to or the deaths of passengers and crew and third parties.

**Accident insurance** covers such things as insurance against burglary and personal accident. There are two main subdivisions.

(a) *Personal accident insurance* covers the insured against partial or total disability arising from accidental causes. Sports stars often take out an accident insurance policy in case they sustain an injury which prevents them from working for a period. Aircraft passengers can obtain short-term policies to cover them for the duration of a flight. Most motor insurance provides cover for injuries received in an accident.

(b) *Property insurance* is another form of accident insurance. Most motorists insure their cars against accidental damage, though they are not obliged to by law. Manufacturers insure their stock and machinery, farmers their animals, and householders their personal valuables. The cover provided is normally for accident and theft.

Property insurance includes *household insurance*, which is itself divided into two parts: *contents insurance* covering such things as furniture, carpets, television sets and jewellery, and *buildings insurance* covering the actual building against damage.

**Liability insurance** provides cover against claims arising from injuries to other people, or loss of or damage to their property. Motorists are legally required to be covered against liability to third parties, and we have already seen that shipowners and airline operators insure against third-party claims.

One important example of liability insurance is *public liability*, covering a company that may have to face claims arising from injuries to people or damage to their property. For example, the emission of dangerous fumes from a factory into the atmosphere may damage the health of people outside. A firm's product may be faulty and cause injury to its users. Insurance cover is essential in such circumstances.

Another example is *employers' liability*. All employers are required by law to insure their liability to compensate their employees for disease or injury arising from their employment.

A rather different liability arises where an employee is in a position of trust handling the employer's money. The employer may feel it sensible to take out a *fidelity bond* to insure against the employee misappropriating the funds. Provided that the insurer can obtain satisfactory references about the employee's character, it will agree to compensate the employer for loss arising from theft by the employee.

## 19.7 The business world and insurance

By now it should be clear that most individuals and all businesses need to be covered by a range of insurance policies. The insurance that might be carried by a business organization is summarized in fig. 19.6.

## 19.8 The importance of insurance

It is not exaggerating to say that the standard of living we enjoy depends on insurance, since it is related to the range of goods and services we can buy. Many of the goods are transported across the world in consignments worth, perhaps, several million pounds. As we have seen, traders could not afford to send these goods unless they were covered by insurance. Without insurance, the loss of the goods would mean bankruptcy.

Similarly, few people would set up as sole traders, investing their life's savings in a business, unless their stock and premises could be insured.

**Fig. 19.6** Insurance for the business organization

The insurance industry is also important to the economy of the whole nation, which it affects in two ways.

(a) A substantial proportion of the nation's savings is channelled through the insurance companies to the capital market, where it is invested in a wide range of enterprises (see Unit 13).

(b) The insurance industry is also important to the country's balance of payments (see Unit 21). In 1990 the total United Kingdom receipts from services (invisible trade) was £29 000 million. Approximately £2700 million of this (9.3 per cent) was earned by the insurance business.

Our conclusion is that insurance as an aid to trade makes an essential contribution to the economic life of the community. Without it, we should lack many of the things that nowadays we take for granted.

## 19.9 Questions

1. Give examples of *insurable risks* and *non-insurable risks*.
2. What is necessary before a risk can be regarded as insurable?
3. (a) Why is insurance sometimes referred to as a 'pooling of risks'?
   (b) Explain how the pool operates in the case of motor insurance.
4. (a) Explain what is meant by the *principle of insurable interest*.
   (b) Why would insurance companies be unable to operate if this principle was not observed?
5. (a) What is an insurance premium?
   (b) Why do insurance companies normally charge higher premiums for motor insurance to 19-year-old drivers than to 35-year-old drivers?
6. (a) What is meant when it is said that an insurance company will *indemnify* a policy-holder?
   (b) Why is the idea of *subrogation* important to the process of indemnity?
7. There are 1000 people wishing to insure their jewellery against burglary. Experience shows that each year 5 per cent of people who have this kind of insurance make a claim, and that the average claim is for £500. Assuming that the insurer expects these figures to be maintained, how much should it charge each person so that the expected claims can just be met?
8. In what respect are the services and policies offered by the insurance companies (a) similar to and (b) different from those offered by Lloyd's?
9. (a) Distinguish between the various kinds of life assurance.
   (b) Why are endowment policies considered an important means of saving?
10. (a) What are the principles of insurance?
    (b) Show how they are important (i) to someone taking out an insurance policy and (ii) to someone making a claim under the policy.
11. (a) What are the main risks undertaken by business people?
    (b) Describe how insurance can help a factory-owner to overcome these risks.

12. John and Mary Jones have recently moved into a new house which they are buying with a building society mortgage of £20 000, having paid one-third deposit. Before this, their main contact with the problems of insurance was in connection with their car, which for a payment of £80 is covered on a 'third party, fire and theft' basis. Now, the building society insists that they take out a mortgage guarantee policy and that they insure the house itself.

   They have also been advised to insure the contents of their new home. They calculate that the contents are worth £10 000, but being short of money they decide to insure them for only £8000.

   (a) What is the proper name for the £80 payment referred to above?
   (b) Explain fully what is meant by the term 'mortgage'.
   (c) Some weeks after moving, John drives the car into a lamp-post and immediately claims £200 from the insurance company for the damage to the car. Draft a short reply from the manager of the insurance company.
   (d) For how much should they have insured their house?
   (e) Unfortunately, a few months later some jewellery is stolen from the house. The items are worth £200. How much compensation can they expect from the insurance company?
   (f)  (i) What is meant by the term 'indemnity'?
       (ii) How is it illustrated in the case of the stolen jewellery?

# UNIT 20

# International trade: exports and imports

No country can itself produce everything that its consumers want or need, so some items – whether basic food-stuffs and raw materials or exotic foods and luxury goods – must be imported from abroad, perhaps from countries that specialize in their production. To pay for these imports, countries must in turn export goods (or services) of their own. Countries are thus economically interdependent on each other.

Each year, probably without even realizing it, you and your family buy a large amount of goods imported from abroad. Figure 20.1 will give you some idea of the nature of the international trade of the United Kingdom.

## 20.1  Imports

Imports into the UK fall into two broad groups:

(a) those items that cannot be produced within the UK, such as copper, or that could be produced only at great expense, such as bananas;
(b) those items that could be produced within the UK but which are nevertheless imported in large numbers. Cars, kitchen equipment and television sets are examples. There may be many reasons for importing these: the prices of imported goods may be lower, their designs may be better or people may believe them to be more reliable.

Recently there have been some important developments in the pattern of United Kingdom imports. First, during the last 25 years the importance of food and raw materials as a proportion of total imports has declined from over half the total to about 15 per cent. This does not mean that the quantity or value of such imports has fallen. There has been a corresponding increase in manufactured goods as a proportion of total imports. The other change has been geographical in that United Kingdom imports increasingly come from other western European countries, over half from the European Community and a further 12 per cent from elsewhere. In 1970 about one-third of imports came

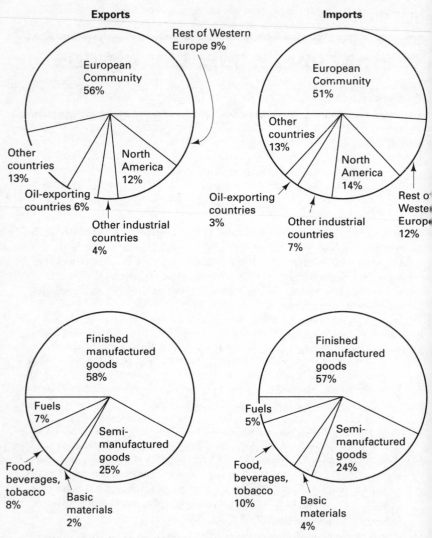

**Fig. 20.1** The structure of the foreign trade of the United Kingdom, 1991

from western Europe and a similar proportion from countries of the British Commonwealth.

## 20.2   The European Community

The growth in trade with European countries is linked to the development of two separate organizations. One is the European Free Trade Area (EFTA). The main objective of this group is for members to establish free trade with each other while making their own individual arrangements with non-members.

The United Kingdom once belonged to EFTA but in 1973 transferred to the larger European Community (EC), now a group of 12 nations. Again a prime objective is to establish free trade between members and it should be achieved by the establishment of the single market in 1993. Beyond that, members agree to adopt a common policy towards trade with non-members. For example, the customs duties imposed on goods imported from the USA will be the same whether the goods arrive in the UK or France or any other EC country.

However, membership of the EC implies the development of more than just trade agreements. These are matters which have great significance for the UK and it is worth recording some of the more important items.

(a) Some of the powers traditionally belonging to national governments become a matter for EC institutions. The main institutions are

   (i) *The European Commission* which has 17 members drawn from all member states. The Commissioners try to adopt a Community outlook and propose and develop policies in the interest of the EC as a whole. Once those policies have been agreed the Commission ensures that they are implemented.

   (ii) *The Council of Ministers* which is the main decision-making body, consisting of one minister from each country. Necessarily the ministers will examine policy proposals made by the Commission from the point of view of the likely impact on their own countries.

   (iii) *The European Parliament* has 518 directly elected members (81 from Britain) and has limited powers to suggest amendments to the Commission's proposals before the Council makes its final decisions.

   (iv) *The Court of Justice* adjudicates on disputes between members over the treaties which established the community. It also deals with complaints against community institutions and enforces community laws.

It can be expected that in time each of these institutions will develop greater powers and that there will be a corresponding reduction in the powers of national institutions.

(b) The development of common internal policies. This has already occurred in the Common Agricultural Policy which ensures that all farmers receive the same price for, say, milk and that they are protected from foreign competition. Common policies for transport, regional development and employment matters are being developed. In the longer term for the single market to operate effectively there will need to be moves towards a common policy on taxation.

(c) Perhaps the most fundamental change that is envisaged is the establishment of a common currency for the European Community. Although there is no set date for achieving a common currency, its introduction would mean that many of the economic decisions normally made by the British Government or the Bank of England would be made by EC institutions.

Thus it can be seen that the European Community will continue to have a major effect on the economic and commercial life of the UK.

## 20.3   Exports

Geographically, exports have changed in the same way as imports: in 1991, 65 per cent of them were sent to western Europe. In the 1960s less than half went to Europe and about 40 per cent to Commonwealth countries.

The nature of what is exported from the United Kingdom has changed substantially too. The development of North Sea oil resulted in fuels accounting for over 20 per cent of exports in the early 1980s, but this figure has now fallen back to 7 per cent. Traditionally the UK has been an exporter of manufactured goods and they still comprise half of the total. Twenty-five years ago the proportion was nearer three-quarters. The change is attributable to increasing competition from abroad, especially from Japan and more recently industrialized countries such as Korea. In 1970 manufactured exports were 50 per cent greater than manufactured imports. By 1991 manufactured exports were 6 per cent less than imports, an indication of the change that has occurred.

The difference between the value of imports and the value of exports makes up part of the *balance of payments*, which we shall examine in Unit 21.

## 20.4   Difficulties facing exporters

Exporters face a variety of problems which are quite different from those experienced in domestic trade. They are summarized below.

**Distance**   For UK exporters the distance involved in exporting is usually greater than in domestic trade, which may necessitate the appointment of overseas representatives. It also makes *transport* more complicated: UK exporters have to use sea or air transport as well as road and/or rail.

**Language differences** may mean that *communications* with overseas traders must be carefully translated, while publicity material and instructions which accompany goods must be prepared in several languages. The increasing involvement of the UK in the European Community has resulted in many companies improving the foreign language training of their staff.

**Cultural differences and local requirements** must be taken into account when exporting, which makes *market research* (see Unit 17.5.4) more important. We shall see that this can be overcome to some extent by using the intelligence services of the Department of Trade and Industry.

**Technical differences** Different governments may have different technical specifications for goods sold in their country. The exporter dealing with several overseas countries may have to produce half a dozen or more different specifications for electrical equipment. One of the objectives of the EC is to establish agreed standards and specifications for the production of a whole range of goods. Eventually goods produced in one EC member country will be suitable for sale in all others. This, of course, will be much more convenient for manufacturers.

**Trade barriers** *Tariffs* are taxes levied on imports (and occasionally on exports too). They are a considerable obstacle to trade, and they can only be avoided by not exporting to those countries which impose them. Instead of imposing a tariff, a country may limit the number of goods imported. This limit is known as an *import quota*. Governments are continually negotiating for the abolition of these and other barriers to their trade. One of the reasons for the rapid growth of trade between EC members has been the removal of tariffs and quotas between members.

**Customs regulations** have to be obeyed, and they create more work for the exporter.

**Documentation** is much more complicated in exporting than in home trade, and requires more work from the exporter. Much of this work can be handed over to a *freight forwarder* – that is, a firm that specializes in making all the arrangements in connection with the export of goods, from advising on packing to collecting payment. Again, the development of the single market within the EC should result in more straightforward procedures.

**Payment** poses an additional problem, because the exporter and the customer use different currencies. Currency must therefore be exchanged in the foreign exchange market. As we shall see, exporters need to make special arrangements to ensure that they receive payment. The establishment of a common currency in the EC would avoid this complication for trade between members.

**Insurance** is also more complicated for the exporter, because the risks are greater. Again, the Department of Trade and Industry helps to overcome some of the problems.

We shall now look briefly at how some of these problems are overcome.

## 20.5   Methods of exporting

Various methods are open to the firm wishing to enter the export market. It may organize the whole project itself with its own employees doing all the work, either from head office or by going abroad, or it may hand over some or all of the work to an outside organization, called an *export house*.

### 20.5.1   Export houses
These are firms offering services in the export trade. They function in several ways.

One possibility is that they act as *merchants*, obtaining orders from abroad and then buying the goods from the manufacturer in this country. The home producer can avoid many of the difficulties of exporting goods by simply selling them to the home-based merchant. Merchants have full responsibility for the goods they handle. If prices fall after they have bought the goods, they may make a loss. Manufacturers need not even know that their goods are exported.

Alternatively, export houses may act as *agents*, looking for customers on behalf of manufacturers wishing to sell in export markets. There are two kinds of agent: factors and brokers. Both are paid on a commission basis.

The *factor* undertakes to find a buyer for the exporter's goods, and meanwhile has possession of them. Factors can sell the goods in their own names and at the prices they think best. They are then empowered to receive payment for the goods from the buyers. *Brokers*, with whom factors are often confused, have none of these characteristics – brokers merely bring buyers and sellers together, without taking possession of the goods.

### 20.5.2  Overseas agents

While a large amount of export business is conducted by merchants and agents based in the United Kingdom, manufacturers often find it preferable to employ an agent permanently based in the country to which they are selling. However good their intelligence services, it is impossible for agents based in the UK to become fully acquainted with the needs of consumers in every distant country to which they hope to sell.

Overseas agents may be natives of the territory in which they are selling, or they may be sent from the exporting country. They may represent one firm or several, but the problem of divided loyalties may arise where an agent represents several firms. It is usually preferable for an individual exporter to employ an agent dealing solely with his own products, paying the agent a salary plus commission rather than just commission. Many overseas agents do represent a range of companies, however, and work on a commission basis.

### 20.5.3  Licences to overseas manufacturers

One way round the problems of exporting is to allow overseas manufacturers to produce goods to your design for sale in their local markets. They then pay you a proportion of the money they earn on each unit they sell. Such a fee is called a *royalty*. Thus the risks of exporting disappear while you, as the original producer, benefit from the successful development of new markets.

### 20.5.4  An export department

Agents of various kinds and locations are especially suitable for small firms to whom exporting is a subsidiary activity. A larger firm, well established in exporting, usually prefers to set up its own export department. This performs many of the functions of an agent.

(a)  It may receive orders direct from abroad.

(b) It may find markets abroad as a result of information provided by Government agencies – the Department of Trade and Industry publishes a daily list of export opportunities, which is carefully studied by exporters.

(c) It may be approached directly by the UK-based representatives of foreign firms or governments.

(d) It will control a team of overseas sales people, often with permanent offices centred in the main overseas markets. These salesmen will be full-time employees of the firm and will be expensive to keep in the field.

Export markets are increasingly competitive, and there is no doubt that the volume and value of the exports of a particular firm depend very much on the effort that it puts into selling its goods. This is why an increasing number of firms establish their own export departments with permanent representatives overseas, charged solely with selling the company's products. It is generally best for the overseas representative to be a native of the area, for such people are more aware of the exact needs of local customers.

### 20.5.5 Manufacturing abroad

In very highly developed export trades there is another possibility, which is to set up manufacturing plant in the overseas market. This, of course, is open only to firms of some substance and is a process usually associated with large companies such as Shell or Ford. In some respects it may not be in the interests of the exporting country, as it may ultimately reduce the level of exports. But to the firm it has the considerable advantages of bringing it nearer to its market and, since it will be employing local labour, of perhaps making its products more acceptable in the host country. In recent years many Japanese manufacturers in the electronics and motor manufacturing industries have established factories in the UK, thus avoiding European Community tariffs.

Companies who develop their overseas sales in this way are known as *multinational companies*. A fuller discussion of their role can be found in the companion volume *Success in Economics*.

## 20.6 Obtaining payment

Two different problems arise here. One is that two different currencies are involved in each transaction. The other relates to the time and distance factors: an exporter sending goods to a perhaps unknown foreign customer needs to be sure of receiving payment, but the customer wants to be sure of receiving the goods before parting with the money.

### 20.6.1 Open account transactions

This method is only used when the exporter is selling to an established and trusted customer. The main UK banks have branches in the leading overseas centres, and in cities where they do not they appoint a bank to represent them. The importer pays the money into the local branch of the exporter's bank, from where it can be transferred rapidly to the exporter's account in the UK.

### 20.6.2   Bills of exchange

'A bill of exchange is an unconditional order in writing, addressed by one person to another, signed by the person giving it, requiring the person to whom it is addressed to pay on demand or at fixed or determinable future time, a sum certain in money to or to the order of a specified person, or to bearer.' This is the definition of a bill of exchange to be found in the Bills of Exchange Act 1882. What it means for our purposes is that a bill of exchange is an IOU in which the purchaser (in our discussion, an importer) promises to settle a debt on a specific date.

For centuries the bill of exchange has played an important part in the commercial life of the United Kingdom. The need for it arises in two sets of circumstances:

(a) where the buyer of goods needs a period of credit before paying, so that raw materials can be converted into manufactured goods and sold, but where the seller cannot afford to tie up capital by giving credit;
(b) where the distance between the supplier and the buyer is so large that there is a delay of perhaps several weeks between the dispatch and the arrival of the goods.

The bill of exchange can overcome both problems, of which the former is more likely to arise in domestic trade, the latter in exporting.

Suppose that Jane Smith Ltd has dispatched goods worth £5000 by sea to James Head Ltd in Brazil. It will be some time before they arrive, and Jane Smith needs early payment. On the other hand, James Head will not be very anxious to pay for the goods until they actually arrive in good condition. Jane Smith Ltd therefore draws up a bill of exchange like the one shown in fig. 20.2.

Note that

(a) the bill instructs J. Head to pay the appropriate sum at a particular time;

```
£5000                          31 Any Road
                               Somewhere
30 November 19..               England


90 days after sight pay Jane Smith Ltd
five thousand pounds at National
Westminster Bank, Somewhere.


To: J. Head        Signed: J. Smith
Rio, Brazil                    Director
```

**Fig. 20.2**  A bill of exchange

(b)  the drawer of the bill is J. Smith, a director of the exporting firm;
(c)  the drawee is J. Head, the importer.

Once the bill has been drawn up, it is sent to James Head Ltd, which accepts the bill by signing it to acknowledge its debt and to signify agreement to the terms of the bill. James Head will not be willing to accept the bill until it is sure that the goods are on their way to it. The bill will therefore be accompanied by a copy of the *bill of lading*, which is signed by the ship's master and proves that the goods are on their way (see Unit 20.7.1). A copy of the insurance policy covering the goods will also accompany the bill of exchange, as will any invoices in connection with the deal.

In practice it would usually be unnecessary to send the bill of exchange and the shipping documents to James Head's office in Brazil. Because of the distance involved, the bill of exchange (now a *documentary bill*, as it is accompanied by the shipping documents such as the bill of lading and the insurance policy) will be accepted by James Head's London agent and re-turned to the exporter. As long as the agent is one of the leading accepting houses (see Unit 12.2.2), Jane Smith can now *discount* the bill: that is, it is passed on to a bank (negotiated) for a sum slightly less than its face value. Jane Smith Ltd now has its money, and the bank makes a profit by collecting £5000 in a few weeks' time. James Head Ltd meanwhile receives the documents relating to the transaction, which will permit it to claim the goods when they arrive. It will then arrange for the £5000 to be handed over on the due date.

There is sometimes a danger that the importer will default. This no longer worries the exporter, as the bill has been accepted by an accepting house, which has thereby guaranteed payment on the due date. But the accepting house must take precautions to ensure that it does not accept bills on which it will be called to meet its guarantee.

*Letters of credit* were devised to facilitate the use and acceptance of bills of exchange in international trade. In our example, James Head Ltd would have instructed its bank in Rio to instruct its London branch to issue a letter of credit to Jane Smith Ltd, stating that £5000 would be paid to the company in exchange for the documentary bill. This provides an extra guarantee to Jane Smith Ltd.

The letter of credit can be *revocable* or *irrevocable*. If it is revocable it may be legally cancelled by the importer. An irrevocable letter of credit can only be cancelled with the exporter's agreement, however, and is thus much safer for the exporter.

## 20.7   Export documents

One of the obstacles confronting an exporter is the formidable documentation that is required. It is extensive for several reasons.

(a)  A written record is essential, as in all business transactions.

(b) The Government needs to be kept informed of the level of exports and imports.
(c) A large number of intermediaries, and often several thousand miles, separate exporters and importers. Detailed documentation of transactions helps to keep track of goods.
(d) Traders have to comply with many legal requirements. As we shall see, importing countries are often very strict about the goods they allow to be imported and they demand written evidence of their nature and origin.

The following are the main documents needed to ensure that a consignment of exports reaches its destination safely.

### 20.7.1    Bill of lading

This is perhaps the most important document in international trade. It contains the names of the consignor (sender) of the goods and the consignee (recipient), full details of the goods themselves, their destination and the name of the ship that is carrying them. The markings on the crates are also given. No goods can be exported by sea without the bill of lading being properly drawn up, usually in triplicate. One copy is kept by the ship's master, one copy is retained by the consignor, and one copy is sent on (usually by air) to the consignee.

When the goods are delivered to the ship, the bill of lading is signed by the ship's master, and serves as a receipt for the goods. If the goods are damaged on arrival at the ship, the bill is endorsed accordingly. Once signed, the bill of lading is evidence of a contract between the consignor and the shipping company for the carriage of goods to their destination, in keeping with the terms of the bill.

Most important, the bill of lading is the *document of title* to the goods. This means that the holder of the bill of lading is entitled to claim the goods from the ship's master when the vessel reaches its destination. This is why the consignee's copy is normally sent ahead of the vessel carrying the goods. Without this copy, the consignee cannot take possession of the goods or remove them from the ship.

In legal terms the bill of lading is a *quasi-negotiable instrument*: this means that the holder of the bill can transfer the title to the goods by endorsing it in favour of someone else.

### 20.7.2    Airway bill

This corresponds to the bill of lading but is used only when good are sent by air. It is made out in triplicate: one copy is retained by the consignor, another by the airline, and one is carried *with the goods* for the consignee. The airway bill differs from the bill of lading in that it is not a document of title and is therefore not quasi-negotiable.

### 20.7.3 Consular invoice
When goods are imported into a country, customs duties are often levied on them, and these are normally calculated from the price of the goods as stated on the invoice. Obviously it would be possible to reduce the duty payable by falsifying the price on the invoice. The prices on a *consular invoice* (or *certified invoice*) are certified as correct by the consul or other representative of the importing country resident in the exporting country, so that this kind of fraud is prevented.

### 20.7.4 Certificate of insurance
A *certificate of insurance* is usually enclosed with the goods. This, together with the other documents, assures interested parties that the goods have been properly insured.

### 20.7.5 Shipping note
When the goods are delivered to the docks, they are accompanied by a *shipping note* formally requesting the port authorities to handle them. This note tells the authorities what the goods are, their port of destination and the ship they are to be sent in. A copy of the note is signed by the port authorities and retained by the exporter as proof of delivery to the port. It is then referred to as a *dock receipt*.

### 20.7.6 Mate's receipt
Sometimes the cargo is delivered direct to the ship and put aboard. In this case a *mate's receipt* is issued by the ship's mate.

### 20.7.7 Certificate of origin
The duty that an importing country imposes on goods varies according to the country from which they have come. Members of the European Free Trade Area (see Unit 20.2) are each allowed to impose their own tariffs on goods imported from non-members, but they impose no tariffs on goods imported from other members. Non-members could therefore be tempted to send all their exports via the member country with the lowest tariff against them, and the goods could then be re-exported from there duty-free to the other members. This practice is prevented by the use of *certificates of origin* which usually accompany duty-free goods to confirm that they were in fact produced, or largely produced, in the exporting country.

There are, as you might expect, many other documents used in exporting, but in this section we have seen the most important of them.

## 20.8 The Government and exporting
The Government is interested in exporting for several reasons. Most important, it must ensure that the nation exports enough to pay for its imports (see

Unit 21), and it therefore takes special steps to encourage exporters. The Government itself provides a wide range of services to promote the growth of exports: it has established certain independent bodies to facilitate trade, and it negotiates continuously for the reduction of tariff barriers against exports. These activities are considered in Units 20.9 to 20.11.

## 20.9    The Department of Trade and Industry

This is the Government department with the main responsibility for exporting. It provides several services to encourage exporters.

### 20.9.1    *The British Overseas Trade Board*
Attached to the Department of Trade and Industry is the British Overseas Trade Board, which has the general task of supervising export promotion. It consists mainly of business people, with representatives from the Department of Trade and Industry and the Foreign and Commonwealth Office. The Board has an advisory rather than an executive role, but many promotional schemes benefit directly from its advice.

### 20.9.2    *Trade fairs and promotions*
A special division of the Department of Trade and Industry supports trade fairs and other promotions, though it does not normally organize them. The Department often rents space at large international trade fairs and sublets it very cheaply to British companies wishing to expand in the areas concerned. More intensive promotions of exports take the form of *British weeks*, where local shops in foreign cities are given every incentive to sell British goods. These are organized by the Department, and wherever possible a programme of sporting and social events is held to boost the image of British goods.

### 20.9.3    *Export intelligence*
Among the special problems facing exporters is the difficulty of learning about opportunities. The Department of Trade and Industry's Export Intelligence Service provides an efficient and economical way of overcoming this problem. For a small annual subscription the Service provides information about a variety of topics, including specific exporting opportunities, conditions in particular markets, import regulations in overseas countries, trade fairs and British weeks. The information is collected by the commercial staff of British embassies overseas and is processed through the Department's own computer, so that subscribers to the system usually receive the relevant information within forty-eight hours of its arriving in London.

The Department of Trade and Industry will also provide exporters and potential exporters with more general information about foreign markets, tariff changes, and export opportunities.

The individual firm hoping to enter the export market for the first time can approach the Department of Trade and Industry for an assessment of the prospects. If the firm provides a detailed specification of its products, the Department will report back on the most likely market for the goods, perhaps suggesting modifications that could be made to meet local requirements in a particular area.

## 20.10 The Central Office of Information

The Central Office of Information provides publicity services for British exporters. Although commercial advertising is not accepted, any newsworthy item – the details of new products, for example, or the execution of an important export order – may well be incorporated in a newsletter, broadcast or film produced by the COI for the benefit of business people and consumers overseas.

*Translation* of documents written in a foreign language sometimes poses a problem to exporters. Similarly, it is important that publicity material that is to appear in foreign countries is properly translated from the English. The Central Office of Information is normally able to suggest a suitable translator. (In fact, several non-Government bodies such as the Institute of Linguists provide a similar service.)

## 20.11 The Export Credits Guarantee Department

This is dealt with separately here, even though it is under the direction of the Department of Trade and Industry, for the ECGD enjoys considerable independence and is run as a commercial enterprise and not as a Government department.

Exporters often send goods to brokers they don't know, in countries where political conditions are unstable and from where it may be difficult to secure payment. Large sums of money may be tied up in an export order and, without insurance, the danger of non-payment would deter many potential exporters from entering the export trade. The bulk of export insurance is provided through the ECGD. The usual principles of insurance apply, and the main policies offered by the Department are these.

**Comprehensive policies** With a comprehensive policy the exporting firm insures all its exports to all markets against non-payment for any of the following reasons:

(a) because the buyer does not want to pay;
(b) because the buyer is insolvent;
(c) because payment is prevented by the buyer's Government, who cannot afford the foreign currency;
(d) because of war; or

(e) because the import licence has been cancelled by the buyer's Government before the goods have been delivered.

The period covered varies from six months for consumer goods to five years for expensive investment goods. The premiums vary according to the duration of cover and the markets to which the trader is exporting.

**Specific policies**   A basic principle of the ECGD is that clients must insure all their exports. This enables the ECGD to pool the risks in the normal way, The Department does, however, issue specific policies for large 'once and for all' transactions, such as the sale of expensive generating equipment for a power station. Because the risks to the ECGD are greater, the premiums are higher.

**Investment insurance**   A departure for the ECGD has been the attempt to encourage overseas investment, especially in developing countries. Some of these countries are subject to quite rapid political changes which can result in an expensive investment being nationalized, with no compensation to the owner. The ECGD scheme normally offers up to 90 per cent compensation for a period of up to fifteen years.

## 20.12   The terms of importing

As you might expect, the problem facing importers are a kind of reflection of those familiar to exporters, and they do not need repeating here. Several points do need emphasizing, however, including the terms upon which the goods are imported. These normally refer to the various costs, other than the price of the goods themselves. The more common terms include the following.

**Free on board (f.o.b.)**   The importer knows that the price quoted includes all charges up to the point where the goods have been loaded on to the ship. Any charges arising after this will have to be met by the importer.

**Free alongside ship (f.a.s.)**   This is not quite so advantageous for the importer, who has to pay the expenses of loading the goods on to the ship.

**Cost, insurance and freight (c.i.f.)**   Here the importer's commitment is quite clear, for the price quoted includes the cost of the goods, the insurance premium, and the freight or carriage charges levied by the shipping company.

**Ex ship**   The importer has to pay for the unloading of the goods from the ship once they have reached the port. All charges up to this point have to be met by the exporter.

**Duty paid** This is not frequently used, but it means that the exporter pays the import duty on the goods as well as all the charges. The importer's calculations are thus much simplified.

There are many other terms on which goods may be exported, but those above are the most widely used and serve to show how the importer's expenses vary according to the terms quoted. When the goods have reached their destination, the agent or merchant will send the importer a bill setting out the details – this will show the cost of the goods and any other charges, including commission. This bill is known by the technical term *account sales*. The importer may already have received from the exporter a *pro-forma invoice*. This is not a demand for payment but a statement showing the goods being sent, their cost and other charges that are going to be made. It serves as an advice note to the importer.

## 20.13 Customs duties

Many of the goods coming into the UK are subject to customs duties, which are taxes imposed to raise revenue for the Government or occasionally to protect home industries. Sometimes an importer will pay the duty immediately and take the goods away. This may present difficulties, however.

For example, the duty payable on a consignment of tobacco or wine may run into hundreds of thousands of pounds. If this had to be paid as soon as the goods arrived in the UK, importers would have to tie up large amounts of capital, even though they might not want the use of the materials for some time. The problem has been overcome by the use of *bonded warehouses*, where imports can be stored until duty has been paid.

## 20.14 Bonded warehouses

Bonded warehouses are owned either by importers or by independent concerns, *not* by the customs authorities. They are normally located at ports, airports or land frontiers; but some large importers have their own bonded warehouses located at their factories. Cigarette manufacturers, for example, who have enormous amounts of duty to pay, do not like to take delivery of tobacco until they are just about to use it. They therefore need the bonded warehouse to be located as near as possible to the factory.

Bonded warehouses are subject to customs supervision and to strict regulation of the withdrawal of goods.

(a) The owner must give a *bond*, which is a written undertaking that goods will be released from the warehouse only in the presence of a customs officer and only when the duty has been paid. If the regulations are broken, the bond stipulates a financial penalty that the owner must pay to the authorities.

(b) Goods may be removed from bond in small lots, and the duty paid on each lot as it is withdrawn. This represents a considerable economy to the importer.

(c) While in bond, goods may be sampled, packed or blended, but they must not be manufactured. They may be moved from one bonded warehouse to another by *bonded carmen*, who are specially licensed to move such goods.

(d) The owner of the goods may sell them while they are in bond, in which case, of course, the purchaser becomes liable for the customs duty.

(e) Once the duty has been paid on the goods, they may be removed on the authority of a warrant issued by the customs officers.

Sometimes goods are imported temporarily, the purpose being to re-export them. In this case they can be stored in a bonded warehouse pending re-export without any duty being paid. In the days when the United Kingdom dominated world shipping, goods for several European countries would be brought from America to London for reshipment to their eventual destinations. With the expansion of international transport, however, this *entrepôt* trade has declined in importance.

If the goods have to be manufactured in some way before they are re-exported, the procedure is different because, as we have seen, duty must be paid before goods can be manufactured. For example, duty has to be paid on imported tobacco; however, if the tobacco is made into cigarettes for export, the exporter is entitled to claim repayment of the duty paid on the tobacco. This is known as *customs drawback*.

## 20.15    The role of the customs authorities

It is appropriate at this point to summarize the role of the Customs and Excise authorities in the import and export trade.

**Statistics**    They compile a wide range of statistics showing the pattern of trade and the movement of goods. (They are not responsible for checking the movement of *people*, however – this is the responsibility of the Home Office and is exercised through the Immigration Department.)

**Control**    They supervise the movement of goods in and out of the country, ensuring that prohibited goods are not imported or exported.

**Revenue**    The duty payable on imports (and some exports) is collected by the customs authorities.

**Bonded warehouses**    These warehouses are controlled by customs officers, although they are not owned by the customs authorities.

**Public health** The customs authorities have certain functions in connection with the control of infectious diseases. For example, they organize quarantine for animals.

## 20.16 The port and harbour authorities

While the customs authorities are responsible for the supervisory functions outlined above, the process of importing and exporting in the United Kingdom could not go ahead without the facilities provided by the docks and the bodies controlling them. We shall confine our comments to the docks, but you should remember that equivalent facilities are provided by the airport authorities for the increasing amount of trade undertaken by the airlines.

In the United Kingdom most ports are privately owned, and most trade now passes through such organizations. The form of ownership is immaterial to the services that have to be provided by these authorities.

**Deep water and clear access** These are the first requirements of any port. The larger the ships that will use the port, the deeper the water needs to be. A port authority has to spend considerable sums on dredging to keep the channels to the port clear. It also provides pilots, with a detailed knowledge of the approach, to take over the steering of vessels entering and leaving the port.

**Wharves** Adequate facilities must be provided for the speedy discharge and loading of vessels – cranes, warehouses and labour should be available to deal with ships as soon as possible. Moreover, provision must be made for ships to refuel and take on any other supplies they need. Dock charges are based partly on the time that a dock is occupied, so a port that earns a reputation of being slow in turning ships round will gradually lose traffic. The development of containerization (discussed in Unit 18.2) has speeded up the handling of cargoes, though it has also necessitated the installation of special and very expensive handling equipment.

**Access** A port must be linked to the road and railway networks by a transport system which is capable of dealing with the volume of traffic generated. Without easy access, the port will lose business to other centres.

**Office space** Shipping companies, customs officers and other organizations using the port all need office space.

**Ship-repair yards** Dry docks and repair yards should also be provided so that routine maintenance can be effectively carried out.

**Special facilities** Certain imports – timber, grain, coal and oil, for instance – require special handling. If ports want to attract trade in these goods, they must provide the special facilities necessary to deal with them.

## 20.17  Questions

1. (a) Name five problems faced by exporters which do not affect people in domestic trading.
   (b) Show how each of the problems mentioned above can be overcome.
2. (a) Describe the structure of the United Kingdom's international trade in terms of what is traded, the main customers, and the main suppliers.
   (b) What are the main changes that occurred in this trade in recent years?
3. Distinguish between the following: (a) merchants, (b) agents, (c) brokers, (d) factors.
4. J. W. Brook Ltd is importing £5000 of cotton textiles from Bombay Weavers Ltd. The transaction is to be financed by means of a bill of exchange.
   (a) What is a bill of exchange?
   (b) Show the stages of the transaction which enable Bombay Weavers to obtain the money for its cotton.
5. Describe the main functions of a port and harbour authority.
6. (a) What is a bill of lading?
   (b) Explain the importance of bills of lading in international trade.
   (c) How does an airway bill differ from a bill of lading?
7. Describe the main ways in which Government departments and organizations can be of assistance to exporters.
8. (a) Explain the meaning of the following terms used in international trade: (i) c.i.f., (ii) f.o.b., (iii) f.a.s.
   (b) Why is it essential for an importer to know the basis on which he or she is purchasing goods from abroad?
10. (a) Describe clearly the main characteristics of a bonded warehouse.
    (b) Explain how such a warehouse is of importance to a manufacturer of cigarettes located in the United Kingdom.
11. What are the principal responsibilities of the customs authorities in the UK?
12. J. Arjan and Co. Ltd manufactures office equipment in London, selling mainly to firms within 100 miles of its factory. It wishes to expand to sell some of the products abroad. Naturally its directors are aware that there are problems concerning language and tariff barriers. However, there are two things in particular that worry them.
    First, they are not certain about the best way of finding overseas customers.
    Second, they are not sure how the company will be paid for its overseas sales.
    You are required to
    (a) Write a report advising the directors on the assistance given to exporters, with special reference to Government departments;
    (b) Write an explanation from Arjan & Co.'s bank manager showing how payment can be facilitated by means of a bill of exchange.

# UNIT 21

# The balance of payments

## 21.1 Introduction

A country's balance of payments is a record of all its financial and economic transactions with the rest of the world. Every time someone in the United Kingdom imports or exports goods, takes a holiday overseas or receives interest from abroad, the balance of payments is affected.

The essential difference between these transactions and purely domestic transactions is that domestic transactions can be settled in currency that is familiar to and recognized by all the parties concerned, while overseas transactions usually involve two different currencies. Suppose you want to import a £10000 German car into the UK: you will find that the German supplier will not have much use for £10000 of sterling. You will have to instruct your bank to buy £10000 worth of Deutschmarks from the *foreign exchange market* (see Unit 21.4), which is the collective name given to the institutions concerned with buying and selling foreign currency. Your bank balance will fall by £10000, but you can now use the Deutschmarks to pay for your car.

Although you will go nowhere near the Bank of England, this is in effect where your Deutschmarks will come from. The real reason for concern over the balance of payments is that if too many people want to buy German cars (or anything else from abroad), the Bank of England's reserves of foreign currency will begin to dwindle. The Government, in conjunction with the Bank of England, keeps a watchful eye on the UK's trading performance, so that if necessary it can take corrective measures to protect the currency reserves.

## 21.2 The structure of the balance of payments

It would be possible simply to lump together all the payments received from other countries and all the payments made to other countries, deduct one from the other and thus determine the balance of payments for the year. However, this would not reveal very much about the causes of the surplus or deficit which was revealed. If there were a surplus, we would know only that receipts exceeded payments; if there were a deficit, only that payments exceeded receipts. We could get a much better picture of our performance by classifying the transactions under several different headings as in Table 21.1, which summarizes the balance of payments for the year 1991. (We will look at the figures for that year in more detail in Unit 21.3.)

**Table 21.1** The United Kingdom balance of payments, 1991 (£ million)

| | | |
|---|---|---|
| Current account: | | |
|   Visible exports | +103 704 | |
|   Visible imports | −113 823 | |
|   Visible balance | | −10 119 |
|   Invisible credits | +117 165 | |
|   Invisible debits | −111 445 | |
|   Invisible balance | | +5 720 |
| Current account balance | | −4 399 |
| Capital transactions: | | |
|   UK overseas assets | −19 128 | |
|   UK external liabilities | +27 948 | |
| | | +8 820 |
| Balancing item (errors and omissions) | | −4 421 |

### 21.2.1   *Visible trade*
We looked at visible trade in Unit 20. The value of imports is subtracted from the value of exports to give the *balance of trade*. You already know about our visible trade, and there is no need to elaborate on it except to say that we often import goods to a greater value than our exports.

Each month a provisional estimate of the previous month's balance of visible trade is made (the *trade figures*) and is well publicized on television and in the press. The monthly figures, and indeed the annual figures, are almost always amended later owing to the late delivery of some of the appropriate documents to the authorities, but they are accurate enough to indicate the broad pattern of trade.

### 21.2.2   *Invisible payments*
The services which we sell abroad or buy from overseas suppliers are part of what is known as invisible trade. As a general rule, where the United Kingdom provides a service, the UK balance of payments benefits because money comes into the country. For example, if an American businessman flies by British Airways, dollars are earned and the balance of payments is helped; converse-

ly, if a British businessman flies on an American airline, sterling is paid out and the balance of payments is harmed. (Of course when Britons fly by British Airways the balance of payments is not affected because the whole transaction is in sterling, rather like paying your train fare.)

Many items contribute to the invisible balance of trade, which, as Table 21.1 shows, makes an important contribution to the current account figures. Most of the invisible items are commercial, and fall conveniently into the three categories shown in Table 21.2.

**Table 21.2** United Kingdom invisibles, 1991 (£ million)

|  | Credits | Debits | Balance |
|---|---|---|---|
| Interest, profits and dividends | 77668 | 76590 | +1078 |
| Services | 32702 | 26712 | +5990 |
| Transfers | 6795 | 8143 | −1348 |
|  | 117165 | 111445 | +5720 |

**Interest, profits and dividends**    The credits shown in Table 21.2 represent the incomes from all kinds of overseas assets owned by British residents. If you own property abroad, this is where the rent you receive on it will appear in the balance of payments. Similarly, if a company in the United Kingdom is owned by Americans, its profits appear here as a debit when they are sent back to America.

**Services**    Whenever someone in one country uses services provided by someone in another country, the payment will appear here. You may take a holiday in Spain – your hotel bill and any money you spend while abroad will appear as a debit in this part of the accounts. On the other hand, many people in Spain run bank accounts in London, and any bank charges that they pay will appear here as a credit. Other services include payments for air and sea travel, insurance and various Government services.

**Transfers**    Some of the payments arise simply because people decide to transfer money overseas, perhaps to relatives. More important recently have been payments made by the Government towards the costs of running the EC, and payments received from the EC.

### 21.2.3    The balance of payments on current account

This is the name given to the visible balance and the invisible balance taken together. Sometimes there is a surplus, sometimes a deficit. The development of North Sea oil was beneficial to the balance of payments in the 1980s since oil imports were reduced and large quantities of oil were exported. In the early years of the decade this resulted in a surplus in visible trade though other factors led to large deficits towards the end of the period. The most recent figures for the current account are shown in Table 21.3.

**Table 21.3**  Recent balance of payments figures (£ thousand million)

|  | 1982 | 1983 | 1984 | 1985 | 1986 | 1987 | 1988 | 1989 | 1990 | 1991 |
|---|---|---|---|---|---|---|---|---|---|---|
| Visible exports | 56 | 61 | 70 | 78 | 73 | 79 | 80 | 94 | 104 | 105 |
| Visible imports | −53 | −62 | −75 | −80 | −81 | −89 | −101 | −122 | −126 | −119 |
| Visible balance | + 3 | − 1 | − 5 | − 2 | − 8 | −10 | − 21 | − 28 | − 22 | − 14 |
| Invisible balance | + 2 | + 4 | + 6 | + 6 | + 7 | + 7 | + 6 | + 4 | + 3 | + 6 |
| Current balance | + 5 | + 3 | + 1 | + 4 | − 1 | − 3 | − 15 | − 24 | − 19 | − 8 |

The importance of these figures is that they show whether the country is managing to pay its way in the world. Table 21.3 shows that while the United Kingdom achieved this from 1982 to 1985 it was unable to do so from 1986 to 1991, mainly because of a steep rise in visible imports.

### 21.2.4  Capital transactions

Table 21.1 shows that many of the transactions between people and firms located in different countries are not covered by the current account items discussed above. This is mainly because they are *capital* transactions, concerned with lending and borrowing, investing and saving. *Overseas assets* are the result of UK residents investing abroad. For example, you might decide to buy shares on the New York Stock Exchange, or a British company may take over a French rival. *Overseas liabilities* arise for many reasons; for example, a foreign bank may lend money to a British company, or someone in Japan may buy shares in a British firm. The money then owed to the overseas organization is included in these overseas liabilities.

For reasons which needn't concern us, the net figure for these capital transactions should equal the current account balance. In practice it never does: there are many items which are difficult to trace. This is why the balancing item in the last line of Table 21.1 is included. You must not regard this figure as an indication of the balance of payments surplus or deficit – the important figure in that respect is the current account balance. The balancing item simply shows the value of errors and omissions.

## 21.3   United Kingdom balance of payments performance, 1991

Table 21.1 summarized the balance of payments transactions for the United Kingdom for 1991. Here we will look at it again in more detail.

Visible imports (money going out of the country) exceeded visible exports (money coming into the country) by £10119 million, which gave a negative balance (a deficit) on visible trade.

Invisible receipts and payments resulted in net inflow of money amounting to £5720 million.

Taken together visible trade and invisible trade showed a deficit of £4399 million on current account (£5720–£10119 million). This term 'current account' includes all items where goods and services are provided for fairly immediate use.

Overseas assets increased by £19 128 million. (The minus sign indicates an increase in assets, because to acquire the assets money leaves the country.) The most important individual items here are the purchase of shares and loans to overseas organizations. One of the advantages of these assets is that they will earn interest, profits and dividends which will help the current account in future years.

Overseas liabilities also rose by £27 948 million (this time the plus sign shows an increase in what is owed, because money is coming into the UK). The main item here is borrowing from overseas. Of course, in future years interest will have to be paid on these loans and this will be harmful to the invisibles section of the current account.

## 21.4 The foreign exchange market

The main obstacle to international trade is the fact that each country uses a currency which is not usually acceptable in other countries. Currencies must be changed before purchases can be completed. It is the function of the foreign exchange market to deal with this problem.

The foreign exchange market has no set geographical location, because it consists of a large number of banks and foreign exchange dealers in the major financial centres of the world. These centres are linked by telex, telephone, cable and satellite, so that prices in one part of the market can be quickly transmitted to the rest, thousands of miles away.

We shall examine the work of the market under five headings, as follows.

### 21.4.1 Counterbalancing transactions

Suppose that we are importing machinery worth £10 000 from America, and that the price includes all charges for freight and insurance. Let us also say that £1 is worth 1 dollar 50 cents. We instruct our bank (or foreign exchange dealer) to obtain $15 000 from the foreign exchange market, for which we must pay in £10 000. Meanwhile in New York an American businessman places an order for British books worth $15 000. His bank puts $15 000 into the foreign exchange market and takes £10 000 out. The company that sold us machinery can thus obtain its $15 000 and the British book exporter can obtain his £10 000 without any money crossing the Atlantic.

Normally, of course, transactions don't cancel each other out in this convenient way, but it is surprising how often they come near to it. When there is a difference in the value of transactions in each direction, the balance is struck by the central banks of the countries concerned increasing or reducing their reserves of foreign currency.

### 21.4.2  What determines the exchange rate?

If each country uses a different paper currency and can print as much of it as required, what mechanism is there to determine the value of one currency in terms of another?

Basically a currency is worth whatever people are prepared to pay for it. If a country's exports are greater than its imports, its currency will be in demand and will rise in value. If its imports are worth more than its exports, its currency will tend to fall in value. If British importers put £100000 into the foreign exchange market to buy dollars, and American importers put in $200000 to buy pounds, the exchange rate will be two dollars to the pound ($2 = £1). A change in the pattern of trade may result in a different exchange rate. For example, if the Americans reduce their expenditure to $150000 while the British importers make no change, the exchange rate would be $1.50 = £1.

### 21.4.3  Problems for traders

We saw earlier that the existence of different currencies poses problems for exporters and importers which do not exist in domestic trade. The difficulty is that the exchange rate changes from day to day and traders cannot be sure of precisely how much they are going to receive, or pay, for goods until the actual day of payment.

Suppose that we agree to sell a £9000 car to an American customer and, knowing that the exchange rate is $1.50 = £1, we invoice her for $13500. By the time the transaction is completed the rate has changed to $1.60 = £1, and the $13500 which the American importer has transferred to the foreign exchange market is now worth £13500/1.60 = £8437.50. We receive less sterling than we had expected. (Of course if the rate had changed to $1.40 = £1, we would have made an unexpected gain.) We *could* overcome the problem by invoicing the customer in sterling, but this only transfers the risk to her: if the rate changes to $1.60 = £1, she must pay more than $13500 to buy the car (the amount will be 9000×$1.60 = $14400).

Traders can avoid these risks by using the *forward exchange market*. When you buy foreign currency for immediate use, you buy it at the *spot rate*, but it is possible to make arrangements in advance to buy at the *forward rate*. Suppose we know that in three months' time we shall need $2500 to pay for goods we are importing, and we fear that the spot rate at that time will be only $1.40 = £1, while it is $1.50 = £1 today. We could agree with a foreign exchange dealer to buy $2500 in three months at $1.50 = £1, paying a small charge for the facility. If in three months' time the spot rate has fallen to $1.40 = £1, we can still obtain dollars at the old rate, and thereby save money. (The risk is transferred to the bank or foreign exchange dealer.) The dealer will meanwhile have concluded a separate contract with someone else who wanted to *sell* $2500 at $1.50 = £1, so the loss made on one deal is balanced by the gain on the other.

In this way, at a nominal cost, the trader can be protected from the risks associated with floating exchange rates, and any adverse effects that they might have on trade are eliminated. This is just one example of the way in which commercial institutions adapt themselves to changing circumstances.

### 21.4.4 Currency speculation

So far we have looked at the foreign exchange market as though only importers and exporters have an interest in foreign currency. In fact there are at least two other groups who can influence the exchange rate and are affected by it.

The first are investors who may be buying or selling shares or other property in foreign countries. The prices of such assets will be affected by changes in the exchange rate, just as the prices of goods are affected.

The second group are people and institutions engaged in currency speculation and hoping to make a profit by correctly anticipating changes in the exchange rate. Basically this works in the following way.

Suppose the exchange rate today is $1.50 = £1 and that you have reason to believe that within one week it will have changed to $1.40 = £1. You could today purchase £1000 worth of dollars ($1500) and, if you are correct, in a few days' time you could sell the $1500 for £1071.43, making a profit of £71.43. (In practice exchange rates do not normally change so much in so short a period, but the principle remains the same.) Of course you would have to pay some commission in respect of your transactions, which would reduce your profit. It is also possible that the exchange rate will move to $1.60 = £1, so that either you would make a loss or you would have to be patient until the rate did move in your favour.

### 21.4.5 The Exchange Rate Mechanism

The Exchange Rate Mechanism (ERM) is part of the European Monetary System. It is regarded as an important stage on the way to establishing a single European currency. The principle is that within the ERM, the extent to which the pound's value against another currency can move, as described in 21.4.2, is limited to plus or minus 6 per cent. Eventually the permitted fluctuations will become smaller until, it is intended, they disappear altogether.

The supposed advantages of the system are that it establishes more stable conditions for traders, reducing the problems examined in 21.4.3, and that it reduces the scope for currency speculation.

## 21.5 Questions

1. Distinguish between the *balance of payments* and the *balance of trade*.
2. Explain what is meant by *invisible trade*.
3. State in which part of the balance of payments accounts each of the following transactions will be included:
   (a) the sale of Ford motor vehicles from the UK to France;
   (b) a British resident taking a holiday in Spain;
   (c) an American citizen telexing her London stockbroker and buying some shares in ICI;

(d) a Dutch shipowner insuring his vessel at Lloyd's of London.
4. The following is a summary of the international transactions of an imaginary economy (£ million):

| | |
|---|---|
| Goods imported | £500 |
| Payments to foreign shipowners | £800 |
| Export of raw materials | £400 |
| Charges for banking services provided for overseas customers | £300 |
| Purchases of shares overseas | £250 |

   (a) Calculate the balance of trade.
   (b) Calculate the balance of payments on current account.
   (c) Calculate the overall balance of payments surplus or deficit.
   (d) How might this surplus or deficit be dealt with?
5. What is the foreign exchange market?
6. What are the main factors likely to influence the rate of exchange between French francs and the pound sterling?
7. On 1 January 199–, £1 was worth $1.45. By March in the same year £1 was worth only $1.30.
   (a) What factors might have caused this change?
   (b) What effect might the change have had on the earnings of a British exporter had he sent an invoice for $1450 to an American customer on 1 January and received the dollars on 1 March?
8. (a) What is meant by the term *currency speculation*?
   (b) Show how a speculator can make a profit by correctly anticipating movements in the exchange rate.
   (c) What happens if his or her expectations are wrong?

**Table 21.4** Balance of payments current account for Agraria (£m)

| | 1st quarter | 2nd quarter | 3rd quarter | 4th quarter |
|---|---|---|---|---|
| Visible exports | +500 | +450 | +760 | +620 |
| Visible imports | −400 | −600 | −800 | −530 |
| Invisible credits | +700 | +640 | +580 | +800 |
| Invisible debits | −510 | −550 | −400 | −630 |

9. Answer the following questions based on Table 21.4.
   (a) What was the largest quarterly visible deficit during the year?
   (b) Calculate the overall current account balance for the year.
   (c) Give two examples of visible imports into the *United Kingdom*.
   (d) Invisible credits can be broken down into three broad groups. What are those groups?
   (e) State with reasons in which of the four groups in the table each of the following transactions would appear:

(i) an Agrarian resident buys a car from the UK,
(ii) Agraria sells 100 tonnes of wheat to France,
(iii) a British tourist pays his hotel bill in Agraria,
(iv) an Agrarian resident travels to the UK in an Agrarian plane.

# UNIT 22

# The Government and commerce

## 22.1 Introduction

In the United Kingdom vast amounts of goods and services are produced each year to satisfy, directly or indirectly, the wants of 57 million consumers. About 25 million people go to work to help produce the goods and services, and they are employed in hundreds of thousands of different businesses whose main aim is to make a profit.

If the Government were to stand back and allow all the individual units in the economy to go their own way, there could be many difficulties. Some services would not be provided at all, others might be available only on a more selective basis than at present; consumers would be in a weak position in relation to producers; employees might be heavily exploited by employers; and so on.

We have seen throughout this book that the Government intervenes through various pieces of legislation to reduce or eliminate abuses. In this concluding Unit we summarize the need for Government intervention in commerce, and examine the forms that such intervention takes.

## 22.2 The need for Government intervention

There are several important reasons for the Government taking a hand in the commercial life of the country.

**Public services** Many services are needed by everyone (or at least by many people) at the same time, yet there is no way of charging individual consumers according to the amount they consume. Defence, law enforcement and street lighting are examples of services which are more or less unmarketable. They have to be provided directly by national or local government, with no direct charge to the individuals who benefit directly. They are paid for by the community as a whole by means of taxation.

**Subsidized services**   Some services which could be marketed in the ordinary way would be too expensive for a large proportion of the population. Education and the health service are prime examples. It is possible to pay for private education and private medical treatment, but both are costly. To ensure that everyone can use these services, education is provided free, as is most medical treatment. This is clearly to the benefit of the individuals who would otherwise not be able to afford to use the services. It is also to the advantage of society as a whole that people should be well educated and healthy.

**Public corporations**   The State itself markets some goods and services, mainly through the public corporations. Most if not all of these could just as well be sold by private enterprise, but by establishing public corporations a government may aim to provide more comprehensive services than would be available if left to the private sector firms.

**Prevention of abuse**   The State frequently intervenes in a supervisory capacity, as we have seen again and again in this book. All kinds of legislation govern the economic and commercial life of the country, mainly to prevent the exploitation of one group by another. We shall remind ourselves of some of them later in this Unit.

**Assistance to industry**   Some firms and industries need assistance if they are to remain in business. It is quite normal for Governments to make grants or tax concessions to them; alternatively subsidies may be given.

Sometimes an industry finds that it cannot compete with the products of overseas rivals: here the Government may impose tariffs on the competitors' products, or prohibit their import altogether. British agriculture and coal-mining have often received this kind of help.

**Government aims**   Every Government has its own economic as well as political objectives, and the achievement of these may require further State interference in commerce. To take one example, the level of unemployment in some parts of the United Kingdom may be significantly higher than in others. To redress the balance, the Government offers special incentives to firms to build new factories in the areas of high unemployment, and it may make special payments to them when they begin production.

Most of these activities are for the benefit of the community in general and they must be paid for by the community. Each year the Chancellor of the Exchequer prepares a Budget containing proposals to generate the necessary revenue while also stimulating particular sections of the economy.

Figure 22.1 shows where each pound of revenue comes from and how it is spent. It is worth looking briefly at the main sources of income and the largest items of expenditure.

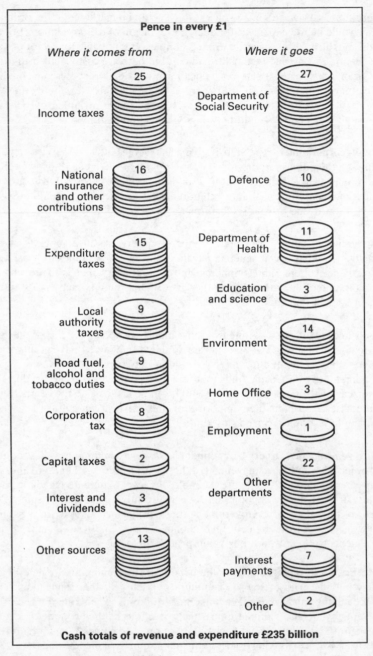

**Fig. 22.1** Government money, 1991–2

## 22.3   Government income

**Income tax**   This is the principal source of Government income, and it is said to be a *progressive* tax – that is, the proportion of a person's income payable in tax increases as the income rises. For a single person in 1992–3, the first £3445 of income is not taxable. In addition a further £1720, married couple's allowance, is tax free. This is normally awarded to the husband but the couple may opt to divide it equally or, if it is beneficial, to transfer it to the wife. Once these and any other allowances have been taken into account the remaining income is taxed at the rates shown in Table 22.1.

**Table 22.1**   Income Tax bands 1992–3

| Band of taxable income (£) | Tax on this band of income (%) |
|---|---|
| 1– 2000 | 20 |
| 2001–23700 | 25 |
| Over 23700 | 40 |

At these rates the maximum rate of income tax for most people is 25 per cent, but someone with a taxable income (that is income after deducting the tax free allowances) of over £23700 will pay at 40 per cent on the excess. On the slices of taxable income up to £23700 tax is always paid at the appropriate 20 per cent or 25 per cent rate.

The outcome is that a single person receiving the personal allowance and earning £10000 per year will lose about 15.4 per cent of it in tax; someone earning £20000 will pay 20.2 per cent; on £30000 it would be 23.2 per cent.

It is generally thought to be fairer to arrange income tax in this way, since the ability to pay rises as income increases. A further advantage is that the system has the effect of reducing some inequalities in income.

Most people pay their income tax through the PAYE (Pay As You Earn) system. Their employer is given a set of tax tables by the Inland Revenue, and each person has a code number related to his or her tax-free allowance. Each week or month the employer deducts the appropriate amount of tax by reference to the code number and the level of the individual's pay.

Although no one actually enjoys paying tax, it is more convenient to pay by this method than by a lump sum every half-year, as self-employed people do.

**National Insurance contributions**   All employees and their employers contribute jointly to the National Insurance Fund by paying National Insurance contributions every week or every month. In this way they finance (at least in part) unemployment benefits, retirement pensions and other Social Security payments. As far as the individual is concerned, National Insurance has the same impact as income tax – it is a deduction from weekly or monthly pay packets which reduces the amount available to spend.

**Value Added Tax** (VAT) is another tax that is ultimately paid by individuals, but it is related to their expenditure rather than their income. In general, VAT is payable at the rate of 17.5 per cent of the value of any good or services purchased. For the purposes of illustration, let us look at an imaginary series of transactions where VAT is levied at 17.5 per cent.

A forester produces timber and sells it to a carpenter for £300. The carpenter makes the wood into tables and sells them to a wholesaler for £500. The wholesaler sells the tables to retailers for £550 and they are finally sold to consumers for £650. This could be summarized as in column 1 of Table 22.2. By the introduction of 17.5 per cent VAT at each stage, each price is increased by 17.5 per cent as shown in column 2, the final price being £763.75, of which the retailer keeps £650 and £113.75 is VAT.

**Table 22.2** VAT at work

|  | 1<br>Basic<br>price | 2<br>Price including<br>VAT | 3<br>VAT sent to<br>Government |
|---|---|---|---|
| Forester sells<br>timber | £300 | £300 + £52.50 VAT<br>= £352.50 | £52.50 |
| Carpenter sells<br>tables | £500 | £500 + £87.50 VAT<br>= £587.50 | £87.50 − £52.50 = £35.00 |
| Wholesaler sells<br>tables | £550 | £550 + £96.25 VAT<br>= £646.25 | £96.25 − £87.50 = £8.75 |
| Retailer sells to<br>customer | £650 | £650 + £113.75 VAT<br>= £763.75 | £113.75 − £96.25 = £17.50 |
|  |  |  | £113.75 |

Since the tax is imposed at 17.5 per cent and the price is £650, £113.75 is the amount required by the Government. If each trader sends off all the VAT that has been collected, however, the Government will receive £350 (£52.50 + £87.50 + £96.25 + £113.75). This is not the intention. Column 3 shows what happens. Each trader sends to the Government the tax he has collected *minus* any VAT he has paid, so the revenue amounts to £52.50 + £35.00 + £8.75 + £17.50 = £113.75.

Most goods and services are subject to VAT – at present at a rate of 17.5 per cent – but some items (such as books) are *zero-rated* (taxed at 0 per cent) and some (such as financial services) are *exempt* from the tax altogether. The difference between these last two categories is that the seller of zero-rated goods is able to reclaim any input tax that has been paid on raw materials or components, while the seller of exempted goods cannot. Thus the VAT on components used in exempted goods is still carried forward to consumers.

**Local taxation**   Local authorities clearly need large amounts of money to finance their activities. Much of this is provided in the form of grants from central Government and conceivably all local government income could come from this source. However, in order to preserve some independence the local councils need some revenues of their own.

Traditionally this was provided by a system of 'rates', a property tax related roughly to the value of the property. It was superseded by the Community Charge or poll tax levied at a fixed amount per person irrespective of income. The Community Charge is itself due to be replaced in 1993 by the Council Tax, which reverts to a property-based system. Under this system domestic properties will each be allocated to one of eight broad tax bands according to their value, in order to determine the amount payable to the local authority. Households comprising two or more persons will pay the full Council Tax for their category; single person households will receive a discount of 25 per cent.

A separate non-domestic rate is imposed by the Government on business organizations to ensure that they make a contribution towards the cost of local government.

**Fuel, alcohol and tobacco taxes**   These are known as *excise duties* and are imposed on home-produced goods (as opposed to customs duties, which are payable on imported goods). All three items are taxed at very high rates, since people continue to buy them in spite of the taxes and the Government can be sure of its revenue.

**Corporation tax**   Limited companies have to pay corporation tax on their profits at the rate of 33 per cent. They are, however, allowed to make several deductions from their gross profits before arriving at their taxable profits, and companies whose profits do not exceed £250000 pay at the lower rate of 25 per cent. If profits are between £250000 and £1.25 million they are taxable on a sliding scale between 25 per cent and 33 per cent.

Oil-producing companies also have to pay special taxes on their output and sales from the North Sea, and although these are separately identified we can regard them as extra tax on the companies' profits.

**Borrowing**   In most years the Government has to borrow in order to cover some of its expenditure. It does this in two ways:

(a) through National Savings – if you have money in the National Savings Bank or have some premium bonds, you are in effect lending money to the Government;

(b) through the issue of Government securities. The Government sells the stock (often called 'gilt-edged stock' – see Unit 13.5.1) to the public in £100 units, guaranteeing a fixed annual rate of interest and repayment in a stated year.

The accumulated borrowing of the Government is known as the National Debt. In March 1992 this amounted to over £160000 million.

**Other income**   The Government also receives income in the form of trading profits (perhaps from nationalized industries), rent on Government property and interest on loans. During the 1980s a significant new source of revenue was developed – the money received from the privatization of many industries, over £35 000 million during the decade.

The Government's raising of money through taxation affects commerce in two ways. First, all commercial organizations have to pay some tax to the Government. Limited companies pay corporation tax, and partnerships and sole proprietors pay income tax on their profits. Second, most firms have to act as unpaid tax collectors for the Government. As we have seen, they are responsible for the deduction of income tax from their employees' wages and salaries, and large firms have to employ staff specially to do this. They also have to keep detailed records so that VAT can be properly assessed, and extra staff may be required for this too.

This problem of unpaid work on behalf of the Government is a serious one for a small firm working on a very narrow profit margin. Nor is it only a question of taxation – the Government often makes enquiries and sends requests for information concerning output. All this takes time, which the small firm can scarcely afford.

Much of the information collected by the Government is ultimately to the benefit of the firms themselves, however, as we shall see in Unit 22.5.

## 22.4   Government expenditure

Figure 22.1 shows in broad outline how the Government spends its money.

**Social Security** is easily the biggest use for the Government income. It covers all kinds of welfare benefits, including retirement pensions and unemployment pay. Since there are going to be more old people in future and it seems unlikely that unemployment will fall by much, this component of expenditure will remain at a high level. We may add to it the third item on the right of fig. 22.1 – Department of Health, the main component of which is the National Health Service.

**Defence**   Ten per cent of expenditure (about £23 billion) is on defence. The political parties have differing views on the need for defence expenditure, and this is one item that depends largely on the policies of the Government in power at the time.

**Education**   Expenditure on education depends in part on the age structure of the population, but the Government can to some extent control the amount spent by, for example, insisting on teachers having bigger classes, or restricting the number of people going to universities.

**Other payments**   You will have noticed that none of these items of expenditure (over half the total) has anything directly to do with commerce! However, the phrase 'Other departments' refers to a variety of Government departments, many of which are closely involved with business and commerce – the Department of Trade and Industry and the Department of Transport for example. This is also true of the ministries covering Scotland, Wales and Northern Ireland. Some of their services are covered in Unit 22.5.

## 22.5 Government services to commerce

Apart from the services provided by the nationalized industries, which we discussed in Unit 9, the Government helps commerce in three main ways: it provides information services, it sets up co-ordinating bodies and it often gives direct financial help.

### 22.5.1 Information services

Government departments are great gatherers of information, much of which they make available to industry and commerce. Sometimes the information is provided directly by a Government department to interested organizations and sometimes a special organization is established. Some of the more important are described below.

(a) The Central Office of Information provides general information services for Government departments and other public sector organizations (see also 20.10).

(b) The Central Statistical Office collates and publishes general economic information and statistics which are made generally available through such publications as the annual Abstract of Statistics, the Monthly Digest of Statistics and Economic Trends each containing a wealth of information of use to trade and industry.

(c) The Department of Employment publishes the *Employment Gazette* monthly, providing continuous statistics on employment, as well as discussions of labour legislation and other developments.

(d) The Government plays an important role in the encouragement of exports through a co-ordinating body, Overseas Trade Services, to which a number of departments contribute. The most important is the Department of Trade and Industry which operates in this respect through the British Overseas Trade Board. The main services are the provision of information about export opportunities, the identification of markets and the organization of trade fairs.

### 22.5.2 Co-ordinating bodies

Apart from providing information services, the Government establishes or encourages the establishment of organizations to supervise or co-ordinate various activities. These include the following.

(a) The British Technology Group (BTG) was established in 1981 to promote the commercial use of technology, especially new processes developed in the universities and polytechnics or Government research organizations. BTG also provides finance to firms in the private sector to encourage innovation. The finance is provided either through loans or by the Group purchasing shares.

(b) The Department of Trade and Industry is responsible among other things for regional development, providing financial assistance to areas with economic difficulties. In Wales the Welsh Development Agency co-ordinates assistance for industrial development, particularly through encouraging investment from abroad. In Scotland, Scottish Enterprise and Highlands and Islands Enterprise carry out a similar role, as well as taking a lead in training. In Northern Ireland these tasks are the responsibility of the Industrial Development Board. In all cases they may be able to obtain assistance from the EC's European Regional Development Fund.

(c) Governments normally involve themselves directly or indirectly in manpower training. Policy has changed frequently in recent years but the main responsibility for industrial training is now vested in a network of Training and Enterprise Councils (TECs) funded by, but operationally independent of, the Department of Employment. The TECs are also responsible for work-related courses in the Technical Colleges, and for Employment Training, a programme for the re-training of the long-term unemployed. Youth Training is designed to enable those school leavers who are eligible to acquire a vocational qualification and this programme, too, is linked to the TECs.

(d) There is no point in training or re-training labour if no jobs are available. Employment Service, an agency of the Department of Employment, has the task of advising the unemployed and where possible of finding them employment through its network of Jobcentres.

(e) The Advisory Conciliation and Arbitration Service (ACAS) is an independent statutory organization whose main purpose is to encourage good industrial relations between employers and trade unions. This may be achieved through offering advice on appropriate systems or by providing a conciliation service to resolve disputes or even by arbitrating on such disputes, whether they involve thousands of employees or a single individual.

The list is almost endless. There are innumerable *ad-hoc* bodies set up to study the problems of particular industries. Normally Government-inspired, these bodies usually include representatives of both sides of industry. Some are established to solve a particular problem such as a wages dispute, while others have a more permanent existence as a kind of standing advisory body.

### 22.5.3    Financial assistance

The Government may provide financial assistance to commerce and industry in several different ways:

**Fig. 22.2** The Youth Training Scheme (YTS) was set up by the Manpower Services Commission (now the Training Agency)

(a) tax concessions to firms investing in new machinery and factories;
(b) subsidies to firms creating jobs in areas of high unemployment;
(c) a contribution towards the cost of training workers in some areas;
(d) grants to firms for particular purposes;
(e) subsidies to enable essential firms to stay in business.

In all these ways the Government pursues the objectives of efficiency and a stable economy. But these objectives cannot be achieved simply by advisory and financial assistance: if businesses are left alone to make profits and follow their own self-interest, distortions appear in the economy which may be to the disadvantage of many people. Sometimes, therefore, legislation is necessary to correct existing abuses or to prevent other abuses developing.

## 22.6 Legislation and commerce

We have seen that legislation is necessary to protect consumers from exploitation, and to control the terms of hire purchase agreements. There are many other areas in which the Government has found it necessary to introduce legislation to safeguard the interests of the public and of the economy in general. Here we will look at just a few of the important areas of Government concern.

### 22.6.1 Regional problems

While unemployment is a nationwide problem it is more severe in some regions than others, notably in the north and north-east where many old industries have declined over the years, while new industries have been established elsewhere. To try to redress the balance, various Acts of Parliament allow the Government to offer grants related to the creation of new jobs. Under the same laws, the Government may also provide factories and workshops in the regions at low rents and makes special grants towards the improvement of the infrastructure (the basic services of an area) and the clearing of derelict land.

### 22.6.2 Monopoly and restrictive practices

A *monopolist* is the single seller of a product who has no competitors. In practice a true monopolist is difficult to find, but Governments have long been on their guard against firms who dominate particular industries. Today in the UK any firm that produces 25 per cent of the output of an industry is regarded as a monopolist. Legislation exists to prevent such firms unfairly exploiting consumers and to prevent a group of firms conspiring to exploit consumers. The Director-General of Fair Trading has the overall responsibility for implementing the policy.

### 22.6.3 Labour

The economy and commerce cannot operate without labour, and there is a mass of legislation to ensure that labour is properly protected. We can note two important aspects.

(a) The *Employment Protection Act 1978* contains many safeguards for employees. They have to be given a written statement of the terms of their employment – pay, conditions and so on – statutory periods of notice are established and there are safeguards against unfair dismissal.
(b) The *Health and Safety at Work Act 1974* covers all aspects of the working environment, imposing on employers of five or more people the duty of establishing, in conjunction with employees, a health and safety policy

acceptable to the appropriate inspectors. With increasing awareness of the danger of many industrial and commercial processes, it is difficult to exaggerate the importance of this Act to almost every employee.

### 22.6.4 Companies

As we saw in Unit 8.5, companies are closely controlled by the *Companies Acts*. The way in which companies are formed, their behaviour once they are formed and their rights and obligations are all carefully set out in the interests of shareholders, suppliers and customers. Company finance is so complicated and the opportunities for fraud are so great that tight control is essential if people are to be persuaded to invest in, and deal with, limited companies.

There are other areas in which the State has to legislate in our system of commerce. We have looked at some of the most important areas, but the whole scene provides scope for more detailed and specialized study. State legislation in commerce can be a controversial matter, and you will learn to form your own judgements. What is quite certain is that without certain rules being made and enforced by the State, our system of commerce could not exist and flourish at all.

## 22.7 Questions

1. State four reasons why it may be necessary for the Government to intervene in the commercial life of the community.
2. In what ways can the Government help to prevent the exploitation of consumers?
3. (a) Name two services which the Government provides for people more or less free of charge.
   (b) Why is it considered necessary or desirable for the Government to do this?
4. In what ways may Government expenditure be of direct assistance to manufacturing businesses?
5. Describe the main taxes by which the Government raises money from individual citizens.
6. In what ways does the Government provide information that can be useful to commerce and industry?
7. It is discovered that an overseas manufacturer is flooding the UK market with attractive but inferior cutlery, and severely damaging the sales of home producers. What steps could the Government take to help the home producers?
8. (a) In what ways do the Companies Acts control the activities of limited companies?
   (b) Why is it necessary for the shareholders of companies to be protected by legislation?
9. Explain what difficulties might occur if the Government did not control the activities of (a) advertisers, (b) road haulage operators, (c) hire purchase companies, (d) food manufacturers.

# New technology and commerce

## 23.1 Introduction

At several points in earlier Units we have taken note of the introduction and the impact of new technology in various areas of commercial activity. While you will probably be familiar with many aspects of this from your own experience, it is worthwhile to categorize some of the developments and to assess their importance from the point of view of commercial organizations.

The prime importance of the new developments derives from the way in which information of all kinds is handled in shops, banks and offices – computer systems enable information to be stored, recalled and processed far more rapidly than before. People and organizations have had to adapt to changes in the way that they conduct their lives. Once a new procedure or product is introduced, it soon becomes the norm and before long tends to be taken for granted. We don't even need to look outside the home to appreciate this.

## 23.2 Technology at home

It is estimated that 98 per cent of UK households possess a television set. An obvious example of the application of new technology is the use of a remote-control unit to operate the television receiver. Increasingly the television is linked to a video recorder, which may also be operated by a remote-control unit. Almost certainly the video recorder can be set in advance to record at least one television programme automatically, and perhaps several on different days on different channels.

Clearly television and video recorders are an important part of home entertainment. Together, from our point of view, they illustrate some of the advantages and disadvantages of the introduction of new methods inside and outside the home.

### 23.2.1   Advantages

(a) Although it is not important in this particular instance, the new technology is obviously labour-saving. You don't even have to leave your armchair to change the station on your television set.

(b) There is greater convenience. If two programmes which you want to watch coincide, you can record one of them and watch it later. Or if you want to do something else while your favourite programme is being transmitted, you can simply record it and watch it at a more convenient time. Thus the system is more flexible – you don't have to plan your time to fit in with arrangements dictated by someone else.

(c) There is also greater choice. One of the expanding parts of the home entertainment industry is the video-tape rental business. This enables you to ignore completely the programmes transmitted by the television companies and watch tapes of your own choice, a facility not available until recently. An even more recent development, known as Direct Broadcasting by Satellite (DBS), enables those with the necessary equipment (a special dish aerial similar to but smaller than that shown in fig. 16.2) to receive television programmes transmitted via satellite from several European countries.

(d) Information is made more readily available. Many television receivers are now equipped to receive teletext transmissions (known as Ceefax on BBC and Oracle on the independent television channels) in which information is transmitted like ordinary television programmes.

In a way these developments have crept up on us to the extent that they are now taken for granted. What a few years ago was regarded as an innovation and a luxury is now commonly regarded as the norm and a necessity. Even so, there are disadvantages associated with these developments, although you may feel that they are outweighed by the advantages.

### 23.2.2   Disadvantages

(a) New technology may encourage dependence. We tend to become increasingly dependent on new equipment – and the more sophisticated it becomes, the more dependent are we on specialists to correct any faults that develop.

Another aspect of this is said to be that people become too dependent on their television and video for entertainment, ignoring what some regard as more worthwhile pastimes – reading, for example.

(b) New technology may lead to a decline in the use of existing products or services. As home entertainment systems have become more popular, other parts of the entertainment industry have suffered. While there can be no single cause-and-effect relationship, the growth of domestic entertainment has coincided with, among other things, a reduction in attendance at football matches and a fall in cinema attendances. A major problem of new technology is the impact that it has on the users of more traditional methods. In particular, it is likely to lead to unemployment, an aspect to which we will return later.

However, it is not only in the field of entertainment that new techniques have affected the household. In the kitchen, microwave ovens conveniently permit the rapid preparation of food, and programmable washing machines and dishwashers are important labour-saving devices. On a broader scale the central heating system and, increasingly, the burglar alarm or security systems depend on micro-electronics, responding to the householder's instructions.

The increasing popularity of personal computers enables the household to store more conveniently all kinds of information previously only available on numerous pieces of paper and probably in all kinds of places: bills for gas and electricity, details of income and expenditure, bank statements, medical and education records and so on.

Now, if the new techniques have resulted in these kinds of changes within the household, how much greater are the possibilities outside, among industrial and commercial organizations? Let us consider these under two headings: the high street (covering shops and banks) and the office (which could include businesses in all sectors of the economy).

## 23.3    The high street

We saw in Unit 3 that the scale of retailing has generally been increasing and that the large retailers can take advantage of many of the applications of new technology. But even the small independent retailer is now likely to use an electronic till for the takings and, where appropriate, an electronic weighing machine.

In small businesses it is not difficult for the owner to keep track of what is going on: he knows roughly how many cans of drink he sells each day, say, and can easily establish when it is necessary to re-order. In large stores this is not so, but the task is made easier by the use of new systems. You may have noticed that in many clothing stores garments have specially perforated tags, called Kimball tags, attached to them. These tags are removed when the goods are sold, and at the end of the day they are sent to head office where a computer decodes them to determine how many items have been sold and their size and colour, automatically placing an order for the re-stocking of the store. The manager or manageress of the store does not have to arrange for the staff to record details of each sale in order to organize the intake of new stock.

Elsewhere, as we have seen in Unit 3.5.5, bar codes are used to achieve the same saving of labour. The code contains information such as the manufacturer and the size and grade of the item, which may or may not be price-marked. The goods are passed over a decoder at the checkout, the total bill is established and the information about the sale is stored in a computer. At the end of

**Fig. 23.1** Bar codes enable details of sales to be recorded automatically and, by eliminating keying-in of prices at checkouts, may provide a faster service for customers

the day the computer totals the sales of each item, communicates with head office and, in effect, makes arrangements for the re-stocking that is necessary as a result of the day's business. Since some large stores may be selling up to 4000 separately identifiable articles, you can imagine the amount of effort that is saved by the introduction of such systems.

If you book a package holiday through a travel agent, you will probably find that the agent has a computer terminal which will give almost instant information about the availability of places and which will up-date this information for other potential customers if you decide to make a booking. Similar systems are used for airline tickets and theatre tickets, where there are obviously only a limited number of seats available for a particular flight or performance and completely up-to-date information is necessary so that none of these seats is sold twice but the customer can make a firm booking on the spot, without having to wait for confirmation.

Some stores with several branches may keep only a display model of large items, like washing machines, in each branch but will have a computer link to a central warehouse so that customers can be given immediate information on availability.

In many stores credit cards are used for payment. Until recently these were manually processed in the way described in Unit 6.3.2. Increasingly, however, such cards are now cleared automatically at the till by passing them through a decoder which records all the necessary details, communicates direct with the

**Fig. 23.2** On-line access to update details of holiday availability is now a feature of many travel agents

bank operating the credit-card scheme (including a check that the customer's credit limit is not exceeded) and issues a printout of the transaction.

It is perhaps the banks themselves that have experienced the widest changes as a result of the use of computerized systems. We saw in Unit 11 how such systems have facilitated the processing of cheques and other instructions, and how automatic teller machines (ATMs) have made banking more convenient for personal customers. There is, too, likely to be an increasingly strong link between the banks and retailers through the development of EFTPOS – Electronic Funds Transfer at the Point of Sale – the procedure through which a customer uses his plastic card and his own Personal Identification Number to pay for goods or services electronically (Unit 11.12.9), funds being transferred from the customer's account to the retailer's as soon as the sale is made.

A further refinement of this system is known as EFTPOL – Electronic Funds Transfer at the Point of Living. Still in its infancy, the system will eventually permit a person to transfer money electronically from his or her bank account to another or even to select (via teletext), order and pay for goods without leaving home.

As is the case with household applications of computer technology, these commercial applications have the principal advantages of speed and convenience. From the point of view of a business organization, they can be expected to lead to greater efficiency – hopefully, costs will be reduced. This is likely to be at the expense of employment – the rise in unemployment in the

1970s and early 1980s had a number of causes, but one of them was the use of computers to undertake work previously done by people.

To some extent, while making some types of personnel redundant, computers may enable a business to expand and take on more workers of other types – and, of course, the computer companies are themselves employers – but the result of computerization is still likely to be a decrease in the overall number of job opportunities, and there will certainly be changes in the pattern of employment.

If the rise in unemployment is one disadvantage of the new systems, another is the need to educate people about their use. There is a suspicion of change in itself. When that change involves computer systems that people don't fully understand the suspicion tends to be even greater. This is particularly so where the transfer of money is concerned – systems such as EFTPOS will expand only as people become convinced of the security of the system, that they cannot be charged for goods or services that they have not received.

## 23.4  The office

Such has been the impact of new technology in offices that the term 'the electronic office' has rapidly established itself in the language. If you consider the basic functions of a business office you will quickly appreciate that there are few office activities that have not been affected by new procedures.

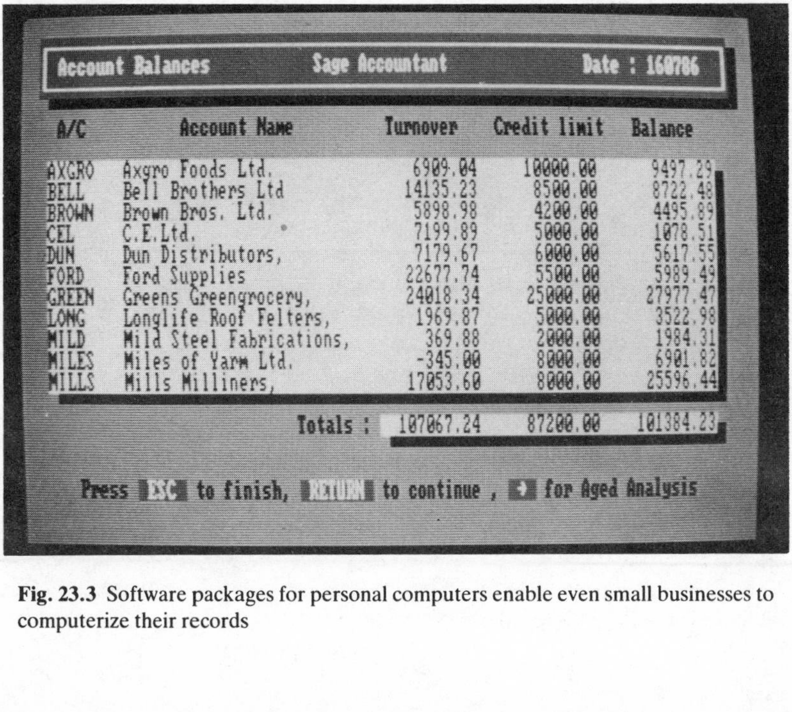

| A/C | Account Name | Turnover | Credit limit | Balance |
|-----|--------------|----------|--------------|---------|
| AXGRO | Axgro Foods Ltd. | 6909.04 | 10000.00 | 9497.29 |
| BELL | Bell Brothers Ltd | 14135.23 | 8500.00 | 8722.48 |
| BROWN | Brown Bros. Ltd. | 5898.98 | 4200.00 | 4495.89 |
| CEL | C.E.Ltd. | 7199.89 | 5000.00 | 1078.51 |
| DUN | Dun Distributors, | 7179.67 | 6000.00 | 5617.55 |
| FORD | Ford Supplies | 22677.74 | 5500.00 | 5989.49 |
| GREEN | Greens Greengrocery, | 24018.34 | 25000.00 | 27977.47 |
| LONG | Longlife Roof Felters, | 1969.87 | 5000.00 | 3522.98 |
| MILD | Mild Steel Fabrications, | 369.88 | 2000.00 | 1984.31 |
| MILES | Miles of Yarn Ltd. | -345.00 | 8000.00 | 6901.82 |
| MILLS | Mills Milliners, | 17053.60 | 8000.00 | 25596.44 |
| | Totals : | 107067.24 | 87200.00 | 101384.23 |

Account Balances    Sage Accountant    Date : 160786

Press ESC to finish, RETURN to continue , F3 for Aged Analysis

**Fig. 23.3** Software packages for personal computers enable even small businesses to computerize their records

Among other things the office will be responsible for the processing of the documents examined in Unit 5 and the kind of calculations considered in Unit 14. We have already seen how various Post Office and British Telecom services enable firms to communicate more easily with each other. The telephone network provides an essential link between offices not only for direct person-to-person contact but also to enable computers to link up with each other. It is this which permits more sophisticated and rapid communication between offices in different parts of the country. The exchange of documents which previously might have taken some days can be accomplished in seconds.

The applications we have discussed have mainly been concerned with improving on systems which were already in operation, but new technology may make it possible to carry out tasks which previously would not have been done, either for lack of time or because the relevant skills were not available. The computer may keep records of past sales or enquiries and use these to generate a mailing list of potential customers for new products. Sales can be analysed in great detail as an aid to market research. There are even 'expert systems' which can analyse problems and provide a 'second opinion' for help in management decision-making.

## 23.5    Conclusion

There can scarcely be an organization mentioned in this book which has not been affected by the introduction of new technology. Invoices and receipts, payments and wage slips, airline tickets and booking systems, these and all kinds of other things are now computerized. Information is more readily available and transactions are more speedily transacted.

The ease with which information about an individual's finances, buying patterns and other affairs may be stored and disseminated by computer has led to fears about possible misuse of this information, and the Data Protection Act 1984 was passed to give new rights to individuals (but not organizations) about whom information is recorded on computer. They are entitled to access to this information, to challenge it if appropriate and to claim compensation in certain circumstances. Those who record and use personal data must be open about that use (through a central Data Protection Register) and must follow sound and proper practices (the Data Protection Principles).

Whatever technology is used, however, the underlying procedures remain the same, as does the overall purpose of commercial activities: to ensure that goods and services are available to customers in the right quantities in the right place and at the right time.

## 23.6    Questions

1. Explain the main ways in which the use of computers has led to changes in the procedures of retailers.

2. It is sometimes suggested that we are becoming a 'cashless society'.
   (a) What is meant by the phrase 'cashless society'?
   (b) What evidence is there to support the statement?
   (c) Why might it be unlikely that we could do completely without cash?
3. Describe ways in which communications between businesses have been improved in recent years.
4. (a) Why do companies install computers?
   (b) What disadvantages might these involve for the company?
   (c) What effect might such systems have on consumers?

# Index